From the East

FROM THE EAST

Conflict and Partition in Cyprus

Costas Yennaris

Elliott & Thompson
London & Bath

A section of photographs appears after page 160

Contents

FOREWORD

Cyprus' recent, painful history has been examined at length. A number of notable works dealing with various aspects of the 'Cyprus problem' have been published, both by those at the forefront of the Cyprus struggle and by scholars making use of first- and second-generation source material. Unfortunately, the Turkish aspect, including positions developed by Turkey on the Cyprus issue and broader Turkish policy on Cyprus, has not been studied to the same extent. It was thus with great pleasure that I agreed to provide this foreword for Costas Yennaris' book, which presents a detailed study of Turkish policy on Cyprus from the 1950s until the present day.

The book is of particular interest because, through the use of material from Turkish sources, it sets out Turkey's policy, which originally aimed at neutralising the insistence of the Greek inhabitants of the island to unite with mainland Greece and to transform the small 18% minority of Turkish Cypriots into a coherent body and to make it a co-founder of any post-colonial political system. The author describes the gradual implementation of a policy the basic aim of which was, and still is, Ankara's political and strategic control of Cyprus, in the context of its broader policy on the Middle East. The various stages have included the recognition and legitimisation of Turkish 'interest' in Cyprus, the securing of Turkey's presence on the island, forcing the Greek Cypriot side to accept a political system that turned Cyprus into a state with limited sovereignty, and creating a 'legal' basis for the Turkish Cypriots' demand for separate self-determination and sovereignty. The Turkish Cypriot leadership has played a key role in efforts to fulfil these ambitions, and following Rauf Denktash's election to the leadership, the Turkish Cypriot community came under Ankara's control and was turned into a 'strategic minority'.

At the same time, those who promoted their Cypriot identity more than their Turkish origins were forced to go along with the situation under the threat or the actual use of violence. TMT (*Turk Mukavemet Teskilati* – the Turkish Resistance Organisation) became active as the main vehicle for Turkish policy on the island and still continues its activities today via illegal and extremist organisations such as the 'Grey Wolves'.

The 1974 invasion, the continuing Turkish occupation of the northern part of the country, the concentration of the Turkish Cypriot population in the occupied areas and the expulsion of the Greek population have led to serious obstacles in communication between the two main communities of Cyprus: the Greek and the Turkish Cypriots. The cultivation of nationalist passions and Turkish claims of a plan by the Greek Cypriot leadership to annihilate the Turkish Cypriots during the 1960s served to reinforce the feelings of mistrust by the Turkish Cypriot masses towards the Greek Cypriot majority on the island.

Nonetheless, the 'Attila Line' was drawn to serve the interests of Turkey, not those of the Turkish Cypriots. Division and segregation on national lines are no solution. They have led the Turkish Cypriots to a state of underdevelopment and poverty which forced many to emigrate from their country. It is no coincidence that, while the Turkish Cypriot population in 1974 was 120,000, today that figure has fallen significantly and, following the mass influx of settlers from Asia Minor, the Turkish Cypriots are now a minority even in the occupied areas. The terrible economic situation in the occupied part of Cyprus was confirmed by the European Commission in its announcement of 'Agenda 2000', where mention was made of the huge gap between the economic and social development of the two communities on the island, with the mean per capita income in the north amounting to just one-third of that in the free areas.

The Greek Cypriots and the Turkish Cypriots ought to be inaugurating a new era of coexistence and cooperation with a new shared vision, that of building a Republic of Cyprus in which the human rights of all the Cypriots are fully safeguarded.

In this context, Cyprus' EU accession prospects present a highly significant, historic opportunity for the reunification of the island as a bizonal, bicommunal federal state under the auspices of the European Union. The main beneficiaries of such a just and permanent solution will be the Turkish Cypriots, since membership will bring them not only security but economic prosperity. Issues such as national, cultural and linguistic identity, the protection of human rights, the safeguarding of the pluralism of the European Union and respect for these principles by all sides will be under the permanent scrutiny of the Court of Justice of the European Communities. The Amsterdam Treaty represents the best possible institutional shield.

Unfortunately, however, the Turkish side in Ankara and its mouthpieces in the occupied areas seem tied to an outdated awareness and continue to ignore the developments that are taking place. It is the hope of all that a new awareness will develop in Turkey to review its medium- and short-term objectives. Its insistence on legitimising the illegal 'state' in the occupied areas is not only preventing the start of a substantial intercommunal dialogue but is leading Turkey into isolation. By contrast with past 'formulas' that have been proposed and, unfortunately, continue to be proposed by successive Turkish governments, Turkey's contribution to a resolution of the political problem and the participation of the Turkish Cypriot leadership in the accession process will act positively on Turkey's own EU membership aspirations.

Over and above the various aspects of Turkey's policy on the Cyprus issue that Costas Yennaris presents to the reader, his study also proves how contradictory and obstructive Turkey's policy has been on Cyprus, culminating in, on the one hand, its attempts to legitimise the illegal state and, on the other, its threats to annex the occupied areas.

Yiannos Kranidiotis
Athens, September 1999

Introduction

There can be no doubt whatsoever that, for the past 25 years, a political and military impasse has been maintained in Cyprus for reasons that have nothing to do with either the substance of the so-called 'Cyprus problem' or the interests of the parties involved. It is a situation fostered by the problem becoming so distanced from its original causes. As a consequence, prospects for a solution have been created far removed from one that represents a natural administration of justice based on international law.

The result has been the prevalence of myths surrounding the historical development of the Cyprus issue; myths which have since led to what I call 'historical distortion', a distortion supported by an almost masochistic tendency to interpret everything within the context of alleged mistakes by the Greek side, to the extent that it has become an alibi for the positions and specific solutions that have been proposed from time to time.

This does not mean that there have not been serious mistakes – fatal ones in some cases – by the Greek side on the Cyprus issue. Many have occupied themselves with these mistakes and omissions, to the extent that the other side has virtually been absolved of its responsibilities for creating the problem and implementing a policy which, by its very nature, falls outside international law and the principles governing international relations.

Without wishing to reduce in any way the significance of the mistakes made by the Greek side and their 'contribution' to the creation of the present circumstances surrounding the Cyprus issue, I shall attempt in the following pages to prove the existence of a conspiracy that Turkey has been hatching against Cyprus – and not only Cyprus - from the 1950s until the present day. A knowledge of the facts – as presented by the Turks themselves – not only removes this distortion of the truth, but leads to a fuller awareness so that any 'historic compromise' may be based on a proper recognition of the mistakes and omissions committed by both sides – and naturally of their consequences – and also to an understanding of Turkey's current policy and the military objectives that this policy serves. The task of shaping a strategy to deal with the Turkish objectives – insofar as their achievement proves to be against the national interests of Hellenism – can only be based on a version of the truth, even if this reveals the extent of the mistakes committed by the Greek side.

This book outlines the tactics employed by the Turks to achieve their military objectives but, above all, it provides evidence of the responsibility of Ankara which, always acting alone, has taken all the decisions, even against the will of the Turkish Cypriots, whose interests it has neglected in order to serve its own military interests. The Turkish Cypriot leadership, moreover, is seen to have been a tool in the hands of every Turkish government, in whose name it imposed from a very early stage a regime of terror and oppression against the Turkish Cypriot community.

Since the 1950s up to the present day, the Turkish government has applied consistently and unwaveringly the formula prepared by Turkish constitutional expert and former Prime Minister Nihat Erim. One can compare the policy implemented by the Turkish establishment throughout this period with the Nihat Erim formula, and it will not show the tiniest deviation from the strategic context proposed in the formula. As a result, one may easily identify the objectives in their various stages: the recognition and legitimisation of Turkish interest in Cyprus; the establishment of Turkey's presence on the island; the creation of a territorial and demographic basis for its claims and of the legal requirements for the demand for separate self-determination and sovereignty; total political and military control of the whole of Cyprus.

Many of the facts included in this study will doubtless be already known. In combination with many others that may not be known, however, and viewed as a whole, they take on a frightening dimension. One is left wondering where any failure to alter the course that Turkey is probably following might lead.

The idea for this book arose from a personal experience, which has left an indelible mark on my mind. In an armed conflict there are always innocent people who pay for the extremes of the two sides. But the picture of three small children and their mother immersed in their own blood in a bathtub is one that can only provoke a reaction of horror. One such photograph has been used ad infinitum by Turkish propaganda to 'prove' the 'barbarity' of the Greek Cypriots and to illustrate Turkish claims of alleged organised genocide plans against the Turkish Cypriots. In the photograph are the wife and children of a Turkish army officer serving the Turkish Contingent (TURDYK) during the intercommunal clashes caused by the Turkish Cypriot rebellion against the Cypriot state at Christmas

1963. I had always believed this horrific crime to have been carried out by Greek Cypriot irregulars at a time when various groups had been formed to deal with the rebellion. Silently, I had always carried the guilt of all the Cypriots inside me. I had looked at the photograph on many occasions and tried to understand how anyone could reach the point of cold-bloodedly executing three small children, even if they were children of 'the enemy'. What purpose could such a crime possibly serve?

In Athens in the 1980s, I got to know many Turkish journalists in my own capacity as a professional journalist. Towards the end of 1985, one of them, Ahmed Baran, was put in charge of the semi-official Turkish news agency 'Anadolu' and he invited me to the official opening. After the ceremony, a group of foreign journalists and I went to a bar. Ahmed, who was a very quiet person, never spoke a great deal, but he smoked and drank a lot. At the bar he listened to the discussions but did not take part. At some point, after quite a few whiskies, Ahmed took me by the arm and we went into a corner. He wanted to talk to me. We had often chatted before and had a mutual appreciation of each other's work and opinions. That evening, however, he rendered me speechless. Without warning, without any prologue or introduction, Ahmed said:

'You know that photograph of the three children and their mother dead in the bathtub? I took it.'

I was literally speechless. It took several minutes for me to register what he had said and to stammer:

'How? Where?'

And Ahmed told me.

He had gone to Cyprus, he said, as a photojournalist to cover the intercommunal clashes of 1963. One evening, when he was drinking with friends in a bar in the Turkish quarter of Nicosia, two armed men entered and asked him to go with them. They took him by car to the house where the crime had been committed. Some armed men were already there, as were officers belonging to TURDYK, who ordered him to photograph the scene – which he did. And then, gun raised, one of them told him to hand over the film and to forget that he had ever been in that house and what he had seen there.

But Ahmed wanted to know what had happened, who had committed the crime in a house in the heart of the Turkish quarter, far from any points of conflict, far from the Greek Cypriot areas. And he found out.

The children's father had gone berserk, killing his children and his wife in cold blood. The killer disappeared, spirited away by the Turkish authorities, only to resurface after 24 years of silence, serving somewhere in the depths of Anatolia, having remarried. In an interview with a Turkish newspaper – his first and last – he recalled, with those who asked him to 'remember', his 'drama'.

Ahmed could not bear to keep the secret. He had always wanted to share it with someone, someone connected to the country. The Turks had lied about the identity of the killer of the three children and their mother. The crime had not taken place at Omorphita, an area where many battles were indeed fought and where excesses were doubtless committed by both sides. No Greeks could have reached the house where the murder actually happened in the heart of the Turkish quarter of Nicosia. Ahmed had lived for many years with this terrible secret.

He begged me not to use it and I am only revealing it now that Ahmed is dead. While researching this book, however, I came across many similar instances which served the objectives that Ankara had set TMT, the main vehicle for its policy on the island.

However much of a cliché it may be, it happens to be true that the Cyprus problem is now perhaps at the most crucial juncture of its history, one that may consequently represent the tragic conclusion of this history. The content of a solution, which is already looming on the horizon, will determine the future and the basis of relations in the entire region. In this respect, the Cyprus issue is a harbinger.

Without an understanding of the inner philosophy behind the policy that the Turkish establishment is following or has ambitions of implementing, the road to what is frequently referred to as 'Turkish expansionism' cannot be blocked, whether this is understood as being decreed from outside or originating from within. And there will be no end to the suffering.

By writing this book, it is my hope that consciences may be awoken and forces activated so as to exclude such a possibility from any solution. Its purpose is also to assist those endeavouring to achieve a substantial understanding of the Turks and, as a result, reconciliation with them. Such reconciliation, however, must be based on a frank recognition of everything that makes up today's historical knowledge and the foundation of any rapprochement. There are many factors to stimulate the reader in this direction.

It would be a mark of ingratitude on my part if I were not to express publicly my thanks for the significant help provided by my colleague Thanasis Haranas, a true son of Imvros. His willingness to translate articles and even entire books for me from Turkish was truly touching. His untimely death has robbed Hellenism of serious access to the Turkish way of thinking.

I must also express my deep appreciation and love for my wife and my two children for their understanding. The hours of family tranquillity and pleasure that I have deprived them of while busy with the writing of this book and related matters cannot, unfortunately, be made up again.

Finally, as the very least tribute, I dedicate the result of this effort to the late Yiannos Kranidiotis. Only days before his tragic death and that of his son Nicholas, he gave me the text he had written (possibly his very last work) for the Foreword of this book. That was our last meeting, at his home in Nicosia, in the presence of his son. I shall treasure the happy memories of the friendship that I was honoured to have been offered and which was based on our shared concern for the future of Cyprus and Hellenism. These memories will stay with me and will grow more vivid as efforts to resolve the Cyprus issue and come to an understanding with Turkey approach a successful outcome. Unfortunately, however, the historical coincidence of the presence in the Greek Foreign Ministry of a personality with Cypriot roots dealing with the Cyprus issue, as in the case of Yiannos Kranidiotis, cannot be repeated. And this makes the loss through his death even greater to Cyprus and Greece.

Costas Yennaris
Nicosia, March 2000

Chapter 1

How it All Began

When Great Britain approached Turkey during the 1950s, in order to provoke its interest in the future of Cyprus, the Turkish establishment's knowledge of the island was minimal. Frequent visits to Ankara by the small Turkish Cypriot leadership elite with the aim of awakening some interest on the part of the Turkish government were viewed more as an annoyance than a reason to instigate any kind of 'nationalist' activity, which was why these delegations always left empty-handed and disappointed. In those difficult times, particularly immediately after World War II, Turkey's military aspirations lay elsewhere. Its identification with the winners of the war – irrespective of and beyond the country's stance for the duration – and its participation in the sharing of the spoils of war took precedence over any other ambition.

The post-war scene had already begun to take shape under the terms and conditions of the Cold War. Turkey, too, had proceeded unhesitatingly with its choices, taking full advantage of its proximity to the Soviet Union and its strategic geographical position close to the energy resources of the Middle East so as to cash in handsomely on the United States' anti-Communist mania thanks to its identification with the Western camp. Its participation in NATO, which had just been approved, had opened doors, and prospects, which needed to be kept open at all costs for any eventuality. If its NATO allies were asking it to play a particular role in Cyprus, one which would be to its gain – at no cost and with no damage – so much the better. Furthermore, it would be seen to be serving its allies, a fact that it could exploit by developing at no cost its own prospects vis-à-vis the island.

The situation in Cyprus was very different then. Relations among the Turkish Cypriots had gone through many stages but they had never reached the point of having Turkish nationalism as their basis. From the signing of the Treaty of Lausanne onwards, the Turkish Cypriots had expressed their intense opposition to Kemal Ataturk and his agenda of reforms. They considered that the provisions of the treaty that Turkey had signed signified their abandonment, and as a result their opposition to Kemal Ataturk gradually turned into deep suspicion, which the British exploited fully for reasons of their own, just as they had exploited the change of tack by the Turkish Cypriot leadership elite towards the new governors of the island in order to maintain their participation in the administration and, consequently, to protect their incomes and, of course, their social position.

After the Treaty of Lausanne, the Turkish Commissioner in Cyprus, Asaf Bey, openly campaigned in favour of repatriation and the return of the Ottomans to Turkey. In the meantime, however, the colonial government in Cyprus became aware of the possibilities that might be offered in the future by a small ethnic minority in Cyprus and from that time the colonial administration began to plan moves that would enable it to control the island without any problems.

The provision in the Treaty of Lausanne for the repatriation of the Ottomans of Cyprus fully served the objectives of Kemal Ataturk at the time. His efforts were aimed at gathering together all the former Ottoman Muslim citizens of the Ottoman Empire who did not identify with one or other of the national states that had been created following the dissolution of the Empire within the geographical boundaries of the new Turkish state, as delineated in its so-called 'National Contract'. This concentration would allow him to get on with his reforms, undistracted by the problems of minorities outside the borders.

Under these circumstances, the Turkish Cypriots had no choice but to fall into the arms of the British, both to protect their religious rights, as they believed, but also in the hope that the new administration on the island would take advantage of their administrative capabilities.

The Arrival of the British

The cession of Cyprus to Great Britain in 1878 was an expression of the gradual decline of the Ottoman Empire. Exploiting fully the serious internal problems of the Ottomans, in particular their inability to control the militancy of the national liberation movements of the subjugated peoples and their unrestrained fear of a potential Russian attack, London revealed itself ready to assist if there were a serious and acceptable recompense. It thus secured Cyprus for a promise of defence aid to the Ottoman Empire if and when it should come under attack from the Russians. In Cyprus the British found a situation the exploitation of which led to choices and political practices in which one can trace the roots of everything that followed, culminating in the Turkish invasion of the island in 1974.

At the time, the Greeks of Cyprus welcomed the British more or less as liberators. This was not only due to the fact that Cyprus had passed from the hands of the Ottomans to those of a Christian state, nor even the prospect of an end to the oppression of the Ottoman establishment. Their enthusiasm stemmed mainly from the fatal participation of Lord Byron in the Greek Revolution, a fact that created expectations in the Greeks of Cyprus of a swift national vindication of their own.

Relief at Great Britain's taking over of Cyprus was also felt by the Ottomans of Cyprus, though for different reasons. The collapse of the Empire had signalled the end of one of the two factors which united the Ottomans. The other factor was religion but this was not strong enough to guarantee the internal continuity of the Ottomans of Cyprus with the new state of Turkey that would be created a few years hence. Essentially forgotten by the Porte during the last years of the Ottoman Empire, they had no social, political or financial ties amongst themselves which would have united them as a community. The elite, who had identified so far with the religion-centred Ottoman administration of the island, in which they participated, felt their position under threat. For this reason they approached the new governors of Cyprus in the hope of being allowed to maintain the privileges that emanated from their participation in the administration.

The miserable Ottoman masses could not identify with the aspirations of the island's elite. On the contrary, the end of the Ottoman government had created hopes and expectations for an improvement in their living conditions.

Contrary to what was happening in the Greek Cypriot community, the Ottoman community had no strong political institutions at the time with which all the Ottomans could identify and which could be vehicles of expression for whatever nationalism they might feel. In any case, they had been transported to Cyprus immediately after the Ottoman conquest of the island from vastly different regions and tribes of the Ottoman Empire. Moreover, even in the rest of the Ottoman Empire at the time, there was no distinct nationalist movement and vision with which they could identify, apart from those of the subjugated peoples. In these circumstances, it was impossible for any political organisation of the Ottomans of Cyprus to develop, especially since their education did not help at all in the cultivation of a 'national identity'. It was restricted to religious matters and provided those who were fortunate enough to receive it only the most basic knowledge required to be able to work in the administration.

The presence of the Ottomans nonetheless satisfied the new masters of the island. The constant activities of the Greek Cypriots aimed at their national vindication were led by the Church, which had a powerful and hierarchical organisation and was the framework within which their political organisation was developing. But the presence of the latter, one which aimed at uniting Cyprus with another state, caused the British to react since they could not control it, and this resulted in disagreements. The rivalry favoured, on the one hand, the development of nationalism among the Greek Cypriots and, on the other, a British change of attitude towards the Ottomans, especially towards their leadership elite, not only so that they might assist in the governance of the island, but also to act as a balancing factor. This was, of course, an instance of the implementation of the classic British formula of 'divide and rule', which was to lead to the phenomenon of British-led reactions by the Ottoman elite against every Greek Cypriot demand for respect for their national rights, for the history, culture and demographic realities of Cyprus. In every case, the British cited, among other things, the reactions of the Ottoman elite, which viewed the activities of the Greek Cypriots as a threat to it too. Their reaction, however, apart from serving the British, was more related to religious rather than political reasons. The prospect of the annexation of the island by a Christian state was not particularly attractive to the Ottoman elite, not least due to the fact that in such a case they would lose the institutional privileges that they enjoyed under British rule.

The reaction of the elite, examples of which can be found in the British archives and which have created the mistaken impression of a universal reaction by the Ottomans against the demands of the Greek Cypriots, had absolutely nothing to do with demonstrations of any kind of nationalism. The Ottoman elite was suspicious of Turkey itself once the Kemalist state had been created and it certainly favoured the continuation of British colonial rule of the island.

Annexation by Britain

The annexation of Cyprus by Britain in 1914 satisfied the Ottoman leadership group. As Michalis Attalides writes, at the time the idea had been circulating in London of turning Cyprus into a British protectorate and subsequently ceding it to Greece. The *kadhiz* (the senior religious judge), the mufti (religious leader) and the senior adviser of Evkaf (the Ottoman religious foundation) demanded the immediate annexation of the island by Britain so as to be freed from the intrigues of the Porte.

The mistrust of Turkey on the part of the island's Ottoman leadership continued after the annexation of Cyprus by Britain and also after the creation of the Turkish Republic by Kemal Ataturk, in other words after the appearance, development, spread and prevalence of Turkish nationalism. A typical reaction of the Ottoman elite is the well-known example from 1931: when the colonial government demanded and obtained the recall of the Greek Consul in Cyprus, accusing him of being involved in activities in favour of Enosis, the Ottomans immediately demanded the removal of the Turkish Consul, accusing him of being 'a nationalist and a Kemalist'.

It is interesting that, on Britain's annexation of Cyprus, the Turkish Cypriot community rejected all national or cultural links with Turkey. Equally interesting is the fact that, even after the foundation of the Republic of Turkey, the Turkish Cypriots viewed the reforms of Kemal Ataturk with mistrust and so chose as the most effective defence and protection of their religious identity – the only thing that interested them at the time – total identification with the colonial power and its local administration.

Turkish writers and scholars have explained this phenomenon as emanating from a feeling of abandonment after the annexation of Cyprus by Britain and an awareness of Turkey's weakness at the time. This argument is not at all persuasive and certainly fails to explain why the Ottomans of Cyprus bore no characteristics by which they might have formed a national identity, one that would have had much in common with a similar identity in Turkey. Nor were there any instances of 'nationalism', the only link with the Ottoman community being a religious one. Moreover, any involvement of this community in the events and developments emanating from the Turkish nationalism of Kemal Ataturk was naturally limited, due to the almost total lack of appropriate education and to the absence of all communication with the centres of Turkish nationalism at the time.

The education system of the Turkish Cypriots, over and above its religious character, did not contain elements that would bring about a spiritual and ideological development that would subsequently cultivate, spread and support a cultural and nationalist identity and, consequently, nationalism, as had happened in the case of the Greek Cypriots.

Only months after the arrival of the British, the Greek Cypriots published their first newspaper. It was an effort undertaken by distinguished members of the Greek community of Alexandria, begun before the British took over Cyprus and concluded afterwards. The first Greek newspaper on the island was called *Kypros* (*Cyprus*). One thousand copies of its first edition were published on August 29, 1878.

The first Turkish-language newspaper was published almost 10 years after the first appearance of *Kypros*. It was a weekly entitled *Sadet* and it came out in Arabic script on July 11, 1889 but ceased publication on November 14 of the same year after only 16 issues.

Prior to 1914, according to Michalis Attalides, the British had registered the circulation in Cyprus of 600 books, of which fewer than 50 were partly in Turkish. The rest were in Greek.

Until the official declaration of Cyprus as a Crown Colony in 1923, the Turkish Cypriot elite had become almost completely anglicised. This fact is acknowledged even today by Turkish Cypriot scholars such as Arif Hasan Tahsin, who notes that members of the elite Turkish Cypriot leadership had made themselves comfortable under the protection of the British and were fanatical supporters of British sovereignty in Cyprus.

An interesting point is the question of the language that many Turkish Cypriots used during British colonial rule. It confirms not only how strong relations were historically among the Greek Cypriots and Turkish Cypriots, but is a measure of the gap that existed between the Turkish Cypriots and the Kemalist state. Based on the population census of 1921 carried out by the British, Turkish Cypriot researcher Ahmed An writes:

> In the Nicosia district, 1,019 Turkish Cypriots had Greek as their mother tongue. In Paphos, the number was 350. According to the 1931 statistics, there were 1,004 Turkish Cypriots in Nicosia whose mother tongue was Greek, while in the Paphos district those whose mother tongue was Greek had increased to 521. In some villages, members of the Turkish population spoke Greek to one another. Moreover, in Nicosia, Famagusta and Paphos, Turkish Cypriots whose mother language was Turkish used Greek words and expressions when they spoke. By 1955, the Muslim villages whose residents spoke Greek were scattered throughout Cyprus. In these villages, the Muslims had the same customs and morals as the Greek Cypriots.

Chapter 2

Turkish Nationalism

The dismemberment of the Ottoman Empire on the basis of the national and cultural identity of its subjugated peoples had created the prerequisites for the success of Kemal Ataturk's nationalist revolution. The purpose of the revolution was not the safeguarding of the Ottoman Empire but the establishment of the Turkish Republic, which Ataturk in no way considered as the successor state of the multi-ethnic Ottoman Empire. At the height of the so-called 'Eastern question' in 1919, Ataturk clearly declared his intention to break the link with the Ottoman state, stating the following:

> The Ottoman Empire, which has lasted more than six hundred years, has reached the end of its life cycle. It is dead and the dead do not live again. The Ottoman governments have neither power nor determination. Consequently the Turkish nation must itself decide on its fate and plan its own future. The only way to achieve this aim is through the foundation of a new state, based on the sovereignty of the nation.[1]

In other words, Ataturk wanted to create a new state on the basis of the ethnic-cultural characteristics of the Turks, that is to say a national state of Turks, and consequently his intention was to separate the Turks from the multi-ethnic Ottoman Empire, irrespective of the fate of the Empire.

The descendants of Kemal Ataturk reviewed this position and they promoted Turkey not only as the heir-state of the Ottoman Empire but also as the heir to all the states and cultures that had preceded the Ottoman Empire in the land it occupied.[2]

Ataturk's nationalism aimed at the establishment of a Turkish state. Its boundaries would include all those who maintained the religious continuation of the Ottoman Empire but did not belong to the formerly subjugated peoples nor identify themselves with any of the national states that were created by the dissolution of the Ottoman Empire. It was no easy task, since a national identity had to be created, cultivated and developed among the Turkish nationals of the new state, a non-existent concept in the Ottoman Empire. This was not simply because the Ottomans identified almost exclusively with the ideological and administrative machinery of the Empire – the other link being religion – but because they were dispersed throughout the length and breadth of the Empire.

And yet Kemal Ataturk succeeded, helped by developments at the time, during which he was promoting his nationalist movement. The creation, on the founding of the Turkish Republic, of a territorial base contributed to this success. All his reforms aimed at the creation of this national conscience, even if it meant the enslavement and total subjugation of the ethnic minorities who found themselves within the borders of the new state (Kurds, Greeks, Arabs, Armenians, etc.). The dilemma they faced was a crude one: integration or annihilation.[3]

Nonetheless, however hard Ataturk may have tried to sever all political and ideological ties or identification with the Ottoman past, the ideological machinery of the Ottoman Empire took root anew and became the axis around which the Turkish state was founded and Turkish national identity developed.[4]

The basic aim of Ataturk's foreign policy[5] was 'the correction of certain problematic aspects of the Treaty of Lausanne'.[6] And this because, according to the long-standing Turkish view, certain provisions of the treaty had been imposed upon Turkey due to its weakness at the time of signing. This situation, according to the Turks, had created specific balances between Turkey and Greece and any upsetting of them would require a complete review of the whole body of the treaty. Among these 'weaknesses' were the 'grey areas' in the Aegean, which Turkish Prime Minister Mesut Yilmaz raised in May 1996, as well as the underhand occupation of Alexandretta in 1939.[7]

As recorded by the Turks, Kemal Ataturk's wish was to restrict 'Turkism' within the boundaries of the Turkish state. 'Although our nationalism,' he is reported to have said, 'loves all Turks with a feeling of deep fraternity, and although it desires with all its soul their fullest development, it recognises that its political activity must stop at the borders of the Turkish Republic.'[8]

Although Cyprus was outside the borders of the Turkish Republic and Turkey had given up all rights over the island, the Turks still noted Ataturk's aspirations in this direction, an expression of the chauvinistic, expansionist ideological machinery of the Turkish Republic. As Professor Dervis Manizade has written[9], in an address to Turkish army officers, Kemal ordered them to 'turn their attention to Cyprus, because this island is important to us.' As the Turkish professor writes, this was a speech given after the annexation of Alexandretta, which is why Ataturk had added: 'Cyprus' turn has not yet come.'[10]

Particularly after the Second World War, when a new burst of 'Panturkism' was noted, those outside the borders of the Turkish Republic were referred to more and more as 'subjugated Turks'.[11]

It is in this context that one needs to examine Turkish policy on Cyprus. It is no accident that, even when Cyprus was still a British colony, Ankara's view was that, if the status of the island were to change through the withdrawal of the British, it should be returned to Turkey as the heir of the Ottoman Empire.[12]

Turkish nationalism began to spread to the Turkish Cypriots when the latter, under British rule, were too weak to resist the modernisation of their education. And it was assisted to the maximum when the religious foundation Evkaf, which was responsible for the education of the Turkish Cypriots, was placed under British control. The British drew its employees of the colonial administration from the Turkish Cypriot community, but its demands and administrative needs could not be satisfied by the religion-centred education provided by Evkaf. Ataturk's educational reforms were used by the colonial government to persuade the Turkish Cypriots to review their stance on the subject of education. And, despite their original reaction and mistrust, more in order to maintain the favour of the British, the Turkish Cypriots gradually began to use Ataturk's teaching materials. Over time, this exposure (and acceptance) of Ataturk's nationalist propaganda in the schools brought about social and poltical results. It filled, effectively the gap between national identity and national identification and gave the Turkish Cypriots an alternative choice to being attached to the British.[13]

This development, combined with the Turkish view of those Muslims outside Turkey who did not identify ethnically with any of the states created on the territory of the Ottoman Empire, is the one aspect of Turkish foreign policy on which the ideology of the Ottoman Empire and Kemalist Turkey still coincide to this day.

These communities of Muslims, found mainly in the Balkans (in Greece, Bulgaria, Romania, Hungary, Yugoslavia and Albania), were considered and are still considered 'strategic minorities' in the sense of the potential right that their existence gives Turkey to 'be interested' in territory outside its own borders. This theory is accompanied by the slogan 'wherever there is a Turk, Turkey must also be'.[14]

Turkish political practice throughout the history of the Republic of Turkey, in relation to almost all the former Ottoman lands, has essentially been guided by this dogma. A consistent aim has been the redelineation of borders and it is promoted with an openness that is hard to believe, especially by the so-called cultured, multifaceted and complex public opinion of the West. Who, for example, could believe his ears on hearing Turkish Prime Minister Mesut Yilmaz stating in English in front of the TV cameras in Brussels on June 4, 1996, that it was enough for someone to declare that 'I dispute the status of Gavdos' for the Greek island to be considered 'an object of political dispute' and consequently 'a disputed area'. By the same logic, why should one not dispute the status of the Aegean islands or the Peloponnese or of Vienna or any other part of the former Ottoman Empire? Turkey feels that it is perfectly entitled to do so, and not only in relation to Greek territory.

Mousouli and Kirkuk, the oil-bearing regions of neighbouring Iraq, have always been in Turkey's sights, on the pretext that Turks live in the area.[15] When, in February 1980, members of the Turkish-speaking minority (of Turkmen) were hanged for revolutionary activity in the area, the newspaper *Terzuman*, a mouthpiece of the former President of Turkey, Suleyman Demirel, wrote:

> Kirkuk and Mousouli are located within the borders determined in the 'National Council' [of Kemal Ataturk]. If by the Treaty of Lausanne we gave up our rights to these areas, we did so because we considered Iraq a fraternal country. Everyone knows that Turkey has a share of the oil of Kirkuk.[16]

This approach was explained in greater detail by the former Foreign Minister of Turkey, Ihsan Caglayangil:

> A million Turks live in Mousouli. It was a mistake to give it up in the past. Because Turkey, in 1925, was not strong, it was forced to give it up to the British. This oil-rich area next to our borders has always been of vital importance to Turkey. There have always been those who wished to change our decision on the abandonment of Kirkuk and Mousouli. Among them Turkes' National Action Party. But today's circumstances are not favourable to Turkey. There are likely to be adventures. We should not have to keep this a national secret.[17]

The evidence behind the Turkish intentions is often provided by Turkish university lecturers mobilised by the Foreign Ministry for this purpose. Aidin Yalcin, a professor of political science and Editor of the magazine *Yeni Forum*, writes:

> The subject of Kirkuk is of particular significance to the recent history of Turkey. For Turkey it resembles the case of Cyprus. It was located within the national borders but in 1925 we were obliged to hand it over to Britain. Now it belongs to Iraq. When the status of an area is altered, there may be a case for reviewing the principles that were accepted in older agreements.

This Turkish philosophy was understood perfectly by a British newspaper, which had no difficulty in concluding that:

> Turkey now sees Cyprus and the Dodecanese Islands as post-Ottoman regions inhabited by Greeks whose status remains vague since they continue to cause politico-military problems to the Turkish Republic.[18]

Only against the background of these realities can one comprehend the developments in Cyprus that have led to the present situation. One might indeed say that, based on this prehistory, regarding which evidence can be presented in greater detail, it is possible to recognise the final objectives of Turkey vis-à-vis the Cyprus issue and to judge various gestures and choices from the standpoint of this final Turkish aim.

Developments in the Turkish Cypriot community, from the moment the British in one way or another exposed it to the nationalist propaganda of Kemal Ataturk, have followed the doctrine of Turkish nationalism to the letter. Its effect, it should be noted, was not only reinforced by Britain's short-sighted policy and by a variety of occasional foreign allies of Turkey for reasons of promoting their own interests, but, unfortunately, by the mistakes of the Greek side and chiefly by its inability, even today, to study and correctly decipher Turkey's intentions. The issue has always been to look for them and to relate them to Turkish practice. The question of containing or preventing the success of Turkey's strategic objectives would be a matter of studying the facts and the drawing up of a strategy that would succeed in its aim; this is an element that continues to be sought, far from the mere handling of problems created by Turkey.

Prior to 1920 the requirements and conditions for the development of Turkish Cypriot nationalism simply did not exist. Beyond the fact that Turkish or Kemalist nationalism had not been expressed previously, the conditions prevailing on the island until that time delayed even longer the expression of any nationalist tendency among the Turkish Cypriots.[19]

On the contrary, these very conditions favoured an alliance between the wretched masses of Greek Cypriots and Turkish Cypriots against the cause of their economic oppression – on the one hand the Church and, on the other, the Ottoman (later British) administration, which was manned by members of first the Ottoman and then the Turkish Cypriot elite.[20]

The conditions in which Turkish Cypriot nationalism could develop came into being with the Turkish Cypriots' acceptance of Kemal Ataturk's educational reforms. The new educational curriculum was based more on political than religious motives. The basic purpose of the history books was 'the development of a strongly-felt Turkish patriotism' and a unified awareness of Turkism.[21]

Many Turkish writers consider that the treatment of the Turkish Cypriots by the British administration of the island at this time contributed to a great extent to their change of attitude towards Kemal's theories. Pierre Oberling writes:

> The British administration took Turkish Cypriot support for granted and in some instances behaved more harshly towards the Turkish Cypriot minority than it did towards the Greek Cypriot majority.[22]

The following are mentioned as examples of such behaviour:

- On the pretext that the Muslims did not have alternative procedures to the appointment of their religious leader by the Ottoman governments, the British took on this responsibility themselves.

- In 1921 they forbade the Turkish Cypriots to import school textbooks from Turkey.

- In 1927 they abolished the post of head *kadhiz.*

- In 1928 they transformed Evkaf into a service of the British administration.

- In 1929 they removed the responsibility for education from the Turkish Cypriot community.[23]

Nonetheless, the state of the Turkish Cypriot masses continued to be one of confusion. The Ottoman Empire had collapsed and been taken apart, Cyprus was occupied by the British and their future was uncertain. Any political activities and nationalist demonstrations were restricted to the circles of the leadership elite, which was expressing its concern about the activities of the Greek Cypriots in favour of *enosis*. An association was founded called *Osmanli Kiraathanesi* in which the leadership attempted to undertake some political activity.[24] Through this association, efforts were made to publish a newspaper in which the Greek Cypriots' activities in favour of *enosis* would be opposed. And indeed, on December 25, 1891, *Zaman* (*Time*) was published, setting out its aims on its first page:

> A struggle against the British colonial government, the maintenance of a national conscience, a struggle against the Greek Cypriot newspapers that print propaganda in favour of *Enosis* and the preservation of the Turkish language.[25]

It is important to note that at this time, between the First World War and the founding of the Turkish Republic, the Turkish Cypriot masses had little to do with the activities of the elite of their community. On the other hand, this elite was being torn apart by factions identifying with opposing groups in the bleeding Ottoman Empire: in favour of the Sultan, the Young Turks, and the British administration.

An article by the chief editor of the newspaper *Islam* describes graphically the situation at the time, by way of an analysis of the inability of the Turkish Cypriot newspapers to survive:

> I have looked into the reasons why the Ottoman newspapers that have been published so far have not affected the Muslims of the island in a positive way, in the same way that the Greek Cypriot press has affected its readership. I have finally discovered why. It is quite obvious that each newspaper belongs to a particular faction. Each newspaper supports its own faction, and always in an

> exaggerated way. It will refer to the donations and the good works of those in charge of the faction it supports, to their successes and the like. If there is any room left in the newspaper, it will be used to attack the opposing faction. If there is still more room, journalist insults journalist. Finally, if there is space, the paper publishes local and foreign news. When there is no news, it publishes jokes… This is perhaps the reason why people have gradually stopped paying attention to the newspapers. They certainly wouldn't pay for them.[26]

This situation within the Turkish Cypriot community, and the disappointment of the Muslims of the island, would grow worse following the signing of the Treaty of Lausanne, by which any political links between the new Turkish state and Cyprus were finally cut and the island became a British colony.

The leadership elite and its attempts to form some kind of Turkish Cypriot political organisation would be frustrated until the end of the Second World War, when these efforts took on a new dynamic.

Chapter 3

First Attempts at Political Organisation by the Turkish Cypriots

The confusion and uncertainty about the future felt by the Muslim population of Cyprus, because of the British takeover on the one hand and the dissolution of the Ottoman Empire on the other, can be seen in the fluctuations in its size. The Muslim population, as registered by the British, fell from 24.4% in 1881 to 18.5% in 1931.[1] During the same period a reduction in the growth rate of the Ottoman population was observed, while before and after it the rate was the same as that of the Greek Cypriots.[2]

This reduction may be considered natural, a result of the change in the island's status and the decision by many Ottomans to leave precisely because of this change. Indeed, it should be considered a particularly small reduction, given the attempts made by the Kemalist state to persuade the Turkish Cypriots to 'return' to Turkey following the signing of the Treaty of Lausanne, and this fact bears yet more testimony to the mistrust that the Turkish Cypriots felt towards the Kemalist establishment.

In reality, as may be seen from articles in the Turkish Cypriot press, many of the 7,000 Turkish Cypriots[3] who, according to the Turks, responded to the Kemalist state's invitation to settle in Turkey later returned to Cyprus because of the poor living conditions they had been forced to endure there,[4] while their expectations of settling in properties that had been abandoned by Greeks after the Asia Minor catastrophe were dashed.[5]

The size of the population then stabilised at more or less the same level. This was partly due to the mistrust the Turkish Cypriots felt for the Kemalist state and Ataturk's reforms, and partly to their adherence to the colonial administration, which, from the outset and for its own reasons and purposes, took care to maintain the privileged relationship that the Muslims had enjoyed under Ottoman rule.

At the start of their governorship, the British more less maintained the administrative organisation of the Ottomans in Cyprus, a fact that, according to Michalis Attalides,[6] contributed to the development of class solidarity between the two communities at various levels – at that of the financial, commercial and administrative elite, and mainly at that of the disenfranchised peasants.[7]

The political activity of the Turkish Cypriots at the start of the British colonial era – if one can refer to it as such – revolved around the business of Evkaf, which identified completely with the new rulers of the island. Immediately after the annexation of Cyprus, the British placed the foundation under their control, with the appointment of a Turkish Cypriot – always someone loyal to them – and a Briton to handle Evkaf's affairs. This led to the Turkish Cypriot masses being alienated from the affairs of Evkaf, for the future of which only the community's small elite in Nicosia worked.

By contrast, the leading role of the Church within the Greek Cypriot community remained untouched, and as a result the phenomenon arose of the colonial administration coming into constant conflict with the Christian ethnarchy (with which the Greek Cypriots identified), both on issues concerning relations between the Greek Cypriots and the colonial regime as well as on the unwavering demand for the national vindication of Cyprus, while the Muslim Evkaf identified completely with the British.

Before it was announced that Cyprus was to be annexed as a Crown Colony, the Turkish Cypriot leadership, comprising the chief *kadhiz*, the mufti and the advisors of Evkaf, requested the annexation of Cyprus 'to save the island from the intrigues of the Porte', and following annexation they visited the British governor in order to declare their loyalty to the crown and their disapproval of the Ottoman government's decision to fight on the side of the Axis powers against Britain and her allies.[8] By then, the Ottoman or Turkish Cypriot elite had reached a point of almost total anglicisation.[9]

This stance would later be criticised strongly by the Turkish Cypriot leadership. Rauf Denktash has complained that 'we did not want to believe that the British would one day leave Cyprus and so we supported a continuation of the status quo.'[10]

This identification was not, as mentioned above, the response of Turkish Cypriot 'nationalism' to that of the Greek Cypriots.[11] Basically that of the elite, it was an act of defence against the Greek Cypriots' demand for the integration of Cyprus with Greece, a Christian state. In other words, the reasons were more religious than nationalist. This can be seen from the Turkish Cypriot elite's demand that British sovereignty should be maintained over the island,[12] as an arrangement that would safeguard its religious interests, not those of a nationalist or racial nature.

Had the opposition to the Greek Cypriot demand for *enosis* been 'nationalist', logically there ought to have been some identification with the Kemalist state, which, at the time, was based exclusively on Turkish nationalism.

1931: A Turning Point

The British found Cyprus in a dreadful economic state, and yet they showed no interest in improving it. Destitution was what united the Greek Cypriots and the Ottomans in joint uprisings against the Ottoman Empire.[13] It also helped that the Turkish Cypriots lived scattered throughout the island, among and with the Greek Cypriots. Poverty frequently overcame racial and religious differences and led to joint struggles for a living wage.[14]

Living conditions, mainly those of the rural population, both Greek Cypriot and Ottoman, were comparable to those prevalent in England during the 15th and 16th centuries. The rural population accounted for 80.5% of the total while arable land represented only three-fifths of the total. The rest belonged to the colonial government, the Church and Evkaf.[15] In 1921, 65% of the population was illiterate. In 1922, the basic daily wage for labourers was one shilling and 8 piastres and for women one shilling. Together, the two wages were enough to buy three or four loaves of bread.[16]

During World War I, the colonial government imposed price controls on agricultural products while leaving all other commerce free. As a result, agricultural debts of £100,000 in 1914 had soared to £3,000,000 by the end of the war, on which farmers paid interest at 12% or more. Between 1920 and 1926, there were 16,559 forced sales of agricultural land totalling 250,000 acres and almost 3,000 homes.[17]

On the other hand, British authority over the island did not permit the creation of political parties if the mission of such parties was to take power, since all authority rested in the hands of the British High Commissioner. Even the legislature, according to the constitution of 1882, was controlled by the colonial government, since on the Legislative Council 'non-Muslims', as the Greek Cypriot majority was described by the colonial administration, elected nine representatives and the Muslims three, with another six members appointed by the High Commission from the ranks of the senior civil servants who were British – with the casting vote in the frequent occurrence of a tied vote between the nine 'non-Muslims' and the nine-vote alliance of the Muslims and the British civil servants[18] belonging to the British governor.

All political activity at the start of British colonial rule occurred within the process of selecting the representatives on the Legislative Council. Any dispute among the Greek Cypriot candidates concerned mainly the intensity with which they pursued the demand for *enosis*, while among the candidates of the Turkish Cypriot elite it was all a question of how opposed they were to *enosis*.

There were two camps among the Greek Cypriots: those who were viewed as 'conciliatory' and those who were 'intransigent' or 'nationalist'.[19] The former supported *enosis* but acknowledged that insurmountable obstacles existed and therefore chose to focus their attention on efforts to increase the freedoms enjoyed by the people under colonial conditions. They were also aware of the presence of the Turkish Cypriots. The demand of those in the second Greek Cypriot camp was immediate *enosis*, and they described the others as 'collaborators with the colonists' and 'the gravediggers of *enosis*'.[20]

Under such circumstances, ordinary people were extremely interested when the Legislative Council dealt with issues that concerned their living conditions. And, despite the difficulties, joint memoranda were issued in 1885 and 1886 on the abolition of the 'tribute', and again in 1903 concerning the tabling of economic demands, and a second joint memorandum was tabled the same year on the divisive policy being implemented by the British.[21]

In the period prior to 1925 the 'intransigents' had prevailed, and this, in conjunction with the return to Cyprus and the activities of many young people who had studied in Athens,[22] where their national feelings had been stimulated, led to a flourishing of the *Enosis* movement.

The same reasons were, to some extent, responsible for the appearance of supporters of Communist ideology around 1922. [23]

In the first issue of the Cyprus Communist Party's publication *Neos Anthropos*, support was expressed for cooperation between Greek Cypriots and Turkish Cypriots, not only against the colonial administration but also in favour of communal justice. The party adhered to this policy in the following years.[24]

It is worth noting how, in 1924, on the initiative of lawyer Kyriakos Rossides, a rural conference was organised at Lefkoniko with the participation of both Greek and Turkish Cypriots as a result of the mass joint gathering in Limassol in 1922 to demand improvements to conditions in rural areas.[25] In July 1925, a second rural conference was organised, at which the Rural Greco-Turkish party was founded and speakers from both communities warmly supported the cooperation between Greeks and Turks on the Legislative Council. This conference also approved a memorandum on resolving serious rural problems, which authorised Rossides to draw up, in collaboration with a Turkish Cypriot of his choosing, a joint ballot paper for the elections of members of the Legislative Council in October 1925.[26]

The Greek military expedition disaster in Asia Minor and Greco-Turkish rapprochement that reached a peak in 1930 demanded a change of climate in Cyprus. On the one hand, efforts were being strengthened for joint Greek and Turkish Cypriot action on the basis of the mutual serious problems they were facing, and on the other the 'intransigents', having realised the unfeasibility in the circumstances of their demand for immediate *enosis*, turned their attention – without abandoning the *enosis* vision – back in the direction of broadening political freedoms, at a time when the authoritarian stance of the colonial establishment was leading to political persecution, excessive taxation and attempts to control education in both communities.

In the 1930 elections to the Legislative Council, a seat was won by Misirlade Necati Noley, a Turkish Cypriot on whom the colonial establishment could not rely entirely. As a result, the balance in the council was upset and a motion for new taxes was rejected. The governor's reaction was to suspend the work of the council indefinitely.[27]

The general reaction caused by the colonial administration's oppressive measures was growing daily and it led to a general outcry, with the first demand, as always, being that of *enosis*.[28]

> On October 21, 1931, the people of Nicosia took to the streets and in front of thousands of residents the priest of Phaneromeni church, Father Dionysios Kykkotis, waved the Greek flag and declared a revolution. The people set off for Government House where demonstrators clashed with the police. Amid the disturbances, stones were thrown and a number of cars were overturned in flames. The wooden-built Government House quickly caught fire and was

> reduced to ashes. The revolt spread to other towns and in the villages the people formed committees. Several more government buildings were set on fire and acts of sabotage were carried out against the government. In all, six people were killed and many others injured. No member of the government was affected, however – all the victims were Cypriots. The government brought in troops from Egypt and in ten days it had stifled the revolution. The revolutionaries were harshly punished. Ten people were exiled and more than 2,000 imprisoned. Harsh, oppressive measures followed. These restrictions applied to Greeks and Turks alike and affected all expressions of individual and social life, education and politics.[29]

In the light of Greco-Turkish friendship, as inaugurated by Venizelos and Ataturk following the developments that led to the 1931 uprising, notable cooperation was achieved between the Greek Cypriot and Turkish Cypriot members of the Legislative Council on the promotion of solutions to the island's serious economic and social problems,[30] a fact that caused the colonial establishment concern.

On the other hand, the extent of the uprising had indicated how far the Greeks of Cyprus were willing to go to fight to throw off their colonial bonds and obtain national vindication.[31]

These two facts contributed to the imposition of a dictatorship in the period after the uprising with strict measures that affected both communities. And, of course, the Turkish Cypriot leadership saw, on the one hand, that it could exploit this fact so as to appear that it was supporting the Turkish Cypriots, who were being punished despite not having taken part in the uprising, and on the other that it could cosy up to the British administration. Thus the same newspapers, for instance, that had praised the cooperation between the two communities were now aggressively attacking the Greek Cypriots. In this, they were perhaps helped by the stance of the Greek government of the time.

The reaction of the Turkish Cypriots, as expressed in the Turkish Cypriot press, is described by Petros Stylianou in his doctoral thesis.[32]

> The first reaction from the Turkish Cypriot side to the events of 1931 came in an article in the Turkish Cypriot newspaper *Masum Millet* that contained a devastating criticism of the Greek Cypriot leadership. The article states,

among other things: 'It is quite clear that these condemnable actions by the Greek Cypriot leadership will ultimately destroy the harmony[33] that exists among people on the island.' The newspapers drew the attention of the Greeks to the fact that the neutral stance of the Turkish Cypriot community between the Greek Cypriot community and the British administration did not mean that the Turkish Cypriots would always remain dispassionate, cool observers of the dramatic political developments in the country, 'ready to accept the discipline of the winner'. Finally, it made clear that under no circumstances should anyone have the mistaken impression that the Muslim community was not interested in taking a stand should the dilemma ever arise between accepting British or Greek administration.

'In reality we are not at all neutral. We are fanatically against *Enosis*. The British administration is sine qua non for us. It is impossible for the Turks to live on the island without the presence of the British.' [...] A few days later, on November 13, 1931, Storrs [Sir Ronald Storrs, then Governor of Cyprus] sent to the Minister for the Colonies, Sir Philip Cunlife Lister, the November 7 article from *Masum Millet*. Storrs took the opportunity to clarify that the Turkish Cypriot newspaper, which had been launched at the beginning of the year, had begun publication with a sort of anti-government policy but in recent weeks had undergone 'a progressive change'.[34] The rapid suppression of this stance, the harsh, vengeful measures on behalf of the authorities, the sending into exile of the leaders of the Greek Cypriot community and the heavy shadow of the colonial troops, would bring the familiar results, consequences and syndromes: the movement to the side of the 'winners', not only by the leaders of the Turkish minority whose collaboration with the Greek Cypriot community had not, in any case, had a chance to develop or become more specific, but also of the leaders of the other minorities, such as the Maronites, for instance, and finally the leaders themselves – those who had not been exiled or isolated to the villages – of the Greek Cypriot side.

Five days after the publication of the article in *Masum Millet*, on November 12, another article appeared in the Turkish Cypriot newspaper *Secuz*. In this piece, *Secuz*, which gave it the title 'Can Hesitation be Overcome?' accused the British administration of encouraging the Greeks' policy for *Enosis*, questioned its ability to secure the lives and property of the Turkish population and predicted a black future.[35]

Munir Bey, a Turkish Cypriot member of the Executive Council, proved to be an expected ally of the colonial administration. According to Petros Stylianou:

> Munir submitted a document to Lister, the Minister for the Colonies via the Cypriot government, in which he stressed the opposition of the Muslim community to any change to the status quo in Cyprus. He succeeded in gathering the signatures of Turkish Cypriots from 218 Cypriot villages which were either exclusively Turkish or mixed.[36]

The First Turkish Cypriot Organisations

It was around Evkaf and its business that the first effort was made to create a communal organisation of Turkish Cypriots, which would not only be a vehicle for its own political expression but would also deal with the economic problems which, in the case of the Turkish Cypriot community, were made more acute by its inability to escape the lazy habits of the Ottoman era.[37] The identification of the wretched Turkish Cypriot masses with the Greek Cypriots was especially worrying to the Turkish Cypriot leadership, whose consistent aim was the reduction of Greek Cypriot influence on the ordinary Turkish Cypriots and an increase in its own.[38]

When the British took over the administration of Cyprus in 1878, Evkaf was controlled by a representative of the British administration and one appointed by the Ottoman government. Following the cession of Cyprus to Great Britain in 1925, Evkaf was turned into a department of the colonial government, administered by a member of the colonial administration and a Turkish Cypriot appointed by the colonial administration who was, in essence, the head of the department. A permanent demand of the Turkish Cypriot leadership at the time was that the administration and control of Evkaf should belong exclusively to the Turkish Cypriot community.[39]

The head of Evkaf had a significant influence on the Turkish Cypriot community, due mainly to his authority over issues of interest to all the Turkish Cypriots. He exercised this influence chiefly through his control of the leaders of the Turkish villages and communities throughout Cyprus.

In 1930, elections were held for the selection of the three Turkish Cypriot members of the Legislative Council established by the British.[40]

In Nicosia a Turkish Cypriot was elected, who would normally have been the candidate proposed by Evkaf, which was controlled by the British. In 1930, however, the Evkaf candidate was beaten by the 'independent' Necati Ozcan, generally considered to have been the first to express Kemalist nationalism in Cyprus. Of course, it was no accident that he was elected in Nicosia, where the Turkish Cypriot elite was concentrated and on whom he could rely for support.

Following his electoral success, Ozcan attempted to form a faction that would oppose the one that expressed itself through Evkaf and was controlled by its British-appointed head. To this end, he organised a conference[41] that took place on May 1, 1931, with the participation of 200 Turkish Cypriots from all over Cyprus.

The previous month, lawyer Can Mehmet Rifat had published a newspaper entitled *Masum Millet Gazetesi* (*Newspaper of an Innocent People*) with the purpose of 'exposing the legal transgressions of the colonial administration'.[42] The newspaper described the conference as 'a national congress' from which a nine-member Central Council emerged with the task of dealing with issues concerning the Turkish Cypriots, and specifically education, Evkaf, the religious Muslim courts and the appointment of the mufti by the governor.[43]

This effort collapsed when the colonial administration reacted by announcing that it did not recognise the Central Council.

The Foundation of KATAK

The 1931 uprising by the Greek Cypriots led to the colonial administration's imposition of so-called 'Palmerocracy', essentially a dictatorship that sidelined the restricted political rights of the Cypriots. The economic problems of the masses worsened under a regime that left no room for reaction. In the years that followed, some Turkish intellectuals appeared on the scene who maintained contact with nationalist Turkey and the ideas of Kemal Ataturk. These intellectuals remained cut off from the mass of ordinary Turkish Cypriots[44] but it is a fact that gradually there grew in Cyprus a hard core of Kemalists who were the vehicle of Turkish nationalism in Cyprus.

Among them were Fazil Kuchuk,[45] Rauf Denktash and journalist Remzi Ocan, the publisher since 1920 of the newspaper *Soz*. When Ocan died in 1940, his newspaper closed, just as *Masum Millet Gazetesi* had done, and this led Fazil Kuchuk, encouraged by the then Turkish Consul,[46] to go ahead with the publication of the newspaper *Halkin Sesi* (*Voice of the People*).

All the indications are that Fazil Kuchuk and the other Kemalist intellectuals changed their tactics vis-à-vis the Turkish Cypriot masses. The initial stance of the Turkish Cypriot elite was one of total identification with the colonial establishment, with the basic aim of securing their religious rights. But now they appeared as defenders of the political rights of the Turkish Cypriots against the colonial administration. And the nationalist propaganda that had been the basic aim and activity of the Turkish Cypriot elite was now, on the one hand, hidden and on the other appeared to offer a way out to the oppressive stance of the colonial administration.

The preparations for the creation of a vehicle of political expression for the Turkish Cypriots took place mainly in Nicosia, where most of the leadership elite was concentrated. These procedures were speeded up by a decision by the British to permit the holding of municipal elections in April 1943. Faced by such a prospect, two groups were formed[47] with the purpose of taking part in the elections for the Nicosia Municipal Council. At the head of one was Fazil Kuchuk and the group adopted the name 'People's Party' without ever actually being formed as a party. Its basic pre-election proclamation was 'to save our national entity and restore the violated rights of the Turkish people'.[48]

The chasm dividing the leadership circle of the elite from the masses of the Turkish Cypriots was noted by Kuchuk himself, who, in a newspaper article, attempted to explain this phenomenon:[49]

> For many years there has been a Turkish Cypriot community whose members are unconnected and disorganised. Who is responsible for this situation? We have to admit that blame does not lie with the [British] government or the other communities. We the Turks are ourselves responsible because we have not managed to benefit from the rights given to us by the government from the beginning.[50]

Heading the other group was Necati Ozcan, who accused his rivals of being indifferent to the real problems facing his fellow Muslims, reminding them that he alone had fought from the beginning of the 1930s for a solution to these problems: 'We alone can support the rights of the Turkish community, which today finds itself in the state of a minority.'[51]

The Kuchuk group eventually won four seats on the Nicosia Municipal Council. This was a serious step in the direction of creating a political vehicle for the Turkish Cypriots.

With his newspaper as his main propaganda outlet and organising tool, Fazil Kuchuk proceeded with other Turkish Cypriot intellectuals to found the minority's first political organisation, *Kibris Adasi Turk Azinligi Kurumu* (Association of the Turkish Minority of Cyprus), known by its acronym KATAK, in April 1943.[52]

The Turkish Cypriot historian and researcher, Hasmet Gurkan,[53] argues that the establishment of KATAK was a result of encouragement by the British who were attempting to use the Turkish Cypriots as a balance against the Greek Cypriots' struggle for *enosis*. The same view is shared by Arif Tahsin[54] and Osman Orek.[55]

As Iacovos Tenedios[56] notes, at the time the colonial administration was represented in Evkaf by the Turkish Cypriot Mehmet Munir,[57] whose requests for 'personal favours' were rejected by the British on account of his reduced influence over the Turkish Cypriots. They proposed that he first regain his standing, evidently through the foundation of KATAK. Despite the mutual dislike between him and the nationalist circles of the Turkish Cypriot elite in Nicosia, Munir approached them and discussed the foundation of KATAK with them. The nationalists responded positively, presumably because Munir had convinced them that the British identified with them in their dealings with the Greek Cypriots' movement for national vindication. And it may be considered a certainty that these nationalist circles were not relying solely on the word of Munir, whom they viewed as a man of the British. They must have received something much more specific from the British themselves which confirmed the mutual nature of their ambitions. This version of events is reinforced by the rapid spread of KATAK throughout Cyprus, while previous efforts had shown that such an occurrence was almost impossible and could only have been achieved with help from the British, who had the ability to move quickly around the island, and, with their permission, through the use of Evkaf organisation.

The very first meeting of KATAK took place on April 18, 1943, with 76 people present. The appearance at the meeting of Turkish Cypriot intellectuals who opposed British administration of Evkaf – through the British representative in

Evkaf – created an image of unity among the elite, which had a positive impression on the Turkish Cypriots in the large urban centres.

At the meeting, Munir promised – presumably after reaching an understanding with the British – financial support for Evkaf's efforts, but he clarified – again, presumably, at the insistence of the British – that this depended on the organisation not going against colonial laws in its activities.

It is interesting to note that the nationalists insisted that the organisation should become a vehicle for political activity and not be restricted to sending off telegrams of complaint about what the Greek Cypriots were up to. They also demanded that the organisation be used as a means of bringing economic development to the Turkish Cypriots.

KATAK was controlled by the conservative group of the leadership elite, which strongly pushed the line of 'loyalty to the Crown' above all. As a result, the image of unity was not only false and misleading but any expectations created by the founding of the organisation were also proved false.

Ihsan Ali[58] mentions that in Nicosia there was strong rivalry between Kuchuk and Necati Ozcan for control of the organisation and both were forced to resign. Kuchuk, however, immediately proceeded to form his own party, the *Kibris Turk Milli Birlik Partisi* (Turkish Cypriot National Unity Party). The party never managed to gain acceptance with the masses of ordinary Turkish Cypriots, but became an outlet for a restricted circle of intellectuals that was trying to work out and determine its 'national role' in relation to Turkey, which was still indifferent to Cyprus and to the Turkish Cypriots. The colonial administration was similarly indifferent to the ambitions and nationalist aims of this elite. Its mission, according to the colonial administration's view of things at the time, was limited to serving strictly local and restricted aims and managing the administration itself. Nonetheless, the party began to create an environment which attracted ambitious young intellectuals of the community who were searching for ways of achieving social recognition and political development.

As Osman Orek[59] has noted, Sir Mehmet Munir was behind Kuchuk's decision to form a party, on behalf of the British.

There followed the founding of the *Istiklar Partisi* (Independence Party) by Kuchuk's political rival Necati Ozcan, who, as Iacovos Tenedios says, was in contact with – and had the support of – Ismet Inonu, leader of the Republican Popular Party in Turkey.[60]

Trade Unionism

One of the young intellectuals rallying around Fazil Kuchuk was Rauf Denktash,[61] who took responsibility for the virtually non-existent trade union organisation that Kuchuk had attempted to found. This organisation remained on the fringe for many years, an indication of the gap dividing the ordinary Turkish Cypriots from the leadership elite. The Turkish Cypriot workers had always preferred to develop their union activities and demand their rights through the ranks of the Pancyprian Labour Federation (PEO) rather than through the union organisation formed by the Turkish Cypriot leadership.

The first attempts at developing union activity were made immediately after World War I but they originated with urban politicians whose main aim was to form associations that would offer them political support.[62] Their activities went no further than issuing worker-friendly statements, which was partly due to the lack of legislation allowing union activity. In essence the jurisdiction of unions over claims to rights was not recognised.[63] There was, of course, a reaction from the employers, who hid behind the veil of the needs of the 'national struggle'.[64]

The first unions started to appear in Limassol in 1917 with the establishment of the Builders' Union. Others followed in Limassol and elsewhere but the effort seems to have taken on particular strength after the formation in 1925 of the Communist Party of Cyprus.[65]

The October Revolution in Russia and the founding of socialist groups contributed to the culmination of efforts to form real unions, especially in Limassol, which was then viewed as the island's 'labour town'.[66]

Turkish Cypriots were active in all these efforts, and several were elected to the union's administrative committees.[67]

During the next phase of the union movement's organisation, the unions were housed beneath the labour centres that had been established in all towns prior to the October Revolution. The dictatorship that had been imposed after the 1931 uprising led to the persecution of the unions and their members, many of whom – Greek Cypriots and Turkish Cypriots – were arrested and imprisoned.[68]

In 1932, under circumstances of general oppression, a law on unions was adopted and, within this illiberal legislation,[69] efforts were made to organise workers on an island-wide basis. In 1939, Famagusta was the venue for the first Pancyprian Trade Union Congress with the participation of 101 representatives of 3,389 regular members of various unions from all over Cyprus. The Congress elected a five-member committee whose task was to prepare a resolution/declaration of the demands and aims of the workers.[70]

In 1941, the second Pancyprian Trade Union Congress was held in Nicosia, with the participation of 194 representatives of 7,500 members belonging to 62 unions, which ended in the formation of the Pancyprian Union Committee (PSE).[71]

Throughout the period of the formation of the trade union movement, working conditions led to genuine conflict between the workers – Greek Cypriots and Turkish Cypriots – and the economic-political establishment, resulting in the victimisation of the pioneers – both Greek Cypriot and Turkish Cypriot – of these movements, such as, for instance, the strikes by Nicosia builders in 1934, by shoemakers in 1935, Limassol builders in 1938 and Nicosia builders again in 1939.[72]

This same period, however, also saw the development of a strong anti-Communist movement on the island, which was particularly encouraged by the colonial administration. Far right nationalist elements associated the struggle for Cyprus' national vindication with anti-Communist hysteria and attempted to undermine the union struggles that were taking place under the auspices of the PSE and later PEO, invoking on many occasions the fact that Turkish Cypriots belonged to the unions[73] and attempting, as early as the start of the 1930s, to form unions that they themselves controlled.[74] When it became clear that it was impossible to control the whole of the union movement, they proceeded to split it with the foundation of the Federation of Cypriot Workers (SEK) in 1944.[75]

During the same period, and using similar arguments, the Turkish Cypriot elite was trying to distance Turkish Cypriot workers from PEO and to found Turkish Cypriot unions.

The policy of the ethnarchy, the main mouthpiece of the Greek Cypriots in their struggle for *enosis*, was to look down on the presence of the Turkish Cypriots, thus assisting the nationalist Turkish Cypriot leadership in its efforts aimed at making the Turkish Cypriot masses share its intolerance.[76]

The climate at the time was such that even AKEL, which otherwise supported the joint struggles by Greek and Turkish Cypriots, overdid the *enosis* demand, which was again exploited by the Turkish Cypriot leadership.[77]

Characteristically, during the fourth PSE-PEO conference, held in March 1946 in Nicosia, Mehmet Emin Helmi, a Turkish Cypriot member of the 17-member board of directors, requested that the union movement show greater interest in the minorities, while another Turkish Cypriot, Cemal Mehmet, wondered why an issue should be made of 'national vindication' since it was being exploited by all those who wanted the Turkish Cypriots to withdraw from PEO.[78] The reply to this question, which was posed frequently, was that the majority of the population were Greeks and, in accordance with the democratic rules and the declarations of war, the will of the majority for *enosis* had to be respected.[79]

In 1942, a Turkish Cypriot union organisation appeared on the scene which, according to statistics kept by the British at the time, had just 43 registered members, as opposed to PEO's 9,507. In 1945 it had managed to count 843 members, but by 1950 this number had fallen back to 130, compared to 13,000 members belonging to PEO and 1,000 and 2,650 respectively to SEK and ihe independent TU.[80]

Turkish Cypriot workers were making a conscious choice when joining the Cypriot union movement, and this emanated from the fact that they identified their interests (better wages, better working conditions, improved social benefits, medical care, etc.) with those of the Greek Cypriot workers. All the more, given that there was no separate Turkish Cypriot economy, while the economic development of the community was limited, and as a result the number of those working in Turkish Cypriot businesses was very small.

PEO actually set up an office for Turkish Cypriot affairs, headed by Mustafa Bitirim.[81] Even a few years ago, Turkish Cypriot journalists researching the participation of the Turkish Cypriots in non-Turkish union organisations, though complaining for obvious reasons about the lack of Turkish Cypriots on the central committee of PEO, had to admit that the Turkish Cypriot members of PEO were satisfied: 'The Turkish Cypriots had no objections, since no one was laying a hand on their bread and they were not losing any of their rights.'[82]

The establishment of Turkish Cypriot unions did not serve any union-linked purpose or need. The motives were purely political, an expression of the chauvinistic ambitions of the Turkish Cypriot leadership. This was precisely why the masses did not follow them, provoking the anger of the elite, which adopted other means in an effort to force them to leave PEO and SEK and to join the Turkish unions. In the prevailing global conditions of the Cold War, which, naturally, had not left Cyprus unaffected, a systematic campaign of verbal misinformation was begun, depicting the Turkish Cypriot members of PEO as undesirables in their own community since they were allegedly agents of Communism. And of course, given the leading role of Britain in the Cold War, it is not hard to work out what role the British played in this, fully exploiting the situation created with the encouragement of the Turkish Cypriot elite.

Two Turkish Cypriot officials of PEO were persuaded to step down from their posts, taking with them a very small number of their Muslim colleagues, a fact that displeased the nationalist centres that had been hoping for a complete split. The fact that many Turkish Cypriots worked for the British administration, which was, of course, willing to recognise the Turkish Cypriot unions, helped the elite's plans.

The right circumstances were created when the Turkish Cypriot employees of the Telegraph Office joined PEO. Among them was Hasan Ali Sasmaz,[83] who was sworn in as their representative. As the Turkish Cypriot journalist Cemal Mapolar writes, Sasmaz 'was a young poet, imbued with the spirit of Turkism, who was interested in maintaining the Turkism of the Turkish Cypriot members of PEO.'[84]

Mapolar argues:

> PEO, on AKEL's orders, attempted to make the Turkish Cypriot workers lose their Turkism. AKEL wanted to take the Turkish Cypriot workers onto its own line and to appear to be a united and unique labour organisation. It had other additional objectives, which it had not yet revealed. AKEL's purpose, once it had won over the Turkish Cypriot workers, was to achieve *Enosis* more easily.[85]

The opportunity was provided in 1944 when, in the atmosphere of demonstrations in favour of *enosis*, PEO sent a telegram to Sir Cosmo Parkinson, then a Junior Minister for the Colonies, who was visiting Cyprus, in which they demanded the implementation of the declarations on the self-determination of peoples, which in the case of Cyprus, was being interpreted as the right to *enosis*.[86]

A copy of PEO's telegram was passed on to Sasmaz by a Turkish Cypriot employee of the Telegraph Office and Bitirim was immediately ordered to hold a meeting of Turkish Cypriot workers at PEO's head office:

> On August 22, 1944, the Turkish Cypriot workers held a meeting at PEO headquarters. It was a Tuesday. The people were in revolt, history was racing ahead.

> This revolution included for the first time the freedom of the Turkish Cypriot workers. For the Turkish Cypriot workers, one era was ending and another beginning. Sasmaz had finished his speech and, addressing the Turkish Cypriot workers, he said: 'I shall proceed, follow me.' No one asked where or why. Sasmaz went in front with other leaders, behind them were the Turkish Cypriot workers with Turkish flags in hand, and they began their march to freedom, to the Turkish Cypriot quarter.[87]

Things had been prepared very well. News of Sasmaz' action spread like lightning throughout the Turkish Cypriot quarter. In one particular garden, a stage had been built for the next phase of the action. Sasmaz climbed onto it and, addressing the people who had gathered to find out what was going on, said: 'Mothers, fathers, brothers and sisters. I have brought your children here before they become Communists. Embrace all those who are now on our side.'[88]

However limited the success of the attempt to create political vehicles for the Turkish Cypriots through which nationalist propaganda could be distributed, the fact remains that an attempt was made, resulting in the actions of the Turkish Cypriot elite, which were always taken in the name of all the Turkish Cypriots, being noted down and shown today as the alleged proof of the competition between the two communities from very early on. However, conditions were very slowly being created for the penetration of the Panturanist ideas that had thrived in Turkey into the elite.

Even in these circumstances, however, collaboration at trade union level did not stop. Joint struggles and shared demonstrations continued despite the difficulties. This culminated in the foundation, in 1953, of PEO's Turkish Office, about which Pantelis Varnavas has provided interesting information:

> The Turkish Cypriot workers who belonged to PEO knew Greek, understood and spoke it. This helped greatly in resolving difficulties regarding contact, the discussion of problems and briefings. When extremely serious issues were at stake and whenever required, those who spoke the most fluent Greek helped with speeches and the publication of leaflets in Turkish.
>
> Amid all this development that the PEO union movement was undergoing, with the help of Turkish Cypriot workers too, in order to improve the work that was being done it was decided that the establishment of a Turkish office

> was essential. The Office was set up in 1954 and its members were Ahmet Sati (in charge), Ferit Uray, Camil Dunzel, Piluz Caglar, Hasan Ibrahim, Mustafa Ali, Ali Mehmet, Ali Hasan and Tilaver Nasir. Others became members of the Office from time to time.
>
> For the more effective operation of the Central office, Turkish offices were established in all districts and all (except Paphos) were manned by paid officials.
>
> With the founding of the Turkish Office, it was also decided to publish a weekly Turkish Cypriot newspaper entitled *Inkilapci* (*Revolutionary*) but publication was suspended because of the murder of the editor, Fatil Onder, by Turkish terrorist elements on March 24, 1958.[89]

By 1945, the number of members of the Turkish Labour Federation had reached 843 but this subsequently saw a sharp fall and, as a result, the federation folded in 1951. It was relaunched in 1954 when, following the infiltration and control of the community by extremist elements under the leadership elite, it was made to succeed at any price.[90] Despite the terrorism…

> …by the end of 1955, according to statistics mentioned at the 10th PEO Congress, 1,400 Turkish Cypriot workers were registered members, while the previous year this number was more than 1,700. From these figures we can see that despite the terrorism, the basic mass of the Turkish Cypriots remained in the ranks of PEO and only around 300 people left.[91]

Chapter 4

Panturanism and Cyprus

The Turks consider Kemal Ataturk's greatest achievement to have been the creation of a 'Turkish nation-state' within whose fixed borders he wished to gather all the Turks of the Ottoman Empire. They also believe that he succeeded in creating a new national awareness in the Turks, free of the burden of their Ottoman heritage, as a starting point for the development of the awareness of the irretrievability of the lost regions of the Empire.[1] Indeed, this philosophy found its expression in international law with the signing by Turkey (by Kemal Ataturk's close collaborator, Ismet Inonu) of the Treaty of Lausanne, by which Turkey essentially gave up all rights to territory outside the borders of the Turkish Republic.

However, the ideas of Panturanism[2] were never dealt with decisively in Turkey. On the contrary, such tolerance was shown that they were transplanted successfully to the new state and expressed through organised groups inside and outside Turkey, at every level of Turkish society.[3] The height of Panturanism, following the foundation of Kemal Ataturk's Turkish Republic, was revealed in the Turkish state's absorption of Alexandretta, the Syrian port that had been under French command at the end of World War 1. Citing reasons of 'national security',[4] Turkey demanded that it be given this Arab area in which a Turkish-speaking minority lived – a minority with a similar history and relative size to that of the Turkish Cypriots. Using methods that recall vividly those it used in Cyprus, Ankara succeeded in 'legally' making the Alexandretta area part of its territory[5] and it is now called Iskenderun.

The Panturanist dimension at the heart of Kemalist philosophy was revealed more openly at the end of World War II[6] when Turkey, despite maintaining a position of an 'evasive neutrality' during the war, demanded that it be honoured as an ally of the victors,[7] particularly in connection with Hellenism, which Panturanism regarded as an expansionist 'terrorist activity of a century' against Turkey.[8] Indeed, Ankara was seen to be adopting a 'defensive' policy against 'Greek expansionism'.[9]

Similarly, Turkey's policy on Cyprus was presented at the outset – and is still presented – as a reaction against Greece' policy of *enosis*. Hellenism and the world have forgotten the subject of *enosis* for reasons that are more than obvious. The Turks, however, maintain the issue as the great alibi for their policy and the tolerance with which it is viewed by the world's most powerful nations.

The truth is that Turkish policy in Cyprus is a reflection of the effect of Panturanism on Turkey's foreign policy and has nothing to do with a possible reaction against Greek irredentism, insofar as this ever existed and was expressed. It is also true that, in the eyes of the Panturanists, a Turk is any Muslim of the Ottoman Empire who was unable to identify with one of the nation states that came about as a result of the Empire's dissolution. Turkish policy on Cyprus, from the moment that British diplomacy stirred Ankara's interest, was characterised basically by its Panturanist philosophy. Based on evidence from Professor Jacob Landau,[10] Panturanism or Panturkism is the most extreme form of Turkish nationalism, its basic aim being the 'transportation' of the Turkish state to anywhere that there are Turks, in other words the integration of Turks, wherever they live, and consequently the areas in which they live, into the authority of the Turkish state.

These 'unredeemed' Turks, the *Dis Turkler* as they have become known in the language of Panturkism, are found in areas that begin in the former Yugoslavia (Bosnia chiefly), Bulgaria, Albania, Greece and Cyprus, stretching to Iraq, Syria and Iran, reaching as far as Azerbaijan, Turkmenistan, Kazakhstan and Uzbekistan, and ending up in regions of China and Mongolia. Their numbers are presented as being in the order of 100 million. The symbol of Panturkism is the Grey Wolf (*Bozkurt*), which is said to have opened the road during the westward push of the Turkic tribes. The symbolism of the Grey Wolf, as explained in the Panturanist magazine par excellence, *Turk Kulturu* (*Turkish Culture*), in 1967,[11] is found in the way it extends its range of influence. There are three basic guidelines to contemporary Panturanism:

Ata Olorak Bozkurt	The Grey Wolf *must* be the father;
Rehber Olorak Bozkurt	The Grey Wolf *must* be the leader; and
Kurtarici Olorak Bozkurt	The Grey Wolf *must* be the saviour.

Theoretically, Panturkism was in conflict with the philosophy of Kemal Ataturk and it is a fact that, while Ataturk lived, Panturkism saw a slight decline. However, after Ataturk's death and to this day, Panturkism, in one or another form, has not only managed to survive but to infiltrate the ideological mechanisms of the Turkish state. It developed especially in the period from the end of World War II to the mid-sixties. Since then it has found expression at political party level through parties such as those of *Netmecin Erbakan* (Islamic Welfare Party) and *Alpalsan Turkes* (Panturanist Party of National Unity).

However much Kemalism rejected Turkish irredentism and attempted to control Panturanism, it promoted a form of nationalism that proved to be fertile ground for Panturkism.[12]

Cyprus and Panturkism

Cyprus, as was natural, could not avoid the attention of the Panturanists in Turkey. On the contrary, from the beginning of the 1940s, as Professor Jacob Landau notes, Cyprus was the Panturanists' favourite topic.[13] In Istanbul in 1946 a Panturanist group was formed that focused its attention exclusively on Cyprus, the *Kibris Turk Kultur Dernegi* (Association of Turkish Culture of Cyprus).[14] The founding of the association coincided with the emergence of Turkish Cultural Centres (*Turk Kultur Ocagi*)[15] and the Association of Turkish Culture (*Turk Kultur Dernegi*).

Among the founder members of the Association of Turkish Culture in Cyprus were two Turkish Cypriots who lived in Turkey, teacher and author Halil Fikret Alasya and lawyer Hasan Nevzat Karacil.[16]

At the start of the 1950s, one of the most active of these Panturanist groups in Turkey was the Association of Turkish Nationalists (*Turkiye Milliyetciler Dernegi*).[17] The organisation had over 80 branches throughout Turkey by the end of 1952, when the movement in favour of *enosis* was growing in Cyprus. During this period, the nationalists were active with regard to Cyprus, promoting the argument that the Turkish minority in Cyprus was being 'threatened with oppression by the majority which is both Greek and Communist'.[18] The nationalists succeeded in rallying around this position many groups to which they managed to pass on their Panturkic philosophy.

The most active of all was part of the Association of Turkish Culture in Cyprus, and it became known as 'Cyprus is Turkish'.

Chapter 4

'Cyprus is Turkish'

Few details exist about the formation of this organisation and those that follow have been gleaned from Turkish press reports and from Christos P. Ioannides,[19] who has dealt extensively with the subject. The organisation's roots may be sought in the activities of the National Federation of Students of Turkey (NFST) and the publishers and chief editors of a number of Turkish newspapers. In April 1954 the federation decided to host Turkish Cypriot students with the aim of reinforcing 'national ties'.

Immediately after the British set out their proposal for self-government in Cyprus, in July 1954, the federation published a booklet, the basic premise of which was: 'a sacred duty to oppose any activity that will disturb the peace on the island which is an integral part of our country and the sacred heritage of our fathers.' This was also the motto of the federation and its activities concerning Cyprus.

At the end of August 1954, the Turkish Secretariat of the European Crusade for Youth, in collaboration with the NFST, organised a seminar in Istanbul on European integration. Journalists from 20 newspapers were invited to the seminar, which coincided with Greece's recourse to the United Nations on Cyprus. On the initiative of the NFST leadership, a special meeting was held on August 24 with the participation of all those who had attended the seminar, as well as the chief editors of the biggest newspapers published at the time in Istanbul. The meeting discussed developments in Cyprus, a decision was taken to establish a committee called 'Cyprus is Turkish' and an executive committee was elected, comprising the following: Hikmet Bil, lawyer and Chief editor of the newspaper *Huriyet*,[20] Ahmed Yalman, a well-known journalist and chief editor of the daily *Vatan* – well-known by his nom de plume Ahmed Emin; Camil Onan, correspondent for the Alexandretta newspaper *Huriyet*; Orhan Birgit, an editor on *Yeni Sabah*; Husametin Gyanozturk, president of the NFST; Ziya Somar; and the Turkish Cypriot Hasan Nevzat Karacil, who was elected committee chairman.

The purpose of the committee, as set out in its constitution, was: 'To brief world public opinion about the fact that Cyprus is Turkish, to protect the rights and privileges of the Turks in relation to Cyprus and to make Turkish public opinion aware of these facts.'

From his study of official American reports and of the charge sheet related to the vandalism against the Greeks of Istanbul in 1955, Christos P. Ioannides has concluded that, from its foundation, the committee developed a three-pronged idealism, which was essentially the result of its founders' ideological views. The philosophy of Panturkic irredentism was marked out by the committee's name, 'Cyprus is Turkish'. Its emblem was the map of Cyprus in green, framed by the Turkish crescent moon. All the founder members had signed the founding declaration of the committee that Cyprus was justly considered an integral part of Turkey. The second aspect was the fanatical anti-Greek feeling that was a complement and/or by-product of the first. The third aspect was a nauseating anti-Communism. Christos P. Ioannides writes:

> What Panturkism feared above all was a Cyprus that was both Greek and Communist. The most venomous anti-Greek propaganda came from the mass circulation newspapers of Istanbul, *Huriyet* and *Istanbul Express*, the serious *Vatan* and *Zafer* of Ankara, which was the mouthpiece of the Democratic Party. *Huriyet* and *Vatan* published highly inflammatory articles against Greece, the Greek Orthodox Patriarchate in Istanbul and Archbishop Makarios. They also promoted the Panturkic view that not only was Cyprus Turkish but so were Thrace and the Aegean islands.[21] All these newspapers devoted entire articles to explaining the great danger to Turkey of a 'Greek and Communist Cyprus'. This was an additional reason, they argued, why Cyprus had to come into Turkish possession should Great Britain decide to abandon the island. In this way, they said, not only would Turkey secure something that belonged to it historically but also it would be doing the Free World a great service, by ensuring that the island would not become a Communist base in the Eastern Mediterranean. Speculating about the consequences if Cyprus were not to become Turkish, Prime Minster Menderes declared in the summer of 1955 that 'Britain's surrender of her sovereignty over Cyprus could lead to the destruction of the entire NATO defence system in the Mediterranean.' In the same way, Ahmet Emin, Chief Editor of *Vatan* and a member of the Executive Committee of the 'Cyprus is Turkish' committee, argued that the *Enosis* movement in Cyprus was inspired and controlled by Communists and by Moscow. He argued that 'the ridiculous implementation of the idea of self-determination in small areas here and there' was a threat to the vital interests of the Free World.'[22]

However foolish all this may seem today, one should bear in mind that it was taking place against the background of the Cold War. Besides, it did not matter how silly or unrealistic the Greeks or any foreigner viewed the situation. What was significant was the promotion of such arguments in the decision-making places of the so-called 'Free World', for reasons related to the strategic designs of the Western alliance on the region at the height of the Cold War, and the fact that Turkey had the longest borders with the Soviet Union. And these arguments, however sketchily drawn, appear to have struck a chord. Moreover, they certainly appealed to a public that was still drunk with its nationalist revolution and in which the fear of a threat from the north had been successfully cultivated. It is, however, ridiculous to argue that the then anti-Communist Makarios and Grivas, praised for his anti-Communist stance, were acting on behalf of Moscow! But in this way another myth was created which would be adopted not only by the Turkish leadership but also by Turkish public opinion, which was now supporting the policy of the Turkish state against Cyprus and Greece, albeit with derogations from the prevailing Kemalist principles. In any case, in this way the interests of the Turkish state were identified with Panturanist views and ideology.

Relations with Turkish Government

Very quickly, as Christos P. Ioannides writes, the activities of the committee were essentially adopted by the Turkish government. The founding of the committee had been covered extensively in the Turkish press, especially in the government newspaper *Zafer*, which wrote in a leader article: 'A Communist base [i.e. Cyprus] under the guidance of the Komintern, sixty kilometres from Turkish territory, will not be accepted.'

Four days after the committee was set up, its leadership was received by Prime Minister Adnan Menderes in the presence of the Deputy Prime Minister and Foreign Minister Fuad Koprulu, Deputy Foreign Minister Fatin Rustu Zorlu and other members of the government. Of significance here is the speed with which the three most important members of the Turkish government gave their blessing to the committee.

Orhan Birgit, a member of the committee, described the importance that the committee itself ascribed to the meeting with the Prime Minister: 'Since we would be providing this national service [i.e. on the Cyprus issue] *under the guidance of the Turkish government* [my italics], which would support its positions at the UN and thus secure success, Ahmet Emin Yalman, one of us, a good friend and a confidant of the Prime Minister – to indicate our status – would speak to Menderes and inform us of whatever was necessary. [...] Ahmet Emin Yalman spoke with Menderes and the Prime Minister, who was pleased by the foundation of the committee, announced that he would receive us.'[23]

The meeting, Birgit writes, was a cordial one, so cordial in fact that Menderes, with whom he sat on the same couch, patted him amicably on the back and told him: 'The Greeks need to see how united the opposition and the government are on the Cyprus issue.'

Menderes' reference was presumably linked to the support offered to the committee by the leader of the opposition, Ismet Inonu, while the committee's contacts with labour unions and other social organisations reinforced the image of national unity and of a single focus on an issue that Panturanism had basically adopted and promoted.

Birgit also reveals that the discussion with Menderes focused on 'matters of a confidential nature', a fact that seems to have caused concern to Koprulu: 'The Prime Minister indicated to Koprulu that he should not worry, saying: 'We have no secrets from our children. These secrets were sacred yesterday and they will be today and tomorrow, but they're forgotten at once.'

It was not revealed, of course, just what issues Menderes might have discussed with the founders of the committee but, to judge from the vandalism that followed against the Greek minority in Istanbul and the proven role of the committee, it is not unrealistic to suppose that some related plan may have occupied the meeting.

What is important is the fact that it was in the context of its internal front that the Turkish government was formulating its policy vis-à-vis Cyprus. And it is now a fact that can be proven beyond any doubt – though that is not the object of this study – that at some level, even if we assume that some people did not agree totally with these developments, the Turkish government and Turkish policy on Cyprus had become trapped by the extreme nationalism and its expressions that they themselves had cultivated in public opinion. This remains true today. The so-called 'national issue' is part of Turkey's partisan politics, especially during election periods.

The Leaders of the Committee

By the first months of 1955, the committee had become one of the most important means of mobilising public opinion on Cyprus. It set up branches in 50 districts, always with the participation of local social, economic and political leaders. The broad publicity given to its activities was such that it had soon become a highly effective pressure group, if such a term may be used to describe it.

To discover the reasons for its success, one can look at the composition of the committee but this is only the start of the trail that leads to the confirmation of the involvement of a partnership of party and government offices in the affair.

In 1955, the committee chairman was Hikmet Bil,[24] chief editor of *Huriyet*, who undertook many visits to Cyprus and openly preached his 'irredentist', nationalist-chauvinist views among the Turkish Cypriots, with the tolerance of the colonial government, of course. A report by the American Embassy in Ankara refers to his contacts with a nationalist organisation that the government had dissolved in 1953.[25] This also explains the extreme nationalist content of articles in *Huriyet* in the 1950s, particularly in relation to Cyprus, since Bil was their author. As chief editor of the newspaper with the highest circulation and the greatest influence, he had direct access to the highest ranks of the leadership of the then governing Democratic Party, including the Prime Minister, Adnan Menderes.

Hikmet Bil travelled abroad a great deal on committee business, which means that the committee was well off financially, a fact that can only be explained by its access to the state coffers. There is convincing evidence that the Menderes government had placed unlimited funds at the committee's disposal.[26]

The committee had close links through Hikmet Bil not only with the government but also with Ismet Inonu and his Turkish Republican Party, a fact that was uncovered during the investigations and trials concerning the vandalism against the Greeks of Istanbul in 1955.[27]

The then general secretary of the committee, Camil Onal, also had some interesting contacts.[28] In early 1950, Onal was hired by the Turkish Intelligence Service and, according to some accounts, undertook many missions gathering information about Armenians, Kurds and Communists in Lebanon, Syria and elsewhere.[29]

When he became linked to the committee at the beginning of 1954, he was working as a journalist at the Ankara Press Agency. He became involved in the committee because it reminded him of the 'union' of Alexandretta with Turkey and he dearly wished his name to be identified with a similar 'national issue'.[30]

Onal was a close collaborator of Bil, whom he accompanied on his trips to Cyprus and elsewhere to promote the objectives of the committee. He was particularly involved in spreading disinformation on the Cyprus issue, 'deliberately making up stories about attacks by Greek Cypriots on Turkish Cypriots, which he passed on to the newspapers throughout Turkey, creating and maintaining the nationalist anti-Greek climate.'[31]

The connections between the Turkish Cypriot leadership and the committee as well as other nationalist organisations in Turkey culminated in the mission undertaken by Hikmet Bil: a visit to Cyprus to help Fazil Kuchuk found his 'Cyprus is Turkish' party.[32]

The parallel development of nationalist activity among the Turkish Cypriots and in Turkey, the relationship created between the nationalist organisations of Turkey and the Turkish Cypriot leadership elite, and the link between the nationalists and the establishment in Turkey were preparing the ground for the strategy that Turkey then developed in relation to Cyprus. Naturally, there were external factors playing their own role in this process. Britain, for example, which as a colonial power occupied Cyprus, had specific reasons for wanting Turkey's involvement in the Cyprus issue. The United States and the NATO alliance saw Turkey playing a particular strategically important role in the region on their behalf.

A role was also played by Greece's almost total national dependence at a time when the Cyprus issue was acting as a catalyst for rallying the Turkish nationalist forces and the official Turkish state was adopting the irredentist basis of its policy on Cyprus. This was a Greek weakness, which was fully exploited, by both foreigners and Turks, in order to create a situation in which the drama of Cyprus was to be played out and for which Cyprus and Greece paid a high price. The essence remains that, through the connections of Panturanism with the Kemalist establishment and the Turkish state, conditions were created for the adoption of an official policy characterised by designs on the island of Cyprus while, at the same time, control of the Turkish Cypriot leadership was achieved and in this way the Turkish Cypriot minority was turned into a strategic tool of Turkish policy against Cyprus. And all this without recognition of Turkey's practice and consequently without any strategy for foiling its ambitions, which, seen from today's standpoint, opened the way to still further designs on other ethnic areas.

Chapter 5

Turkey Centre Stage

At the beginning of the 1950s there was no such thing as a 'Cyprus problem' as far as the rest of the world was concerned. The international press paid no attention to the subject. The post-war situation was in the process of being consolidated and it was this that monopolised interest, in relation to the ideological clashes of the Cold War that had already begun. A real war between the two ideological camps was already raging in Korea[1] and Indochina.

British interest, especially with the prospect of the Conservatives coming to power, was focused on the Middle East and the crisis in Egypt, and on Iran.[2]

In the Greek camp the idea was maturing of a recourse to the UN over the Cyprus issue.[3] The *enosis* referendum had been held in the meantime and national representatives of the Greek Cypriots had been sent abroad to hand over the results of the referendum and to promote the demand for national vindication.[4]

In Turkey virtually the whole of the press was involved in a crusade aimed at mobilising public opinion on the Cyprus issue, based on the nationalist, expansionist positions of the 'Cyprus is Turkish' committee.[5] By taking such a stance, the Turkish government was partly satisfying a need to deflect public opinion from its pressing internal problems and at the same time pleasing London, whose support for Turkey's participation in the Baghdad Pact and NATO made Ankara a good receiver of British suggestions regarding Turkey's stance on Cyprus.[6] In the climate that was being formed by the Cold War and the ideology of the allies, of whom Turkey was one, the Turkish press crusade revolved around the 'bogey' of the Communist threat.[7]

Nevertheless, the main characteristic of the Turkish press crusade was its anti-Greek wrath. E. N. Tzelepis writes:[8]

> On the pretext that Greece's claims on Cyprus revealed a renaissance of the 'Grand Idea' (the return of the Greeks to what had been Constantinople), some of the more serious commentators in the Turkish press dug up from the archive of Turkish nationalism some old claims that one would have imagined to have been buried for ever beneath the newly carved monument to 'Greco-

> Turkish friendship'. Thus talk began of handing over to Turkey territory in Thrace as well as the islands of Samos, Chios, Mytilene, Rhodes and others.

In Cyprus itself, every time the leaders of the Turkish Cypriot elite approached the colonial government to state their positions on the maintenance of British sovereignty over the island or on the 'return' of Cyprus to Turkey should there be an end to British rule, the reply was always the same: 'Ask Turkey to take an official and direct interest.'[9] At the same time, the Foreign Office was making its own direct efforts to 'persuade' Ankara to show an interest 'in the future of the island'. A typical instance of these approaches to Ankara were the orders given by the Foreign Office to the British Ambassador to Ankara on February 11, 1954:[10]

> Her Majesty's Government note with concern that there has been no abatement of the Greek agitation about Cyprus and that there are signs that it may be intensified in the near future in the United Nations and by other methods. *We believe that the Turkish Government share this concern. We fully understand the Turkish position, as explained on several occasions to your predecessor, and we are sure that the Turks agree with us on the desirability of damping down the Greek agitation.* We should of course be grateful for any direct action which the Turks might feel inclined to take vis-à-vis the Greek Government. *But we wonder whether in present circumstances the most effective course might not be if the United States Government could be induced to express to the Greek Government their fear that the Greek campaign, if continued, will prejudice political and strategic stability in the Eastern Mediterranean as well as the development of the Balkan Alliance* [my italics]. We have already let the United States Government know that we should be grateful for their good offices in discouraging Greek agitation. But we think that if the Turkish Government would, on their own initiative, speak on similar lines in Washington, this would greatly help to convince the United States Government that it is necessary to counsel restraint in Athens.[11]

Britain was proceeding systematically to set the scene that would 'justify' its decision to hide behind Turkey's involvement in the Cyprus issue in order to implement its own policy of 'divide and rule', to reject the demand for *enosis* and safeguard its presence in Cyprus. Again taking full advantage of the Cold War atmosphere, it cited reasons of strategy for the so-called 'Free World' wanting to involve Turkey, indifferent to the consequences, of which it was given a timely warning by its Ambassador in Turkey:[12]

> The conception which prompted our proposed approach to the Turks is that the Cyprus dispute is no longer purely an Anglo-Greek matter. *It has become one of political and strategic concern to all the Western powers, which are interested in Balkan and Eastern Mediterranean security* [my italics]; and it would be proper for such powers to state their view. [...] The Turks would be more likely to show such an interest *if the Cyprus agitation came to a head and forced the Turks, for internal as well as international reasons, to take up a public position*' [my italics].

It was clear by now that Britain's intention was to legitimise and give official acknowledgment to Turkish interest in Cyprus, despite the accurate warnings of its Ambassador in Ankara of the consequences of such action. The British attempted this by inviting Greece and Turkey to take part in a Tripartite Conference in London. The text of the invitation, which was very revealing of their intentions and crucial to all the developments that have occurred up to the present day, was as follows:

> Her Majesty's Government has studied further the strategic and other problems affecting not only the United Kingdom but also Greece and Turkey in the Eastern Mediterranean. The government believes that cooperation among the three countries in this region, based on mutual trust, is essential for their mutual interests. Consequently, Her Majesty's Government invites the Governments of Greece and Turkey to send representatives to confer with it in London at an early date on political and defence matters affecting the Eastern Mediterranean, including Cyprus.[13]

Greece's participation in such a conference would legitimise Turkey's presence, while Turkey's presence would legitimise its interest![14]

Britain's tactics were later interpreted by the British Prime Minister, Antony Eden: 'I considered it capital that we should carry the Turks with us in any new move […] We could not afford to take Turkish friendship and understanding for granted. […] The Cyprus dispute could never be settled until the importance of the Turkish position was understood and accepted.[15]

Sir John Harding, colonial governor in Cyprus from 1955 to 1958, who was asked to implement the internal aspects of this policy on the island by military means, explained in an interview how the British viewed Turkish interest in Cyprus:

> The geographical distance between Cyprus and Turkey determines the extent of Turkish interest in Cyprus. Beyond the proportion of the population of Cyprus that is Turkish and in whose future Turkey is definitely interested, the country could not remain indifferent to the future of an island so close to its shores. America, for example, was always interested in neighbouring Cuba, as is the case of Britain and the Isle of Wight. We did not create Turkish interest in Cyprus. It was always there. And it was quite right and just and legitimate for Turkey to show such interest in Cyprus.[16]

The question that is still being asked today is why Britain chose Turkey in order to secure control of Cyprus. Was there no other way? Could it not, for example, have taken up Greece's offers, which even concerned places beyond Cyprus?

The British journalist Robert Stephens has attempted to give a reply, or rather an analysis of Britain's reply to the question:

> At this time, the government saw in the political scene at Westminster and in the Middle East reasons which were political rather than military for trying to hold on to Cyprus. The new agreement with Egypt had aroused bitter opposition from the 'Suez rebels' on the Conservative back benches. A further concession in Cyprus would, it was thought at Westminster, be interpreted as a sign of weakness, not only by Conservative members of parliament, but also by Britain's remaining allies in the Middle East – especially Iraq, which was being groomed to replace Egypt as the main prop of British influence in the Arab world.
>
> Turkey, too, was becoming of increasing importance in British as well as American plans for the Middle East. The US Secretary of State, John Foster Dulles, wanted to switch the emphasis in the strategy for this area away from

> the British obsession with the Arab states and toward the new concept of the 'Northern Tier'. He wanted an American-backed alliance between Turkey, Iran and Pakistan to close the gap in the ring of containment around Russia. Eden seized the opportunity to combine the American and the British concepts by encouraging the creation of the Baghdad Pact, signed in March 1955.[17]

From this point of view, consequently, Cyprus and its people were being sacrificed in order to serve the interests of the Western allies in their clash with the socialist camp.

The London Conference

Turkey's response to London's instigations that it take a more active interest in matters concerning Cyprus was, of course, as expected. London provided Turkish diplomacy with all the strategic reasons it needed to argue on a new basis, above and beyond Britain's alleged contractual obligations to 'return' the island to Turkey, beyond the nonsense about eastward expansion and nationalist revenge attacks, on a basis which, in the Cold War conditions of the time, was to the liking of many.

Through the London Conference, Britain gained the ability to act as a referee on the Cyprus issue, which it skilfully transformed into a Greco-Turkish dispute.

The London Conference gave Turkey an opportunity to develop not only its unlawful, unfounded and immoral demands on Cyprus but its strategy too.

The 'evidence' backing Turkey's interest in Cyprus at the London Conference followed the formula used in previous instances of expansionist activity, such as that of Alexandretta, but also, later on, in Cyprus and elsewhere. Arguments using this 'evidence' were attempted on different levels: historical, legal, geopolitical and pure incitement.

The Turks were naturally under no illusions about the reasons for their involvement in the Cyprus issue, which flew in the face of all reason and even against the principles of Ataturk, on which their foreign policy was supposedly based.

A Turkish diplomat, Mahmut Dikerdem, provided a characteristic picture of the Turkish view of the Cyprus issue. He considered that the Greek Cypriots' campaign was heading for success and that Britain was contriving 'various ways of delaying its departure from the island so as to benefit from the interest which Turkey is belatedly showing with regard to its nationals in Cyprus.'[18]

Having described the situation inside the Turkish Foreign Ministry at the time, he notes that nothing noteworthy was known about Cyprus, beyond that it had once been an Ottoman dominion which had been ceded temporarily to Britain in exchange for other benefits and that, by the Treaty of Lausanne, all its sovereign rights over the island had been transferred to Britain.[19]

Precisely how Ankara acted in the face of British insistence that it show an interest is revealed below in full, including the important footnotes, from Neoclis Sarris' description:[20]

> Fatin Rustu Zorlu's first action was to form a special committee at the Foreign Ministry, the mission of which, as Dikerem explains, '...was to study the Cyprus issue in all its various aspects and at the same time to determine the view of Turkey and the government stance. Zorlu had laid down two main principles which would form the basis of the committee's further work: 1.We must persuade with evidence that we have rights in Cyprus, at least as many as Greece has, and make this fact known to world public opinion. 2.By providing every type of required assistance to the Turkish Cypriots, we must increase their ability to withstand pressure.'[21] [...] The first action of the committee was to draw up a 'white paper' in which the Turkish views were set out and which was distributed via Turkish diplomatic representations all over the world.'[22]

The London Conference perfectly served the purpose for which the British had called it. Turkey, in the most official way, set out its demands and its positions in the presence of Greece, a fact that made it a 'legitimate interlocutor'. This, for the time and for Turkey's designs, was sufficient. The foundation for everything that was to follow had been laid.

The first claim made by Zorlu, the Turkish Foreign Minister and head of the Ankara delegation to the London Conference, was that the 1878 alliance agreement between Britain and Turkey 'stresses clearly the importance of Cyprus to Turkey's defence' and that 'the fate of the island is exclusively a matter for Britain and Turkey'.[23] He also claimed that any attempt to alter the Treaty of Lausanne was 'tantamount to reviewing' it and, consequently, he argued, if there were to be any change in the status of Cyprus, it would have to be 'a return to Turkish sovereignty'.

The political-military 'arguments' put forward by Turkey were equally provocative. The importance of Cyprus to Turkey, said Zorlu, 'emanates from the requirements of history, geography, the economy, military strategy, the right to security and the existence of Turkey.'

Turkey's arguments were fully within the context that the British had set out so as to justify Ankara's involvement and to secure its role as referee in an issue 'of strategic interest to the West'. It is important, however, to note that the Turkish theory of a 'vital Turkish region' was set out so openly for the first time at the London Conference: 'Cyprus,' Zorlu said, 'is above all of vital importance for Turkey's defence, to such an extent that it is impossible to calculate its defence resources and capability in the event of war without taking Cyprus into consideration.'[24]

Basing his arguments on such logic, Zorlu concluded that: 'from a military standpoint, Cyprus has to belong to Turkey or to another country that is interested in both Turkey and the Far East.' And he explained this by saying that, in the event of war, Turkey would not be able to use its ports for resupplying if Cyprus was not under its occupation.

There was, of course, no shortage of Turkish incitement, all springing from the disinformation that was being channelled to the pages of the Turkish press. The Turkish Cypriots, they argued, were endangered by 'bloodthirsty Greeks'. Moreover, they said, the Turkish Cypriots had the right to their own separate self-determination and consequently the greatest 'concession' that they could make would be to accept partition. Historically, they insisted, Cyprus was an extension of the East and had never belonged to Greece, while it had belonged to Turkey for 400 years.[25]

Chapter 6

The Strategy is Codified

Turkey's presence at the London Conference, the truly impassioned cultivation of an anti-Greek climate among Turkish public opinion, together with the parallel development of activity – with government blessing – by the committee of the 'Cyprus is Turkish' association, plus the international realities stemming from the Cold War, with which Turkey was to be totally linked, had essentially trapped the Ankara government within a policy from which, even if it wished to, it could no longer escape. Turkey now had to draw up its policy so as to be able to respond to the requirements of the situation in which it found itself, trapped by its own international choices, which imposed a second self-entrapment on the subject of Cyprus. It was a dead-end policy, which, however, served the interests of its major allies. Turkey's internal structure, with the army playing a leading role in all areas, was the key link between the international element, which affected policy, and internal elements, which channelled this effect to the level of decisions concerning 'national' policy. The general orientation, which had essentially been determined by British diplomacy and which Ankara had been eager to follow, could no longer satisfy Turkish ambitions. But the course of events and developments led Ankara into situations which it was not ready to face.

At the London Conference, the British government acted evasively so as to show the extent of 'Greco-Turkish differences on the Cyprus issue',[1] in order to appear as a mediator. And the 'mediator' showed its 'impartiality' in its proposal for the participation of Turkey in the administration of the island. The way was being opened wide for Turkey, even though the London Conference did not lead to any decision. The tabling of the issue, the presence of Turkey and the acceptance of Turkey's presence by Greece were the basic ambitions at that moment of both London and Ankara – for different reasons – and in this sense the conference achieved its aims. Now Britain could leave the initiative to Turkey.

Towards the London Conference

The notorious London Conference began on August 29, 1955. London's aim was to gain acceptance by the three participating powers of criteria for the drawing up of a framework within which a solution to the Cyprus issue would later be sought. In other words, not on the basis of the principle of decolonisation and the right to self-determination, but on that of serving allied interests.[2]

By convening the London Conference, Britain appeared to be responding to the demands of the international community for a dialogue on Cyprus. But at the same time it was attempting to determine who would be the main participants in such a dialogue. As Makarios had noted in his letter to the Greek government, 'The British invitation purposely placed the Cyprus issue in the context of broader, unconnected interests in order to use it as an excuse. On the one hand so as to invite the Turks and on the other so as not to invite the directly interested Cypriots.'[3]

Britain still cherished the hope that the holding of talks in London, a global centre of political and diplomatic activity, far from the 'provincial, sick atmosphere of Athens', would help the Greek leadership to negotiate on the Cyprus issue from a 'better international perspective'.[4]

The political leadership in Athens did not appear to be aware of the serious consequences of its decision to respond positively to London's invitation. It did not understand that:

> It became an accomplice in the execution of an act which had disastrous consequences on the national Greco-Cypriot level. It did not even suspect that Turkey's agreement to be the third party in discussions about the Cyprus issue meant not only that it was being recognised as an 'interested party' with the same interests in Cyprus as Greece, but that circumstances were being created under which the Cyprus issue would one day degenerate into a Greco-Turkish conflict with all the dangers inherent in such a development.[5]

The British invitation naturally satisfied Ankara, which formed a special committee for the preparation of its positions and the strategy that it would follow. The requisite preparation of public opinion was carried out by a section of the Turkish press.[6] At the same time, the Turkish press cultivated the impression that the situation in Cyprus itself had reached a crucial stage, with the Greek Cypriots 'slaughtering' the Turkish Cypriots.[7]

The Turkish Prime Minister, Adnan Menderes, took care to publicise Ankara's objectives, which determined the stance it would take at the London Conference. In statements on August 24, 1955, to members of the Turkish delegation to the London Conference, he expressed his concerns about 'the tragic events that the Greeks are expected to provoke today or tomorrow' and added:

> I wish to state clearly that this country will not show the slightest tolerance of any change in the status of Cyprus against Turkey's interests. [...] the principle of self-determination supported by a majority of the population in order to determine the fate of an area is not implemented partially like this anywhere in the world. A homeland is not like a piece of cloth that a tailor may cut where he chooses. [...] A large part of Turkey's coastline is besieged by threatening platforms and watchtowers that belong to another country. Only the area of Cyprus looks safe today. In this sense, Cyprus is a continuation of Anatolia and is one of its security points.[8]

What Turkey Gained from the London Conference

At the start of the conference, the British Foreign Secretary Harold Macmillan attempted to create a climate that would facilitate the positions that his Turkish counterpart would develop later. From the outset he restated the British position that territory under its jurisdiction could not be the subject of discussion with foreign powers and he set out the purpose of the conference as the 'reconciliation' of Britain's two allies, Greece and Turkey, whose 'differences over Cyprus' were endangering the 'joint defence' of the three countries and threatening regions far beyond Britain's authority. He did not omit to note the strategic importance of Turkey to the Western alliance and the British-Turkish alliance of 1878. At the same time, he criticised 'those responsible for terrorism in Cyprus'.[9]

These points were taken up at once by the Turkish Foreign Minister, Fatin Rustu Zorlu, who also took care to 'remind' everyone that the British-Turkish alliance of 1878 had underlined the importance of Cyprus 'to the defence of Turkey'. He naturally recognised that the fate of the island was exclusively a matter for London but he argued that any attempt to change the status quo in Cyprus 'amounted to a re-evaluation of the Treaty of Lausanne and, consequently, any change must mean the return of Cyprus to Turkey.'[10]

Neoclis Sarris[11] sums up the 28-page speech by the Turkish Foreign Minister in the following eight basic points:

1. Cyprus is important to the defence and security of Turkey. It is unthinkable for Turkey not to count on the island in case of war. In any case, that is why, in 1878, its transfer to Great Britain took place.

2. The Cyprus issue is one that interests only Turkey and Great Britain. This is due to the fact that the provisions of the Treaty of Lausanne referring to Cyprus were drawn up between Turkey and Britain.

3. Despite the clarity of the provisions of the Treaty of Lausanne, the idea that Cyprus is an island whose status may be changed is a mistaken one because that would mean a change to the entire system that the treaty established. If this were to happen it would have innumerable consequences and Turkey might proceed with justified demands while Greece could come away worse off.

4. The view promoted by Greece that by the Treaty of Lausanne Turkey gave up all its rights on Cyprus hangs in the air, because Turkey has not cut itself off from the Ottoman Empire.

5. The reasons why Turkey is adamant over Cyprus are supported by historical, geographical, ethnological and military evidence. Geographically, the island is only 40 miles from Turkey while it is 1,000 miles from Greece. It is a geographical extension of Anatolia and, throughout history, the civilisations that ruled Asia Minor also ruled Cyprus. [...]Cyprus must belong to a country like Turkey, which is interested in the fate of the surrounding region.

6. On the issue of self-determination, it is not a principle that may be implemented everywhere at all times.

7. On the issue of autonomy: before proceeding with such a solution, there must be guaranteed order and security, which has been undermined by the

Greek government and the Orthodox Church. Subsequently, the future of the Turkish Cypriots must be secured and their lives and properties guaranteed.

8. The final Turkish view: the status quo in Cyprus must be maintained. In other words, Great Britain must not withdraw from the island. Turkey, which fought against Greece for its liberation, gave up its sovereign rights on Cyprus only in favour of Great Britain.

The First Nihat Erim Report

Ankara did not waste the opportunity it had been given at the London Conference. It began to construct – on the basis of the 'legitimisation' of its interest in the future of Cyprus and the 'recognition' of its strategic interests in the region – a new strategy with objectives that it was in the meantime elaborating.

On November 16, 1956, the Prime Minister of Turkey, Adnan Menderes, proposed that Professor Nihat Erim[12] take up the post of special adviser on Cyprus. Erim would study the Cyprus files and propose to the Prime Minister the policy he should follow, based on specific issues that required answers:

1. If the British remain in Cyprus.
2. If they leave, the island should be given to us.
3. If this is not possible, it should be partitioned.
4. Self-government.[13]

The choice that was definitely discounted was that of the island being handed over to Greece.

Erim dealt substantively with the legal and political problems created by Turkey's involvement in the Cyprus issue, at a time mainly characterised by the liberation of the colonies and the exercise of the right to self-determination by the former colonial peoples. The support, for example, of the maintenance of British sovereignty over the island was tantamount to supporting the perpetuation of colonialism, a situation that the post-war international community rejected. The position of the 'return' of Cyprus to Turkey was viewed merely as a change in its colonial ownership, a change that was equally not acceptable to the international community. The demand for partition was not accepted for demographic, legal, political and economic reasons, as well as due to the traumatic experiences of previous cases such as India. Separate self-determination could not be supported in any specific instance, beyond the fact that it conflicted with the prevailing view in the United Nations and with the declared principles of the world body. Moreover, this prospect worried most countries with minorities, since the recognition of separate rights for a minority could create a precedent capable of disrupting the whole world.

It was on these matters that Nihat Erim had to come up with some answers, and he attempted to do so in the report of November 24, 1956, which he submitted to the Prime Minister and which stated:[14]

> Support for keeping Cyprus in its present form in the hands of Britain will not gain us friends at the United Nations. The slogan in international relations since the end of the Second World War has been the abolition of colonialism. Moreover, article 73 of the UN Charter obliges Great Britain to secure self-determination. In any case, from the beginning of the crisis, Britain had quickly changed its stance and accepted self-determination in the form of self-government. *It is not right for Turkey, with geographical, historical and military rights on Cyprus, to argue the position that the island should remain a British colony* [my italics]. When supporting this view, Turkey must state the following: the sovereignty of Cyprus should remain with Britain with the presupposition that it must recognise the right to self-determination of its people.

In this way, Nihat Erim attempted to align Turkey's objectives with the spirit of the time. Without modifications to Ankara's ambitions, a position could be found that could win support for Turkey on the international stage. As for the form of self-government supported by Ankara, there was no reason, Erim said, for that to be revealed at this juncture. He was concerned about this, however, and in his report he examined various possibilities:

> It is possible that Britain could give Cyprus to us alone.
>
> This view has been supported from the outset by our government. The geographical, historical and, above all, military arguments are reasonable. The

importance of the island for our land, naval and air forces was shown mainly and actively during the Suez crisis. Turkey's security, the operations of the Baghdad Pact and of NATO are closely related to the possession of Cyprus.

The legal structure based on the Treaty of Lausanne looks weak. Article 20 of the Treaty indisputably hands sovereignty over Cyprus to Britain. Even without referring to article 16, as Greece has done, article 20 closes the way to Turkey's legal arguments. Against this, one may argue in favour of an opposing view, which is difficult to accept. Moreover, there are disadvantages to examining the whole issue within the framework of the Treaty of Lausanne: the Treaty cannot be modified without the agreement of the other parties to it. In other words, it is not merely a matter for Britain, Turkey and Greece. In spite of this, if Cyprus is handed over to Greece, there is a very strong argument from the standpoint of political opportunity that the political and military balance established by the Treaty of Lausanne will be completely upset against the interests of our country. In the present circumstances, this position acquires great significance. Our government, by making this clear from the start, has acted most correctly. It is very positive *that his excellency the Prime Minister mentioned on June 29, 1956 to the British Ambassador that since a change in the balance created by the Treaty of Lausanne is being requested, bilateral negotiations should be held with Greece in order to discuss all issues concerning Greco-Turkish relations.* This demand has since been clarified further to the British and the Americans: we have informed them that *we shall be dealing with the issues of Western Thrace, the Patriarchate, the Greeks of Istanbul and certain Aegean islands.* This is viewed as very constructive. Our greatest weapons against the Greeks are these issues. The time has now come for us to become clearer on these matters [...]

Having noted above that the Treaty of Lausanne cannot be promoted to our benefit as a legal foundation of the Cyprus issue, I do not mean that we should abandon everything that we have done so far. At the 9th session of the United Nations General Assembly, the British representative set out his views in accordance with Turkey's position. As our Head of Delegation notes in the detailed report that he has sent to the Foreign Ministry, this view has created a negative feeling towards Greece in certain Latin American countries.

Since the United Nations is not a court, similar manoeuvres can still prove to be strong and useful. But we should not forget the substance of the issue.

Our Head of Delegation has proposed obtaining a ruling by other legal experts in the country on articles 16 and 20 of the Treaty of Lausanne.[15] I have asked the employees involved but such opinions have not yet been sought. Such a ruling will definitely be useful and might forestall the discussions that will take place in the UN General Assembly.

The most effective argument against Turkey's proposals concerning the return of Cyprus to Turkey, on moral grounds, is self-determination, which is a globally accepted principle that has the force of a doctrine. Since the Greeks form the majority in Cyprus today, the obstacle that makes the return of Cyprus to Turkey quite impossible from the UN General Assembly's standpoint is self-determination. On the other hand, since self-determination is still a vague concept regarding its definition and implementation, it is not so powerful as to abandon the fate of Cyprus to the mood of the Greeks. [...]

The cession of Cyprus to Turkey is not supported by legal arguments but by political ones; that is, political rather than legal consequences will ensue. Turkey must maintain its demands to the very end. It must be stated that if Cyprus is handed over, the island's people will enjoy equal rights, without discrimination over religion, race or family background.

Union of Cyprus with Greece, or a return to Turkey: these are two distant possibilities. If the status quo cannot be guaranteed, Britain will want to bring a temporary end to the issue through self-government. *But since the Cyprus issue has been opened, not by Greece or Turkey, it will end with self-government.* For this reason, relations between the three countries will be poisoned constantly. Finding a solution and settling the problem with an agreed middle-course solution will, on the one hand, be in accordance with the principles of justice but, on the other, under the present circumstances, it will not be the only politically feasible way out. It is an arrangement which approaches realism and Britain's effort to resolve the issue. And this middle-course solution is the partition of Cyprus.

The idea of partition has been discussed and examined in a number of secret, official and unofficial negotiations among Turkey, Greece, Britain and the United States.

The Belgian Foreign Minister Spaak has proposed himself as mediator for this idea. From what I have learned through my examination of the files, Greece is thinking of leaving to Turkey a narrow corridor in the north of the island. The Deputy British Foreign Secretary, Sir Ian Kirkpatrick, with a line drawn from north to south, wanted to split the island in half and to give the Eastern part to Greece and the Western part to Turkey. His Excellency Prime Minister Menderes told him that he is of a mind to demand partition into two equal halves. He put this problem to General Holms [later head of the CIA during the Nixon presidency] who had come here [i.e. Ankara] as Dulles' representative, in extremely apprehensive language as if it were possible to bring it about. The partition of Cyprus between Greece and Turkey, perhaps with an area being given to Britain for military bases, means the implementation of the principle of self-determination in a just manner. And here's why: let's say that the population of Cyprus is 481,000 Orthodox Greek-speaking Christians and 100,000 Turkish Muslims. The remainder make up another 10,000. Consequently, there are in Cyprus two different communities, two different unities, two entities, one within the other. When a proper partition is made, each of the two distinct communities is likely to prefer the rule of the country it considers to be its motherland. That is to say that both the Greek and the Turkish community will make free use of their right to self-determination. In this way, a minority which is a completely separate entity will not be forced to live under the sovereignty of whatever state has authority over it because it happens to be the will of the majority.

At the Lausanne conference, Venizelos rejected Turkey's proposal for the holding of a referendum in Western Thrace, on the pretext that the population of the area was not of the same descent but mixed. If the mentality at the United Nations accepts the implementation of Venizelos' position at Lausanne, it will lead to the cession of Cyprus to Turkey without a referendum. But today it looks impossible for us to impose a solution that is opposed to the principle of self-determination.

Consequently we must maintain the concept of self-determination to the end and secure justice. The question will be put to the two communities separately and to those remaining in the Greek region of Cyprus it will be:

1. Independence?
2. Union with Greece?
3. Acceptance of British administration?
4. Another preferred solution?

The Turks in the Turkish area will be asked the same things, with modifications to the second question. In this way, the theoretical principle of self-determination is given its most advanced practical implementation.

The various problems arising from partition may be resolved in a liberal and broad-minded spirit. We can say that if a similar proposal were put to the General Assembly of the United Nations, provided that it had the direct support of the interested countries, it might be totally acceptable. Otherwise, a resolution of the problem is also feasible following agreement among the interested states. Greece is unlikely to go for the 'half and half' solution. Against this there are sound arguments.

The principle of self-determination will be implemented for all the Greeks concentrated in the same area where life under the administration of their choice will be guaranteed. An exchange of population is unavoidable, which, if carried out on a small scale and over small distances, will secure the same environment and climatic conditions. It is not pointless action to transfer a group of people with the aim of not violating the right to self-determination by the Turkish community, which today finds itself a minority, and of providing ways of defending Turkey's security and removing a pending crisis which could cause trouble in the future for the same reason. Especially if one bears in mind that the proposed transfer of population will be carried out with today's technical means and existing conveniences [sic!].

Support for the idea of the partition of Cyprus comes with the legal and human principle of self-determination. The political expediency that reinforces this plan is the need for the island's military power to be in firm and superior hands, for the protection of Turkey's interests and security, the Baghdad Pact and NATO. *Bearing in mind the possibility of acceptance of the proposal for the partition of Cyprus, Turkey must henceforth determine through the relevant authorities which form of partition offers most, taking into consideration its military and economic interests and the interests of the Turkish population of Cyprus. Turkey must participate in the security of the area that will be given to the Greeks of Cyprus since it is linked to the security of Turkey and the Near East. It is not possible for Greece to ask for this right over the Turkish area because the island is 45 miles from the Orient but 600 miles from Piraeus* [my italics].

*

The Radcliffe Proposals

On November 13, 1956, Lord Radcliffe[16] set out his proposals for Cyprus before the British government. In his report, Erim notes:

> The constitution has been drawn up by Radcliffe with the aim of securing self-government. In any case, the stalled negotiations between Archbishop Makarios and the Governor of Cyprus Sir John Harding revolved around this subject. The British government has stated openly that after a certain period of time, it will provide an opportunity for self-determination. It may not seem reprehensible that the constitution will not contain an article that refers clearly to the right of the Turkish community to self-determination. Nevertheless, this must be anticipated through the following measures:
>
> a) The first condition for self-government, as has been demonstrated from the outset by our government, is an end to terrorism by the Greeks. There has to be period of peace before self-government is implemented.
>
> b) The fact that talks are not being held with the representative of the Turkish community violates article 73 of the United Nations Charter.
>
> c) The implementation of self-government must be overseen by a committee made up of representatives of Turkey, Britain and Greece.
>
> d) Regarding self-determination, we must insist on the return of Turks living abroad to Cyprus. This, of course, will also be accepted for the Greeks. If, during an examination of the issue, it is noted that the provision of this right will increase the Turkish population more than it will the Greek population of Cyprus, we must insist on our demand for it.
>
> e) This right is very important for the future referendum on self-determination. In the referendum, which will take place in ten years' time and on condition that we act cautiously, taking our precautions, the number of Turks can be increased to a number equal to what it was under Ottoman rule.[17]

Then we will not worry about the referendum, which will be held either with a view to determining the fate of the island as a whole or implementing partition. As for the constitution of the self-government, we can benefit from the report drawn up by the Institute of International Relations at the School of Political Science [of the University of Ankara]. [...]

The scenario that Turkey will never accept is the opening of the way to ceding the island to Greece on the pretext of giving the residents of Cyprus the right to self-determination. We are so obviously the guarantor of Cyprus, both materially and spiritually towards our country, that the abandonment of the island to Greece, solely on the pretext of implementing self-determination, amounts to ignoring, indeed shaking, Turkey's vital need for security which today may have a population of 25 million but in the near future will have one of 30-40 million. In order to prevent something of this sort, the following is considered expedient as a political measure: a memorandum to our allies and friends, of whom the Americans are the first and best, on the following points:

The abandonment of Cyprus to Greece, or a change in the present status of the island without the previous approval and agreement of Turkey, will bring about a need to review the Treaty of Lausanne in the light of relations with the Greeks. Since the defence of the Orient will be impeded, all our international obligations will have to be re-examined, as will the measure of our military capability.

As regards the clarification of the principles that must govern the future of Cyprus:

a) There is no rule of international law which abandons the fate of the island to the wishes of the Greeks, who form a majority today. The majority on the island in history has been at various times Turkish and at others Greek. Over the past 50-60 years, since the Greeks were protected and due to the injustices against the Turks, they felt a need to abandon the island en masse. If rights are recognised, the Turkish community can increase rapidly and it must grow.

b) Self-determination is an ideal principle: it has been included in a dubious and vague way in the aims and principles of the UN Charter (article 1, para. B). In the part of the Charter that refers to colonies (article 73, para.

> B) self-government is cited, not self-determination. On self-government, the following condition has been added: *the particular circumstances of each territory* must be taken into consideration. In Cyprus, the first of these 'particular circumstances' is the existence of two different peoples. The population comprises two different communities. If the Turkish community is left to the will of the Greek community, which at present is the majority, and is placed under the sovereignty of a governorship it does not want, this goes against the 'particular circumstances'.

Moreover, the fact that it is very close to Turkey and is of vital importance to our security is another 'particular circumstance' which cannot be ignored by anyone and which has to be considered in order that the implementation of article 73 is possible.

Since Cyprus is a place that, only for self-government, is considered to fall under Chapter II of the UN Charter, if we remain true to the letter of the Charter, the General Assembly is not obliged to acknowledge self-determination for the island. If this is attempted it will be violation of the Charter. Because according to the Charter, self-determination, i.e. independence, has been reserved in countries that are protectorates (Chapter XII, article 76, para. B).

The UN Charter can be implemented exclusively and only in the case of self-government. But in this case, the circumstances provided for in article 73, para. B must be considered. In Cyprus, article 76 cannot be implemented since it is not a protectorate.

Both article 73 and article 76 make mention of *the particular circumstances of each territory and its peoples.*

We must insist carefully on this wording. In articles 73 and 76 of the UN Charter mention is made of each territory (in the singular) and 'its peoples', which means that it has foreseen the possibility of more than one people living in a country and granted these self-government or self-determination. If it only had one community and one people in mind, it would not have used the phrase 'territory and its peoples' but 'territory and its people'. It is known that every word and every point of a basic document such as the Charter of the United Nations has been determined after extremely long discussions. The word 'peoples' has not been used by chance. In any case, while initially the singular form of 'people' was used in the preparation of article 76 (minutes of the

San Francisco conference, Volume 10, page 453) following an American proposal, it was changed to the plural. Consequently, the General Assembly may be asked to approve self-government but not self-determination. And whatever principle is implemented, since the Turkish population of the island makes up a different entity, it opposes any attempt to be dragged along by the Greek majority.

Turkey Adopts a Strategy

As was only natural, Erim's proposals were accepted as a whole by the Turkish government, Thus, for the first time, Turkey now had its own policy on Cyprus, with military objectives that in many instances went beyond those of the British and in the name of which London had brought about Turkey's involvement in the Cyprus issue. And this was confirmed by the British Ambassador in Ankara who had warned London that, by instigating Ankara's involvement in Cyprus, it would be encouraging Turkey to demonstrate its own claims on the island.[18]

Thus, while it had previously been indifferent to whatever was happening in Cyprus, Turkey now changed its position from demanding the continuation of British sovereignty over the island instead of its 'return' to the 'heir' to the Ottoman Empire, i.e. Turkey, to that of supporting partition because of its military designs on the whole region and in order to satisfy its ambition of holding sway in the area.

Partition became the means to Turkey's designs on the island. The tactics proposed by Erim involved recognising the right to separate self-determination for the Turkish Cypriots, the provision of 'evidence' for Turkey's military reasons for wanting control of Cyprus and, of course, the integration of the whole issue into the context of the Cold War mentality of the time.[19]

In founding this Turkish strategy, Nihat Erim set out from that time the issue of reviewing the Treaty of Lausanne so as to serve Turkish military ambitions. International law and international principles on which international relations are based could be interpreted – or misinterpreted – in such a way as to serve Turkey's strategy while the proposed solutions (transfer of populations, geographical division, changes to population ratios, etc.) would be implemented on the ground 20 years later.

Chapter 7

ESTABLISHING TMT AND ITS ROLE

Turkey's creation of a strategic framework for its policy was its first step towards drawing up a specific tactical and political method on the Cyprus issue. Its second, and perhaps more significant step, was the subjugation of the Turkish Cypriot leadership and the control of its activities so that there was total support for the strategic objectives set out by Ankara and for the tactics it would choose in order to achieve them.

Turkey had to gain – by any means – the trust of the Turkish Cypriots, who, beyond their distrust of Kemalist Turkey, had attached themselves completely to the colonial government, especially since Ankara had been cold in its response to every effort by the leadership elite to get it interested in what was happening in Cyprus. British intervention had been required to persuade Ankara to show such an interest, which emanated from the fears that the British were cultivating in Ankara. Any concerns, genuine or otherwise, about the future of the Turkish Cypriots were of secondary importance to the Turkish government.[1]

On the island itself, efforts by the leadership to gain the trust and the support of the Turkish Cypriot masses focused on their tactics of securing rights from the British, which would place their community affairs under its control. And the British responded positively. In April 1948, with the blessing of the governor, Lord Winster, a committee formed exclusively of Turkish Cypriots was set up to look at their complaints. One of the committee members was Rauf Denktash.

The committee operated in such a way as to create opportunities for the leadership elite to come into contact with the Turkish Cypriot communities on the island and situations in which it could impose its 'guiding' role on the masses. It dealt with real problems that the Turkish Cypriots were facing, such as their education. Nonetheless, it is impossible that the British did not realise that, through the control of education, which the leadership was asking for, it could create the conditions that would assist it with its nationalist aims, particularly since they showed great sensitivity to similar issues concerning the Greek majority.

The committee's report, 'although of no political significance, was the first step in the gradual orientation of the Turkish Cypriot community towards Turkey'.[2]

The committee's proposals included celebrating the founding of the Turkish Republic, importing school textbooks from Turkey and electing school councils.

In the political field, the participation of the mass of the people remained limited. Fazil Kuchuk himself mentions that, despite his creation of the first party in 1942, the Turkish Cypriots did not become involved in any political activities until 1955. 'Within the next three years, a community political structure was developed as a result not only of efforts of Turkish Cypriot leaders[3] to oppose *Enosis* but also of encouragement from British and Turkish officials who were seeking to safeguard their countries' strategic interests.'[4]

In 1955, Turkey finally having responded to Britain's urging that it show an interest in Cyprus,[5] Fazil Kuchuk's party, under the guidance of Hikmet Bil, changed its name to 'Cyprus is Turkish', thereby fully revealing Turkey's intentions. The colonial government did not object to the party's new name, for all its connotations, and, of course, did not express any concern over the fact that a citizen of a foreign nation was involved in the foundation of a party whose name revealed its purpose to be that of changing the country's establishment.[6]

Armed Groups

At the same time as it was developing effective political organisation, the Turkish Cypriot leadership was also involved in the organisation of armed groups, always on the basis of its opposition to *enosis* – at least, this was the main argument put forward by the leaders to the masses. In fact, the target of these armed groups was always those Turkish Cypriots who refused to serve causes in which they neither believed nor saw any interest.

The first armed Turkish Cypriot organisation appeared in 1945:

> The first secret armed Turkish Cypriot organisation emerged from the ranks of the Turkish Cypriot labour movement and was founded in the winter of 1945. Its founder was the General Secretary of the Turkish Cypriot Labour Unions, Hasan Ali Sasmaz. Within the movement's ranks there was already a 'protection force' which Sasmaz nonetheless considered inadequate.'[7]

Sasmaz made contact with Sergeant Hikmet Hasan Bairam of the British army, to whom he gave the task of setting up the organisation. Its members numbered 50 and their arms had been stored in a Nicosia coffee shop.[8]

Although no information exists about this organisation or its activities, if indeed it undertook any activity, in 1955 Sasmaz called Hikmet Hasan and showed him a letter:

> We appreciate the national effort that you have made until now and your successes. We congratulate you and your comrades on this success. However, you must dissolve your organisation immediately and integrate with us. The foundations have been laid for an organisation that will gather in its ranks the whole of the Turkish Cypriot people and it will begin the struggle. All Turks who love their country, believe in the cause and respect their flag will gather in this organisation and will continue the struggle for salvation as one body.[9]

The letter came from *Volkan*, the armed wing of the Turkish Cypriot leadership elite. *Volkan's* basic aim was, on the one hand, the forcible alignment of the Turkish Cypriots with the policy and practices of their leadership, and on the other the creation of conditions of conflict with the Greek Cypriots:

> The Turkish Cypriots were even asked to stop their age-old social and financial ties with the Greek Cypriots from December 20, 1955 and this declaration was made: 'From now on, it is forbidden, we repeat, strictly forbidden for any Turkish Cypriot or even any Briton to enter the Greek neighbourhoods, Greek cinemas and generally their places of entertainment. Anyone who does not obey this order will be considered a traitor to his country and we shall not be responsible for the catastrophe that will befall him from the acts of vengeance that we carry out. We are certain that with God's help and the succour of the great Turkish nation, we shall achieve our aim very soon.[10]

In parallel with *Volkan*, other armed groups were also operating,[11] such as *Kara Cete* (the Black Gang) and KITEMB (Union of Turkish Cypriot Resistance – September Front). The head of the latter was named as Ulus Ulfet, who, together with two colleagues, was blown up at his home in the Nicosia suburb of Kaimakli as they were making bombs.[12]

Who founded and who controlled *Volkan*?

Specific information answering these questions does not exist. It appears that, at least until the creation of TMT, Rauf Denktash had links with this organisation. He himself says that, at the time when *Volkan* was active, everything was under the control of Fazil Kuchuk. Frequently, however, members of the organisation asked him for advice and on his orders stopped their activities. He also says that the British considered him to be the leader of the organisation and often asked him to mediate so as to bring about an end to its activities.[13] He has also stated that *Volkan* consisted of volunteers who did not cooperate with the Turkish Cypriots' political leadership and, as a result, their activities took place against the wishes of the leadership. When the situation eventually got out of hand after the foundation of TMT, *Volkan* was dissolved on Turkey's orders.[14]

Other sources[15] state that the *Volkan* leadership was made up of a number of Turkish Cypriot policemen, guided by their British officers, and they argue that the organisation's activities were restricted to setting fire to Greek Cypriot properties.

The Arrival of TMT

With the arrival of TMT on the scene, the various other groups and organisations disappeared after being integrated into TMT or dissolved.

TMT was most likely founded in January 1958 and many have claimed to be its founder over the years. Denktash himself, in statements to *The Times*,[16] argued that:

> I founded the organisation with some friends of mine in order to organise the people who had nothing better to do than wander around aimlessly. When TMT took over from *Volkan* and circulated its first proclamation, Dr Kuchuk wondered who these crazy people were. We hadn't told him anything about TMT. He had been happy with *Volkan*. But he could not accept being left out. For two or three years he was bothered by it. [...] Everyone thought that I was the leader of TMT but they were wrong. I was merely its political adviser. Once I had founded TMT I handed it over to others. Even the American and British intelligence services thought that I was the leader of the organisation.

In other statements,[17] Denktash has said that he formed TMT with Burhan

Nalbantoglu and Kemal Tanrisevdi (a Turkish diplomat who served as an attaché at the Turkish Embassy in Nicosia) on November 15, 1957.

Tanrisevdi also claims that TMT was not founded by Turkey[18] since he had no such order at the time. Moreover, he has said that the aim of the organisation was to publicise the 'suffering' of the Turkish Cypriots in order to provoke the interest of the Turkish government.[19] Other information provided by the Turkish diplomat claims that TMT was founded in a house in the Nicosia suburb of Aglandjia, where its first proclamations were written. Burhan Nalbantoglu was in charge of executions.

Ismael Tansu

In August 1995, the Turkish newspaper *Miliyet* published a special feature about TMT, based on a narrative by Colonel Ismael Tansu of the Turkish army. His story is of particular interest for many reasons, especially regarding the foundation of TMT and the organisation's substantial control, the training of its members and the provision of battle supplies, but mainly as regards its plans. None of what the Turkish colonel said has been officially denied or questioned. For this reason, we reproduce below a lengthy extract from his narrative.

The Turkish newspaper began its special report on TMT as follows:

> One day in November 1957, Danis Karabelen, Head of the Mobilisation Control Committee, invited Major Ismael Tansu, whom he knew from the Korean War, to discuss a very delicate case. And he knew exactly how to broach the subject. After his briefing at military headquarters, he was concerned about where and to whom he should address himself. He wanted people who would even sacrifice their lives rather than reveal the secret. Secrecy was a basic principle in this case. On the face of it, they appeared to be alone. The involvement of the government had to remain secret at all costs. For precisely this reason, the case had been handed to the Mobilisation Control Committee. The slightest mistake, the smallest leak could harm the government's foreign policy. The officer who would undertake the leadership and the responsibilities had to be a bold, extremely trustworthy patriot with good organisational skills.

> The first person he thought of was officer Ismael Tansu, with whom he had fought closely in Korea. When he had been given the task of organising the Special War Service, he had called upon Tansu to assist.
>
> He was thinking about this while talking about various insignificant matters with Major Tansu. Suddenly he decided to get straight to the point:
>
> 'Major Tansu, I am going to reveal to you a very important secret but you will not tell anyone, not even members of your family. It is a very sensitive issue. I have been called by headquarters. We have to create an organisation in Cyprus against EOKA. Do you accept?'

For the first time, it was revealed by authoritative lips that the decision to found TMT was taken at Turkey's military headquarters, a place which then, far more than today, was the centre for basic decision-making on the important issues of Turkish policy. Indeed, the task of implementing the decision was given to the Mobilisation Control Committee – the service which was later renamed the Special War Service – whose mission was to create the necessary conditions in which, in case of a Soviet invasion and occupation of Turkish territory, it would be possible to wage a guerrilla war from behind the Soviet lines.

Ismael Tansu accepted the proposal immediately and eagerly. He says:

> Karabelen went straight to headquarters and told them that we were ready to start. That's how TMT came about. Later I found out that the first person to know about the matter had been the then Chief of Staff, General Rustu Erdelhun. The Foreign Minister, Fatin Zorlu, had asked to be briefed on whether we were capable of setting up a secret organisation in Cyprus against EOKA. The Chief of Staff delegated the task to his deputy, General Salih Coskun, who expressed the opinion that something like that was possible but he reserved the right to take advice from our service, which had the technical know-how and the right people to deal with such matters.

This decision had the political blessing of the then Turkish government, as confirmed by Ismael Tansu. However, from what Tansu says, it is clear that, while the orders for setting up TMT had been carried out properly, the drawing up of plans and initiating of action by the organisation were delayed by seven months. The Turkish Prime Minister, Adnan Menderes, delayed giving his final approval, hoping that he would be able to reach an understanding with Greek Prime Minister Constantine Caramanlis. Menderes was finally convinced after certain events in Cyprus, which, as will be seen later, were not at all accidental. On the contrary, they were planned in order to persuade Menderes, should this be necessary.

What is clear from the Turkish and Turkish Cypriot press is that Turkey had begun to prepare for action on Cyprus even before informing the Turkish Cypriot leadership of this. Indeed, it appears that the key events that led to the joining of forces of the Turkish Cypriot leadership's secret and illegal organisations with the group of the Turkish military headquarters to whom the mission had been entrusted were those of 1958.

The then governor of Cyprus, Sir Hugh Foot, had launched a 'peace offensive'. On his orders, hundreds of Greek Cypriots had been freed from detention camps, schools that had been closed down were allowed to operate once more and regulations making certain villages off-limits were lifted. Moreover, orders were given to British soldiers to behave in a less brutal manner.

These measures were accepted with relief by the Greek Cypriots, who saw a better climate being created, one in which an agreed solution could be discussed. The same was not true of the Turkish Cypriot leadership and Ankara, however. The Turkish side considered Foot to be a philhellene and saw his measures as a prelude to *enosis*. The press in Turkey and the Turkish Cypriot leadership launched a campaign of disinformation and incitement, the result of which came in the form of clashes between Turkish Cypriot demonstrators and British soldiers, in which dozens of Turkish Cypriots were injured and seven killed.[20] This event fuelled Turkey's domestic propaganda machine and reinforced the efforts of the Turkish Cypriot leadership to cause such fear – based as always on disinformation – in the Turkish Cypriot masses that they would follow its orders blindly. In this it was undoubtedly helped by EOKA's attacks on Turkish Cypriots who were collaborating with the British but, as will be seen below, also by Britain's policy of forming a special police body made up exclusively of Turkish Cypriots, to be used in curbing the Greek Cypriots' demonstrations in favour of *enosis*.

Turkey had invited Denktash and Kuchuk to Ankara for talks. Officially it was announced that the two Turkish Cypriot leaders had decided themselves to visit Ankara to ask for assistance. Denktash himself says that the visit took place in January 1958 after it was agreed that Kuchuk would ask for funds for his newspaper and Denktash for arms and military leaders for TMT.[21]

The first Turkish head of TMT, Riza Vuruskan, believed that Denktash had placed his hopes in arms while Kuchuk rejected this means[22] and believed in a political and diplomatic struggle.

Denktash then had his first meeting with the Turkish Foreign Minister, Fatin Zorlu, who is said to have asked him whether there was a Turkish Cypriot organisation that could receive arms if Turkey decided to respond to his request. Subsequently he passed him on to Colonel Tansu.[23]

The First Plan

Ismael Tansu has admitted that the Turkish officers in his service did not know anything particular about Cyprus, just as they knew nothing at the Foreign Ministry. Their information, he says, came from reports in the Turkish press but such facts were not a basis on which to establish a secret armed organisation. A meeting was thus arranged between Generals Danis Karabelen and Tansu with Fazil Kuchuk and Rauf Denktash, which took place at the Palace Hotel in Ankara.

> For this reason we arranged the meeting, so as to ask for the information we required. We learned about EOKA's activity, the stance of the British police towards the Turkish Cypriots and in particular about the positions on the north coast of Cyprus. We asked how many weapons they had at their disposal. Their reply was unbelievable. They had only one revolver and one automatic. [...] So we had to start from scratch.

Tansu undertook responsibility for the preparations and drew up a plan codenamed *Kibris Istidrat Plani* (*Reconquering Cyprus Plan*). Lists were prepared of 'volunteer' officers from the Special War Service, those who had knowledge of guerrilla warfare, and a statement was drawn up:

1. Due to developments in Cyprus, it is considered necessary to establish a secret organisation on the island.

2. The name of the organisation will be *Kibris Turk Mukavemet Teskilati* (Turkish Cypriot Resistance Organisation), TMT for short.

3. The government of Turkey will support TMT as much as possible, securing arms, equipment and money.

4. The establishment of TMT will be kept secret from both international and Turkish public opinion. There will be no written communication with the state services.

5. If the existence of the organisation should become known internationally, the government of Turkey will remain outside the issue and the impression will be given that the organisation is the exclusive creation of the Turkish Cypriot community.

6. The organisation will be administered from Ankara by General Karabelen, assisted by General Ismael Tansu.

7. The leader of TMT in Cyprus will be officer Vuruskan, who will have total freedom of movement in his activities, within the framework of the orders he will receive. He will be answerable to General Karabelen.

8. The organisation will be founded and will operate in total secrecy. Under no circumstances must the organisation and its activity become known.

9. Members of the organisation are divided into separate core groups and do not know the other members apart from those belonging to the same core group.

10. The organisation will be run in accordance with all the special rules of secret organisations and its members must be individuals who can respond to these requirements.

11. The name and the activity of the organisation will be revealed when the order 'Start on Day X' is given and on condition that it has been approved.

12. Young people, men and women aged 18 to middle age, will be drafted into

the organisation. All members will receive special training in Cyprus or in Ankara.

13. Some members will be taken to Ankara for training in groups of 25. The necessary preparations must be made so that these groups arrive in Turkey as tourists.

14. The aim is to mobilise 5,000 at first and later 10,000 members and the creation of an armed organisation that will cover the whole island.

15. The necessary weapons and ammunition have already been procured and will be sent to the island when the required preparations are complete.

Organisation and Structure

Information provided by Ismael Tansu and that published in the Turkish Cypriot press confirms TMT's acutely conspiratorial and illegal character and structure.

In 1958 the organisation comprised three ranks. The highest was *otag* (meaning a camp of large tents), which controlled the *oda* (a room) consisting of *cadir* or five-member groups whose members were called *ari* (bees). These names were taken from the terminology of the Turkish nomads, with the tents symbolising the nomadic hierarchy.

Following the military coup of May 27, 1960, the structure of TMT changed. All names with connotations of Turkish nationalism and Panturkism were avoided. Names were used which had more to do with the organisational structure of TMT, which resembled that of a beehive. Thus *otag* became *petek*.

Prior to 1960, when Cyprus gained independence on the basis of the Zurich and London Agreements, six *cansak* or regiments had been set up in six districts. They were originally called *yayla* (plateaux). Each district had three or four groups of 50 well-trained and disciplined members. The head of each group (*serdar*) was known only by his pseudonym, usually the name of a bird of prey such as *kartal* (eagle) or *sahin* (vulture). The leader of the organisation was *bozkurt* (grey wolf), the symbol of Panturkism, with whom only the higher officials of the organisation came into contact. The members were called *kurt* (wolves).

Depending on the mission, they might also have an alternative name.[24] Those sent to Turkey for training were called 'cleanliness wolves', those involved in transporting arms were 'abundance wolves' and those dealing with information gathering were 'oracle wolves'.

At the height of its organisational development, TMT had 10 sections: personnel, information, operations and training, administrative welfare, forwarding and communications, sanitation, finance, social services and public relations, legal and special missions.[25] *Bozkurt* was in charge of headquarters while the *bayraktar* (standard-bearer) was the military leader of TMT.

The oath sworn by members was the following:

> Of my own volition I hereby join TMT, which was founded with vigour and determination for the survival of Cypriot Turkism, against the Greeks, if necessary against the British, and if necessary against Turks who betray the cause.
>
> I give my word of honour that I shall not reveal to anyone the duties I am given or anything I am told about the organisation and that I shall not use arms and equipment for any purpose other than carrying out the orders and fulfilling the objectives of the organisation.
>
> I know that any betrayal means death. Disobedience and carelessness could cost me my life.
>
> I declare that I place myself under TMT's orders and I mark this oath with my honour and my name.

The First Members

One may be certain that, after the first meeting of the two Turkish officers to whom the establishment of TMT had been entrusted with Fazil Kuchuk and Rauf Denktash at the Palace Hotel in Ankara, Kuchuk kept his distance from the practical steps being taken to form the organisation. Denktash, however, upon his return to Cyprus, must have started talks with his close advisers on the creation of TMT, not as he had founded it himself earlier but based on Ankara's plans.

Without knowing from where approval came for its establishment, Kemal Tanrisevdi argues that the organisation was founded in a house in Aglandjia – and he is not mistaken. He is referring, however, to the first core leadership of the organisation, not knowing that the real brain behind TMT was at Military Headquarters in Ankara, abiding by all the rules of illegal activity.

This core leadership took a different form on the arrival of the first *bayraktar* in Cyprus.

The first group of leaders in Cyprus comprised Denktash, Kemal Tanrisevdi[26] and Burhan Nalbantoglu,[27] while the *bayraktar* was Lieutenant General Riza Vuruskan.[28]

Ismael Tansu says that the first people to swear the TMT oath were Denktash, Kuchuk and Nalbantoglu. Indeed, he says that the oath was sworn in a bare room, in the middle of which stood a table with a copy of the Koran on it. A large blanket hung from the ceiling, behind which was the *bayraktar*.

Kuchuk adopted the pseudonym 'Agri', Denktash was 'Toros' and Nalbantoglu became 'Osman Orek'.

Vuruskan arrived in Cyprus in July 1957 under the name Ali Conan, supposedly an inspector from Is Bankasi, the Turkish bank. Tansu says that this was achieved by arrangement with the deputy governor of the bank in Istanbul, Bulent Osman, who undertook to cover all Vuruskan's transport and accommodation costs in Cyprus. Vuruskan was accompanied by another Turkish officer, Mehmet Ozden, who was there as a 'deputy inspector'. Five more officers followed, posing as state schoolteachers, and they were actually appointed to Turkish Cypriot elementary schools, where they are supposed to have taught. These, too, were paid from Turkey.

The specific objectives and 'principles' of TMT, as its propaganda in Cyprus stated, were:

1. Securing the lives and properties of the Turkish Cypriots.

2. Dealing with terrorism by the *enosis* movement.

3. Preventing attacks on Turkish Cypriots.

4. The security of the Turkish community and the struggle against Communism.

5. Safeguarding the rights of the Turks from any Greek or British threat.

6. Strengthening ties between the Turkish Cypriots and their mother country and promoting unity between the Turkish Cypriots and the motherland.[29]

Citing information from an article by Denktash, a Turkish researcher30 says that TMT's objectives were the following:

1. To fill the gap in the Turkish Cypriots' defence, which was becoming more and more evident as EOKA gained strength.

2. To unite all the illegal Turkish Cypriot forces and to coordinate the activities of the *mujaheddin* ('fighters for Islam', or in this case the Turkish Cypriot guerrillas).

3. To create contacts with supporters in Turkey.

4. To create trust among the Turkish Cypriots.

The reference to 'fighters for Islam' is, of course, not accidental. It symbolised, if nothing else, the link between TMT and all the Panturanist, nationalist centres in Turkey. And this link, TMT's ideological Panturanist orientation, was all too obvious from the emblem it adopted: *bozkurt,* the grey wolf, with the map of Cyprus and the Crescent Moon in the background.

TMT's first proclamation was similarly revealing of its true objectives:

> Oh Turkish Youth!
>
> The day is near when you will be called upon to sacrifice your life and blood in the Partition struggle – the struggle for freedom. [...] You are a brave Turk. You are faithful to your country and nation and are entrusted with the task of demonstrating Turkish might. Be ready to break the chains of slavery with your determination and willpower and with your love of freedom. All Turkdom, right, justice and God are with you.
>
> Partition or death![31]

Thus, in 1958, the scenario that the Turks wished to play out in Cyprus had almost taken on its final form, roles had been determined and delegated, the leads and the secondary players alike had taken up their positions and all were waiting for the right opportunity to act within the framework of the military formula that Nihat Erim had proposed.

The British now had the choice and chance to handle the Cyprus issue in the context of the realities as they had developed following the dynamic emergence of the Turkish element, not only in the diplomatic field but also in that of illegal, armed terrorist action.

Chapter 8

Intentions are Revealed

To better understand the importance of TMT's activities and Turkey's strategic objectives in Cyprus, it is necessary to move forward in time to the years immediately following independence.

The Zurich and London Agreements were worked on and turned into a constitution whose provisions served Turkey's strategic objectives.

At the start of their involvement in the Cyprus issue, Turkey's demand was the maintenance of British sovereignty over Cyprus. It then changed the demand for the 'return' of Cyprus to the 'heir' to the Ottoman Empire, i.e. Turkey, and by independence it had become a demand for partition.

The Zurich and London Agreements left Ankara's strategic objectives intact, as determined and analysed by Nihat Erim and as accepted by the entire Turkish political and military leadership. One could even argue that the agreements had created a new political scenario in Cyprus, and had shaped – legally now – Turkey's relations with Cyprus in such a way as to form perfect conditions for the future promotion of its strategic plans against Cyprus. The Turks saw the agreements as a springboard for further pursuits.

In order to understand Turkey's attitude and policy, two Turkish documents are presented below. These were found in the office of the Turkish Cypriot Minister of Agriculture Fazil Plumer following the Turkish Cypriot rebellion in 1963. They analyse the situation that had been created from a Turkish standpoint and the new Turkish objectives are set out. Copies of these documents were also found in the office of the Turkish Cypriot Minister of Defence, Osman Orek.[1]

The first document is undated but it is thought to have been written during the last week of October or the first week of November 1960, three months after the declaration of Cypriot independence.

The second document is dated September 14th 1963,[2] just three months before the Turkish Cypriot rebellion, and is signed by Fazil Kuchuk as vice-president of Cyprus and by Rauf Denktash as president of the Turkish Communal Chamber. It is entitled 'a brief résumé of the policy of the Turkish community regarding the future of the Republic, on the occasion of the third anniversary of its foundation'.[3]

The First Document

The text is presented in full as it is especially revealing, particularly in conjunction with the Nihat Erim report and with Turkish activity from that time until the invasion, as well as later. The Turks never challenged the authenticity of the document. They claimed it was only one of a series of 'working documents':

1. We accepted the Zurich and London Agreements as a 'transitional phase', which is why we signed them.

   If it had been stated that it was not a 'transitional phase' but the 'final solution', we would not have accepted them, but would have continued the intercommunal dispute for longer and left the UN face to face with partition, which they described as 'unfeasible and not practical'.

   As regards the administration of the Republic as set out in the Zurich Agreements, which we accepted as a 'temporary phase':

   a) The rights of Turkey would have gained international recognition.

   b) In the time we would have gained, through better preparation we would have benefited from the mistakes and superficial actions of the Greek Cypriots and in time, by accusing them of violating the agreements, we would have won our complete independence.

   During the 'temporary phase', our whole behaviour and all our actions would have been directed towards the situations described in a) and b) which are accepted by us as the 'final aim'.

2. The reasons for which we cannot accept the Zurich Agreements and the Republic that was created by these agreements as the 'final solution' are the following:

   a) This administration, which is based on a 7:3 ratio, despite the existing guarantees is a *Greek Cypriot administration*. Under this administration, the Turkish structure, which is already weak, is condemned to be wiped out in time.

b) The Turkish Cypriots will remain without a national issue because the process of 'unification' has already started to 'weigh' on the Turks. That is, *maximum cooperation with the Greek Cypriots, no opposition to the Greek Cypriots, smooth coexistence and a show of understanding of their every whim so as not to provoke difficulties.* The result of this process is the neutralisation of the Turkish Cypriots as a separate community.

c) The lack of financial possibilities and existence of material difficulties are such that they are reducing our status as a 'separate community' in the least possible time to zero.

d) The agreements are the result of the principles of mistrust between the communities, hostility and the fact that they can live together only as '*separate and equal communities*'. From the viewpoint of the final solution, the principle of equal communities is condemned to collapse *if we do not maintain it scrupulously or fail to create a climate of mistrust and hostility.*

e) The aim of the administrators of the community, who have not allowed the people to raise their heads for twenty five years during British rule, was to leave the community behind, 'always obedient, loyal and giving in to everything so as not to give the British government a reason to oppress the community'.[4] And now those who consider these agreements to be the final solution are inviting the community to 'always give in to the Greek Cypriots so as not to create difficulties', and as a result there is no longer a community issue. If the Republic is the final solution as far as these proposals are concerned, the Turkish Cypriots' confidence in their community and, later, in Turkey will be shaken. Because of factors such as unemployment and the lack of credit, everything will fall into the lap of the Greek Cypriots. In these circumstances, our acceptance of the Zurich Agreements as 'a final solution' will mean that we are condemning ourselves to the disappearance of the Turkish Cypriots.

It was for this reason that, *before the agreements, an understanding was reached with the Turkish government that these agreements were a transitional phase, that during this period financial and other assistance would be forthcoming and that, in order to achieve our final aim, we would continue to promote the issue of the 'separate community' as a national issue.*

Furthermore, with satisfaction we declare that during our last contact with his excellency Gursel Pasha, the head of our revolutionary government [a reference to the government that was formed after the coup that toppled Menderes on May 27, 1960], '*agreement was reached on the same principles and it was made absolutely clear in the most categorical way that the agreements were merely a phase for us and Turkey*'.

3. There is a major reason for the Turkish Cypriots' acceptance of the agreements and the establishment of the Republic as one phase, and for them keeping their eyes open and not being lulled into negligence. The reason is that the Greek Cypriots as a whole have also accepted the administration of the Republic as a transitional period. From the first day, all their activities have been directed at destroying these agreements.

   a) Through their newspapers, through official or unofficial comments, they have let it be understood that the agreements are transitional, that they cannot become accepted by any free individual and that they have been imposed from outside. Foreign journalists who visit the island accept this propaganda and consequently the idea that 'the Turks need to abandon the technical rights which were secured artificially' has started to take root.

   b) The Greek Cypriots (left- and right-wing) are arming at an unprecedented rate.

   c) The organisation of the Police and Customs and administrative mechanisms is being carried out in such a way as to asphyxiate the Turks. Essentially none of the rights given by the Zurich Agreements to the Turks has been ceded. The Greek Cypriots, through their political delaying tactics, are busy weakening and dividing the Turks, creating Turkish leaders who accept that these rights were exaggerated:

i) The municipalities have not been divided up. The redefining of terms can continue for years. Significant obstacles and irregularities are expected to come up which may make necessary a community revolution. As a result of the 'regular weakening' of the last eighteen months, the fighting spirit of the Turkish Cypriots is fading.

The issue of separate municipalities represents a basic element of 'our status as a separate community'. Even if this separation causes material difficulties for the Turks, it is necessary for this separation to continue at any cost and for us to continue the question of 'separate municipalities' as an issue.

Today the few who have suffered personal damage because of the separation of the municipalities and those 'anti-nationalists who blindly accept the argument that we must coexist harmoniously with the Greek Cypriots at any cost' have begun to act for the removal of the division and the unification of the municipalities. Messrs Ahmed Mouzafer Gurcan and Ayhan Hikmet, who appear as 'anti-nationalists', have stated to foreign journalists that the unification of the municipalities is necessary and that the reason for Denktash and Kuchuk's insistence on separate municipalities is the continuation of the policy of *taxim* [partition].

We request clear guidance on whether the question of separate municipalities should be maintained as our issue. We are of the opinion that, if the way towards unifying the municipalities is followed based on the logic of material interests, the strong foundation on which our demand for 'a separate community status' is based will collapse.

ii) The difficulties that we have faced on the issue of the 70:30 ratio are known to you. Two and half months of the five months during which this ratio was supposed to be implemented have already passed. The Greek Cypriots have no intention of ending the task within five months. The 'method and timetable for implementation' agreed by Makarios and Dr Kuchuk are on the verge of being thrown into the rubbish bin by the Greek Cypriot members of the Public Service Committee. Makarios has reached the point of saying that 'this agreement has no binding value.'

If, at the end of the five-month period, the 70:30 ratio is not adopted, what will the Turkish side do? Will it appeal to the Constitutional Court where it will fight for five more years? Or will it be able to choose the path of securing our rights as a community?

We should not forget that the 70:30 ratio should have been implemented during the period between the London Agreements and the creation of the Republic. We have been sacrificed because of the peculiar behaviour of the Greek Cypriots and, by following the advice of 'for God's sake don't create difficulties' we have been unable to fight for a feasible right at the appropriate moment. The result has been that this very right has been shaken. If this question is not settled by the end of these five months, 'Dr Kuchuk and his friends who promised that it would be implemented within five months will find themselves in a very difficult position!'

iii) In the ministries, at the instigation and under the control of Greek Cypriot civil servants, Turkish issues are being held up. The Greek Cypriot police and employees do what they can to create the impression that we are living under a Greek Cypriot administration. The principle that 'the Turkish Cypriot employees will serve the Turkish villages', which is one of the prerequisites for the status of 'separate community', is not being implemented anywhere.

Must we insist on its implementation? The Turks at Chatos did not pay their taxes to Greek Cypriot tax-collectors who visited them. Now they are being taken to court. Our demand that 'we want Turkish employees' is one that will again incite the Greek Cypriots.

We believe that we must insist on this demand and that we should not give up any of our rights as a community.

iv) Cooperation among the Greek Cypriots in the House of Representatives so as not adopt anything for the benefit of the Turkish Cypriots has reached a maximum.

Everything is being done to create a Cypriot army. The salaries offered to the army commander and his deputy are lower than those of the Chief of Police and his deputy. It is said that the soldiers' salaries will be ridiculously low.

They have no intention of adding a single cent to the sum of £400,000 as the minimum central government aid guaranteed by the constitution, in relation to the community budget of £800,000. On the other hand, £6 million of British aid has been distributed through 'private channels' to the Greek Communal Chamber.

We believe that in view of the path being followed by the Greek Cypriots with the aim of neutralising the Communal Assemblies, which are the only symbols of the 'status of a separate community', the government of the motherland will make the greatest sacrifice and support us materially.

If we reach a situation in which we cannot continue the operation of the Communal Chamber, we shall tear up the existing agreements, which will be in accordance with the wishes of the Greek Cypriots.

v) Development investments from the budget are being distributed secretly to Greek Cypriot villages. No Turkish Member of Parliament can obtain money for investments that are considered necessary. The maximum effort is being made to turn the Turkish MPs into puppets.

vi) Appointments in the police force have been carried out in such a way that the Turkish commanders are ineffective. The Turks of the island are being turned into pawns in the hands of the Greek Cypriot commanders.

4. The way out of the situation, in our view, is the following:

a) The reality that the agreements represent a transitional stage and the conviction that our separate status as a community is vital to the fulfilment of our objectives must be acknowledged by every Turk and this conviction must be spread throughout the whole island in such a way as to pass from generation to generation.

b) To react to the maximum against every activity and effort by the Greek Cypriots to destroy our status as a separate community. We believe that it is our right to react in order to safeguard our constitutional rights.

c) The main lines of the 'national issue' *must be imposed on those who love to play the opposition within the community. They must be prevented from proceeding with publications and propaganda that could harm the national cause.*

Dr Ihsan Ali, who admires and adores the Greek Cypriots and has proven links with the British secret service and extremist Greek Cypriot *Enosis* leaders, and his collaborator, the sexually perverted Muzafer Yurcan, and Ayhan Hikmet, who has documented connections with Communists, must be obliged to abandon their activities and their article-writing, which serve the purposes of the Greek Cypriots. If they do not believe in the existence of a national cause, they should close their mouths.

Today the Turkish Cypriots find themselves at an impasse. The community does not know what to do due to the everyday problems of unemployment, the lack of credit and the lack of jobs. And the inability to gain work with the Greek Cypriots is raising questions in the community and questions about the existence or not of a national cause. Faced with this situation, the people will choose to doubt those who speak about our 'rights as a separate community'. It will be argued that 'there is no separate community when there are no institutions for dealing with unemployment and that only those who trust the Greek Cypriots can survive, that the possibilities of survival for those who support moving away from the Greek Cypriots will be wiped out.' We are face to face with the need to counteract this view and create a society that believes in itself and in the years 1955-1958.

> In short, a national plan must be put to the governors and we must adapt our words and actions to the provisions of this national plan. If the basic lines of the national plan are '*the continuation and spread of the status of a separate community and the prevalence of Turkism in Cyprus one day*' [my Italics], then we must continue the struggle and we shall win public support. But if this plan falls within the framework of 'we have reached the goal, collaborate with the Greek Cypriots, don't destroy the collaboration, don't insult the Greek Cypriot friends to whom you are obliged to open your arms, and don't cause any disturbance because one little right has been neutralised,' then it will be necessary to review the situation and to think about how to take on this responsibility in such circumstances.'

The author is unknown but the text is filled with the philosophy that Denktash has been expressing for decades, one that means scuppering any effort that tends to create a unified political, social and economic environment in Cyprus, the neutralisation of the 'anti-nationalist' Turkish Cypriots, the safeguarding and maximising of the chances of separating off the Turkish Cypriots with the aim of recognising that they comprise a separate entity with a separate status.

The Second Document

The second document, which is also of particular interest, is signed by Denktash and Kuchuk and dated September 14th 1963, just three months before the armed Turkish rebellion against the Republic of Cyprus.

The document is entitled 'A brief look at the general policy of the Turkish community in relation to the future of the Republic, on the occasion of the third anniversary of its foundation'. Its contents are as follows:

> Three years have passed since the establishment of the Republic of Cyprus. Upon the signing of the Zurich and London Agreements which form the basis of the constitution, the Turkish community abandoned its basic aim for union with the motherland and agreed on the founding of the Republic, while the Greek Cypriots for their part abandoned their own basic aim of *Enosis* and

agreed to become partners with the Turks in the administration of the Republic. It was agreed that the newly founded Republic, based on the Zurich Agreements, would have a particular character (*sui generis*) and it was accepted from the very first days that the viability of this Republic would be based on good will, understanding and cooperation between the two communities making up the Republic, with a show of faith in the promises that were made and in the agreements drawn up.

Unfortunately, from the very first days, the Greeks showed that they had not signed the agreements in good faith and they began attacking the Zurich Agreements in the press and other media. Even Makarios, who had personally signed the Agreements, could not help admitting on the April 1, 1960, EOKA anniversary (when the constitution had not yet officially come into operation) that the Zurich Agreements were a springboard for new victories.

From the proclamation of the Republic, the Turkish community made it known in various ways that the Greek Cypriots had no intention of accepting and implementing these agreements with honesty and dignity and it has published articles and prepared reports which prove that, regarding the implementation of these agreements, the Greek Cypriots have resorted to every trick in the book so as to invalidate certain provisions that recognise even the most insignificant rights of the Turks.

It has become quite evident and beyond any doubt that, for the present, the Greek Cypriots have no intention of forming separate municipalities or setting up a Cypriot army, they will never implement the provision for Turkish civil servants to be employed at a ratio of 30% and they will not be considering the Turks' right to a voice thanks to their veto on aspects of such vital importance to the Turkish Cypriot community such as foreign policy, defence and internal security. The most important aspect of the issue for the Turkish community is the fact that the Greek Cypriots have started to question even the agreements on guarantees, which are the only basis for the implementation of the constitution, as well as the fact that Makarios, without feeling the need to obtain the views of the Turkish community, has taken the status of head of state and has the impertinence to declare blatantly that the Greek Cypriots will not recognise the agreement on guarantees. For this reason it is not necessary to explain in this report the injustices, pressures, threats and blackmail with which the Greek Cypriots have treated the Turks since the implementation of the constitution. (We have already sent reports on this matter.)

The real aim of this report is to determine the counter-policy that the Turkish community should be implementing in the face of the de facto situation that the Greek Cypriots have created *through a systematic policy*.

Undoubtedly, when referring to the principles of a policy to be followed, it is necessary to define the real objectives of this policy. Until now, the basis of the policy followed by the Turkish community was the need for the full implementation of the constitution of the Republic. This policy satisfied the needs of the Turkish community as long as the Greek Cypriots were stubbornly avoiding the de facto implementation of the constitution, but it proved to be ineffective in the face of the Greek Cypriots' policy of reviewing or postponing the constitution.

In our view, especially after Makarios' statements that '1964 will be a decisive year for the review of the constitution', the Turkish community needs to follow a more proactive policy. What should be the basic objectives of such a policy? The answer to this question depends on the Greek Cypriots' possible choices:

1. The Greeks may eventually attempt to abandon the constitution and invalidate the Zurich-London Agreements.

2. They may continue with their three-year old policy of de facto 'recognition' of the constitution without allowing its implementation and the de facto demotion of the Turks to a minority with the broadening of the constitution.

   If the Greeks should officially abandon the constitution or attempt to review it, it is our opinion that the Turkish community should do one thing only: take its fate in its own hands, *by founding a Cypriot Republic outside the Zurich Agreements and in accordance with the saying that 'when the obstacle has been overcome, you can take refuge in the forbidden'*. The success of such a move imposes a need for a hard struggle by the Turkish community and depends on many internal and external factors. Without doubt, the most important external one will be the material and moral help from the motherland. Practically, there is no possibility of the Turkish community fighting in the present circumstances *without first having*

> *obtained the approval and consequently the support of the motherland.* It is thus necessary that we agree in advance with the motherland on a line of action, which will be based fully on a detailed plan. *Makarios has not yet made a serious attempt to review or abolish the constitution.* There is plenty of time for the preparation of a plan and we must take advantage of it.
>
> It is true that, according to the Treaty of Guarantee, the motherland may intervene alone if the constitution is officially rendered void. But the only result of such an intervention would be *a return to the legal framework that was put in place through the Zurich Agreements.* Since the Greeks are determined, despite the threat of intervention, not to allow the legal framework to survive, and bearing in mind the negative consequences that such an intervention would have on the UN and international public opinion, it is a matter of working out whether it would be worth taking on the dangers that such a unilateral intervention would cause the motherland. Consequently, should the Greeks officially abolish the constitution, the Turkish community, taking its future in its hands, must proceed with the establishment of a Turkish Republic and thus, if nothing else, the dangers of an intervention would be avoided, at least in the beginning.

To summarise, the main points of such a plan are the following:

1. The Turkish vice-president of the Republic will be accepted by the Turkish community as president of the Republic and he will form a government comprising only Turks, in accordance with the provisions of the existing constitution.

2. The motherland will immediately recognise the government that has been formed and the latter will immediately request assistance from the motherland.

3. The motherland's intervention will follow the request for assistance and, if necessary, the rights of the Turkish Republic will be recognised for those Turkish Cypriots living in Turkey (this right exists in the present constitution in the form of ratios), who will be given passports in the name of the Turkish Republic and in this way their passage to Cyprus will be secured.

4. The Turkish members of the House of Representatives and members of the Turkish Communal Chamber will make up the Republic's parliament and will approve the provisions of the existing constitution for the establishment of a Republic which will consist entirely of Turks or, as an alternative choice, a provisional constitution will be drawn up.

5. Following recognition by the motherland, the Turkish Republic will immediately sign trade agreements with the motherland, via which the Turkish community will cope with its material needs in the conditions that will be created. There can be no doubt that the aim of such an agreement will be to legitimise any assistance from the standpoint of international law.

6. There can be no doubt that this move by the Turkish community will cause a reaction and countermoves from the Greek Cypriots, and the Greeks may undertake a de facto raid on the Turks. As a result of such aggressive moves by the Greeks, a struggle will begin between the two communities and this struggle will judge the final outcome.

7. When the struggle begins, the Turkish community, *which is spread across the whole island, will be forcibly concentrated in one area, which it will be obliged to defend. The choice of area will depend on the strategic plan, which the experts will prepare. Before the struggle starts, it will be necessary to prepare detailed plans for increasing the military mobility of the Turkish community and for the transport of provisions, war supplies and reinforcements from the motherland.*

8. Detailed schedules must be prepared from now and the necessary financial budgets completed. A core staff must be formed from now in the Turkish Communal Chamber so that the civil servants who are now manning the administrative mechanism can continue their work without a break from the first day of their transfer to their new administration.

The above form the outline of the plan and, prior to the preparation of a detailed plan of all aspects, it will be necessary to take a specific and final decision on the basic idea. We are certain that the Turkish community will make every possible sacrifice on this issue.

Regarding the policy that must be followed, should the Greek Cypriots insist on the present situation, i.e. the continuation of the de facto recognition of the constitution: in our view, *if the Greeks continue with this policy, the aim of the Turkish community will again have to be the foundation of a separate Republic. The Turkish community cannot tolerate the continuation of this situation any longer. Nonetheless, since the constitution is going to be violated by the Turks, the Turkish community is obliged to proceed towards the final goal at a faster pace.* For this reason, the following plan comes to mind in relation to the second possibility:

1. The plan that will be implemented in the first case must be prepared as quickly as possible.

2. A movement of violent pressure in all areas must begin so as to force the Greek Cypriots to implement the constitution. The most natural outcome of such action will be that the members of the Turkish civil service will have to go against the Greek Cypriots within the framework of their duties, basing their actions on the constitution. The result will be a need to appoint such elements to the Turkish Communal Chamber so as to comply with point 8 of the first plan.

3. From an economic standpoint, if the Turkish community is to become self-supporting so as to secure the success of the first plan, we shall have to set up useful industries. Since the Greek Cypriots will fight these industries, we shall secure markets in Turkey so as to be able to survive.

4. With the aim of reviving the Turkish community's economy and preparing to implement the first plan, it is necessary to create rapid and frequent communications between Cyprus and the motherland, especially maritime (with ferries, etc.), and *to increase to the maximum the Turkish population of the island, by the arrival of people from Turkey as tourists.*

5. The Turkish community, having fully prepared itself economically, militarily and morally, must put the first plan into operation, taking advantage of the possibility that the Greek Cypriots will cause a constitutional crisis.

> Until now, the Greek Cypriots have given us many chances on this subject and it is clear that they will offer us even more chances, due to their behaviour.
>
> Nicosia 14.9.1963
>
> (Rauf Denktash) President of the Turkish Communal Assembly
>
> (Dr Fazil Kuchuk) Vice-President of the Republic

Observations and Conclusions

The Nihat Erim report and these two Turkish documents provide plenty of information that make clear Turkey's objectives in Cyprus, as determined in the 1950s and at the start of the 1960s, which have a direct link with the situation prevailing on the island today. The internal continuity of the Turks' actions from the middle of the 1950s to the present day stands out when one makes a combined study of the Nihat Erim report and the two Turkish documents, in conjunction with the practice followed in Cyprus since then, which is presented in the next chapter.

A careful study of these three documents reveals how Turkey's national strategy in Cyprus was determined in accordance with Nihat Erim's codification of the situation. The Turkish professor and politician's approach to the Cyprus issue is a pragmatic one that takes into account the legal framework and the concepts prevailing at the time on basic principles such as that of self-determination, and ignoring the groundless position, as he sees it, for the return of Cyprus to Turkey as the heir to the Ottoman Empire.

He begins by recognising that Turkey gave up all legal rights to Cyprus with the signing of the Treaty of Lausanne. But he then proceeds to present the treaty as the basis for a specific balance in the region, particularly between Greece and Turkey, and he argues that any change to the status of Cyprus will disturb the balance enshrined in the Treaty of Lausanne. If one discounts any change in the balance that the Turks claim to have been created by the Treaty of Lausanne, Cyprus is far away from the Greek mainland and is exposed to the guarantorship and the bulk of Turkey. If, on the other hand, Cyprus changes its status without being 'returned' to Turkey, the question of reviewing the treaty for other regions remains open for Turkey. Erim argues that no change to the treaty can take place without the consent of Turkey and that, from the moment that this becomes a topic for negotiation, any changes should be total, so as to restore the upset balance with another, mutually acceptable balance.

Moreover, since it was the British who, through the London Conference, had added the dimension of regional security to the Cyprus issue, Erim, so as to secure international recognition for the 'legitimacy' of Turkish interest in the future of Cyprus, puts forward the arguments for Turkey's strategic security in the region so as to justify the demand for Ankara's control over Cyprus.

He nonetheless recognises that the population and demographic realities on the island – in other words the dominance of the Greek element and the dispersed Turkish minority – in relation to views on the implementation of the principle of self-determination do not allow Turkey to justify its demands. And he proposes a change to these realities through the forcible transfer of populations, by reinforcing the presence of the Turkish element on the island and, from then on, recognising the separate right to self-determination for the Turkish Cypriots. This is precisely what Denktash is asking for today, following the Turkish army's forced segregation of the population and the reinforcement of the Turkish element through the mass settlement with people from the depths of Anatolia.

From that time, as Neoclis Sarris writes, Nihat Erim had supported the creation of a separate Turkish Cypriot statelet within the context of aligning Turkish objectives with international law, and his reports make this clear.

By the Zurich and London Agreements, which led to a truncated Cyprus Republic, Turkey managed to create the conditions for the further promotion of its strategic objectives. Specifically, the Turks obtained through the agreements:

1. Recognition of its role as the 'protector' of the Turkish Cypriots.

2. Recognition of its legal right to intervene in Cyprus under certain circumstances.

3. A legitimate presence for the Turkish army in Cyprus in the TURDYK contingent.

4. Recognition of the Turkish minority in Cyprus as a separate entity.

5. Separate institutions (separate municipalities, a separate Turkish Communal Chamber, separate elections, etc.) for the Turkish Cypriot community.

6. Integration into the system created by the agreements of processes and rights which would enable Ankara, through the total control of the Turkish Cypriots, to control the Cyprus Republic (the vice-president's right to exercise a veto, a separate majority in Parliament, a massive participation by Turkish Cypriots in 30% of all basic services, etc.).

A basic prerequisite for exploiting all the advantages that Turkey had secured was the complete control of the Turkish Cypriot community. This control came through TMT, as will be revealed by evidence presented in the next chapter.

Nonetheless, from the tone of the two reports by the Turkish Cypriot leadership, it is obvious that the leaders could not take any decision without Ankara's approval. The two reports resemble reports from employees to their superiors, especially regarding the choice of policy and practice.

The important thing is that events and developments themselves show that Ankara had adopted in full the proposals of the Turkish Cypriot leadership concerning the strategic objectives after independence and the tactics it would employ to achieve them.

From that time, for example, the aim of segregating the population was taken up and promoted so as to create a pure Turkish Cypriot statelet, 'outside the Cyprus Republic', as it is described, and based on the Zurich and London Agreements. There is, of course, a contradiction here since the agreements discount partition and the withdrawal from the Cyprus Republic. The fact remains, nonetheless, that, straight after the 'compromise' solution in Zurich, the Turkish leadership was preparing to exploit all the divisive elements in the agreements so as to advance its plans.

And Turkey's plans, from the moment Ankara was prompted by London to show an interest and to assist the British government in coping with the problems being caused by Cyprus, had taken on a life of their own, independent of British intentions but also independent of the presence of the Turkish minority on the island, which was merely a pretext. A pretext that the Turks attempted every so often to reinforce with the myths they were cultivating regularly.

'Once', says Melih Ezenbel,[5] 'the Turks there [i.e. in Cyprus] were the majority.

Later, as a result of the policy that was implemented, they became scattered. Whatever the situation, from 1570 they lived there *as remains of the Turkish domination* [my italics].[6] And thus, in the view of the Turkish Foreign Ministry, Turkey had an 'obligation' to protect its 'domination' in Cyprus.

Ezenbel also gave his assessments of how Turkey arrived at the Zurich and London Agreements and what it gained from them:

> The way to the Zurich and London agreements opened as the result of growing Turkish interest. From the moment Turkish interest increased, from the moment Turkey openly and gradually demonstrated that it would protect its strategic interests, it was accepted as an interested party and the idea was conceived for the resolution of the problem, satisfying Turkey too. [...] First the London conference was convened[7] in 1955 and Turkey was invited to take part as an interested party. [...] Then Turkey made efforts, especially to force Britain to recognise its rights. The result was that Britain tabled different but nonetheless similar plans. [...] From 1955 to 1956, we covered a significant distance. And this shows in the fact that in the Radcliffe Plan the principle of separate communal assemblies was accepted. [...] Not only did it recognise a separate identity for the Turkish community but it also provided for the resolving of problems through the participation of Turkish and Greek Cypriots in a council and also proposed an operational system, based on which, under the Chairmanship of the British Governor, Turkey and Greece would collaborate. Turkey reached this point in 1954 when it had no say, and obtained the right to participate in the search for a settlement. From this point the process of recognition of a separate identity for the Turkish community and the establishment of separate municipalities began.[8]

The same Turkish diplomat made a public assessment of the links between the Zurich and London Agreements and the 1974 invasion and all that followed:

> The Zurich and London agreements created a new situation in Cyprus. The most important aspect of this new situation was the 'right of intervention'. To think of the Zurich and London agreements and believe that there would not be an intervention one day would have made the agreements worthless. In concluding the Zurich and London agreements, we knew that one day the

> opportunity to intervene would present itself. Our intervention was carried out in stages. In 1964 we intervened from the air.[9] In 1967, 10,000 Greek soldiers were expelled from the island,[10] but the real intervention took place in 1974. The 1974 *intervention was the intervention we had in mind when we concluded the Zurich and London agreements in 1958-1959* [my italics]. This intervention was made possible in 1974. Another important point is the landing of Turkish troops after the agreements.[11] And this was one of the basic objectives pursued in the Zurich and London agreements.[12]

It is thus no surprise that the Turks insisted on the total implementation of the Zurich and London Agreements, irrespective of the problems that this would cause to the running of the state. Implementation for the Turks represented their victory through the particular agreements.[13]

The Turkish Cypriots, led by Ankara and fully aware of the support of the Turkish army (which, according to the agreements, could set foot on Cypriot soil), 'were intransigent in claiming their full rights as a separate community, even where these rights were likely to be unworkable in practice or to conflict with the interests of the state as a whole'.[14]

It is also a fact that, with Turkey providing support, the Turkish Cypriot leadership became provocative in the positions it was adopting, to the extent that it openly threatened a solution based on the Alexandretta model: 'Cyprus cannot in any way be different from Mersin, Alexandretta or Adana. Those who wish to create problems will not succeed. You can be sure that, if necessary, the Turkish army and Turkey's youth will stand up to their attempts and will cause them injury there and then.'[15] Moreover: 'Whether the Greeks want it or not, Cyprus will be dismantled one day and then they will realise who is really dreaming.'[16]

Exploiting the difficulties and the practical problems created by trying to implement the provisions of the constitution that had arisen from the Zurich and London Agreements to the letter, the Turkish Cypriots began straight after independence, as Turkish writers have admitted, to try and transform the Turkish Communal Chamber, which had been set up in accordance with the constitution with Rauf Denktash as president, into a separate legislative body for the Turkish Cypriot community:

> Thus, the fulcrum of power in the Turkish Cypriot community shifted from

> the Council of Ministers and the House of Representatives to the Turkish Cypriot Communal Chamber. Two other factors accounted for the growing importance of this body: it had become the only tax-collecting agency in the Turkish Cypriot community as a result of the failure of the House of Representatives to reach an agreement on tax legislation, and it was ably led by its president, Rauf Denktash, who had been one of the chief architects of the Constitution and was now reluctantly assuming many of the responsibilities of a chief of state for his politically ostracised people.[17]

Also significant is the fact that, in their reports, Denktash and Kuchuk ask for Ankara's consent for the neutralisation of the anti-nationalist Turkish Cypriots, something which, as we shall see later, TMT achieved while, from the descriptions in the reports, it is evident that the mass of Turkish Cypriots were forced under conditions of terror, as we shall also see, to follow their leadership:

> For example, a Turk working with a Greek could be shot, a Turk shopping from a Greek could be terrorised, a Turk speaking Greek could be beaten up, a Turk getting on well with his Greek neighbour could find himself facing masked men and, finally, a Turkish journalist supporting a peaceful coexistence with the Greeks could be murdered in his bed next to his wife. In order to increase distrust between the communities – and it is this that feeds division – provocateurs could organise bomb attacks.[18]

From the two reports by the Turkish Cypriot leaders, it is also clear that a systematic disinformation campaign was being waged, aimed at the Turkish government and combined with the disinformation being channelled towards Turkish public opinion by the Turkish press, with the declared intention of creating the necessary popular climate so that decisions taken would be those desired by the Turkish Cypriot leadership. The mythology developed and supported by the Turkish Press is well known, with its stories of the 'genocide' of the Turkish Cypriots, of 'massacres' and other 'crimes' contrived to incite the Turkish mob and to 'force' the Turkish leadership, 'justifiably' now, to proceed with decisions that were all a part of Ankara's strategic planning. In one particular instance, if a proposal was not chosen, the threat of resignation was used.

The truly horrific characteristic of the two reports to Ankara, however, is the detailed description of the plan for forcibly imposing a separate regime on the Turkish Cypriots, one which gradually would be upgraded to a 'state' which would ask for 'assistance' from Turkey so as to become consolidated as a political reality. The demographic change with the transport of settlers from Turkey dates back to this time.

The important thing is that, from the moment the political practice of the Turkish Cypriots and TMT coincided with the provisions of the plan, it was revealed that the proposals had been adopted by Ankara and thus had become Turkish policy, the implementation of which was delegated to TMT and the Turkish Cypriot leadership. It is perhaps a unique example of one government working out such a detailed plan for the annihilation of another in an independent, sovereign state, with the aim of taking over territory and wielding political control.

This plan had nothing to do with the activities of the Greek Cypriots, which were, however, used as a pretext. No action and/or major mistake by the Greek side could have brought about such planning and such Turkish ambitions. It was a conscious choice on the part of Ankara, irrespective of what the Greeks were or were not doing. Greek responsibility lies in the fact that they failed to analyse the situation properly and to reach correct conclusions regarding Turkish intentions and take measures to develop a policy that would act as a deterrent towards Turkish intentions

Chapter 9

TMT
IN ACTION

The task of implementing the Turkish government's decision to form TMT was given, as has already been mentioned, to the special war department at Turkish army headquarters, and specifically to Colonel Ismael Tansu. The first strategic plan was drawn up, the oath of the terrorist organisation was prepared, the first leading members were recruited and the first commander of the organisation was sworn in. In 1958 he travelled to Cyprus using a false identity, ready to begin action.

This fact alone left the governments of the superpowers totally exposed. They had shown themselves exaggeratedly willing to demonstrate their 'concern' about the 'future' of the Turkish Cypriots, as Ankara presented it on the international diplomatic scene at the time. The ease with which they accepted the Turkish arguments encouraged Ankara, and their tolerance, on which Turkey based the advancement of its plans against Cyprus and the Cyprus Republic, became elements in a political adventure concerning which the international community and its leading members will one day have to explain their stance. Unfortunately, however, the situation has not altered to this day, since the Turkish leaders still declare blatantly that, even if there were no Turkish Cypriots on the island, Turkey would still strive for its political and military control.[1]

The formation and operation of TMT was an expression of the political will of the Turkish government, which bore the whole financial cost of the organisation's activities. It provided TMT with arms, manned the organisation with officers from its own armed forces and trained the members in its own installations.

The most important aspect was that the activity of this illegal organisation was not being carried out on Turkish soil but on territory under foreign sovereignty – British in this case – the regime of which it wanted to take over for Turkey! This is akin to France founding a similar organisation with the military aim of taking the island of Jersey away from Britain and annexing it.

Who would ever accept such an act?

Training and Arms

The first concern of those entrusted with setting up TMT was the training of members in the use of weapons and the secret dispatch of arms and ammunition to Cyprus for the needs of the organisation. Ismael Tansu reveals:

> The training of the Cypriot TMT members took place in Ankara. For this purpose a special military training camp was set up in the Sincan area of Ankara, again in total secrecy. The individuals chosen by the leader in Cyprus arrived in Ankara as tourists; they were received immediately and given military uniforms so as to appear as soldiers of the Turkish army in a normal training camp. Each group comprised 25 trainees and training lasted 30 days. It started with theoretical preparations on the principles of the organisation and the basic points of the whole operation that they were undertaking. There followed practical training and shooting practice. Once training was completed, the members of the organisations returned to Cyprus in civilian dress and continued their practical training there.[2]

The secret and illegal mission to send arms and ammunition to Cyprus was also one of the first concerns of the military in Ankara. While rapid preparations were under way for the creation of the first core TMT units on the island, the arms and ammunition mission was being delayed. Ankara was searching for the safest way to send the material and to this end, as Ismael Tansu reveals, even smugglers were approached. Shipowners were also mobilised to offer ships for the transport of ammunition.

> One day we were informed that three youths had arrived by boat to pick up arms. We discovered that they were acting on their own initiative. At the time, Dr Burhan Nalbantoglu [a close collaborator of Denktash] was in Ankara. We immediately went to Mersin, Nalbantoglu questioned the three young men and concluded that they were trustworthy patriots. We gave them eight automatics, 20 pistols and 6,200 bullets. It was the first dispatch of arms to Cyprus. We loaded them onto an old boat after covering them with a special plastic substance resembling wax to protect them since they were going to be hidden in the ground.[3]

The three young men were the brothers Vehbi and Celal Mahmutoglu and a friend of theirs. Their first mission was carried out on August 16, 1958. By January 1, 1959, they had carried out a further nine missions of transporting arms from Anemurio to Kokkina. Then came Asaf Elmas who carried out four missions. During the fifth, on November 9, 1958, Elmas' boat *Esther* sank in bad weather and thereafter Ankara decided to use larger vessels. The aim, as Tansu mentions, was to transport arms and ammunition for 10,000 men, a difficult task in small fishing boats.

> We put the matter to Fatin Zorlu [the then Turkish Foreign Minister!] and at once a 25-ton fishing vessel was requisitioned, called *Elmas* after Asaf Elmas, who had drowned when his boat sank. The first mission with this boat was carried out on March 24, 1958. Henceforth they could transport 15-20 tons of arms to Kokkina.[4]

Tansu mentions that, on the subject of the transportation of the arms, 'the Prime Minister Adnan Menderes was very interested', which is why the army and police stores were opened up.

The *Elmas* or *Deniz* was it was still known at the time, carried out 15 missions, transporting weapons and ammunition to the Turkish Cypriots. On the 16th, in the autumn of 1959, a British patrol boat spotted the vessel seven miles off the north coast of Cyprus. Tansu states in his narrative that the crew had contacted him and that, when it was realised that the ship could not escape the British patrol boat or return to Turkey, the order was given to sink it with its cargo, which consisted of 6,000 bombs, bullets and rifles. In the end, however, the British authorities arrested the ship and its crew, an event that caused a major upset in Turkey, as Tansu mentions:

> [...]The Chief of General Staff wanted to interrogate me because I had given the order to sink the *Elmas*, a vessel under state ownership. He was, of course, mistaken. Firstly because the vessel did not appear to be state-owned, but apparently belonged to *Kibris Turk Dernegi* (the Cypriot Turks Association). Our plans always provided for the possibility that the ship would be sunk, should its mission be discovered. And we had prepared for such an eventuality. If it had fallen into the hands of the British, things would have been much worse.

It is worth noting that the crew of the *Elmas* were viewed by the British colonial authorities with visible embarrassment and treated far more leniently than they deserved, as Tansu describes the episode – a fact that fully confirms the Anglo-Turkish partnership against Cyprus:

> To secure the freedom of these brave boys (Captain Resat Yavuz, engineer Oyuz Kontoglu and Petty Officer Leved), I had approached Zorlu. This was his answer: 'Don't worry, I shall do everything to save these brave young men. Indeed, today I shall write to the British Foreign Secretary.'
>
> The British prosecutor had called on Denktash to persuade the accused to plead guilty to one of the three charges so that he could close the case. Denktash was of the opinion that the British were setting a trap. He must certainly have thought this. But knowing the actions of Zorlu, we contacted Vuruskan [the Turkish officer in charge of TMT in Cyprus] to accept the British prosecutor's proposal. A new signal from Vuruskan said: 'Denktash tells us that he knows the British well, having worked for them as prosecutor, and he was certain that they were setting a trap so he was not willing to accept their proposals.' We replied thus: 'You must definitely accept the British prosecutor's proposals. Certain actions have taken place that you don't know about while we are aware of the reasons behind the proposals. We shall brief you in time. This is an irrevocable order.'
>
> The order was carried out. The court condemned the sailors to nine months' imprisonment, but the British Governor asked that they serve their sentence outside Cyprus. Thus, the next day our sailors reached Esebogha airport, Ankara, where we welcomed them, without any press coverage of the event.[5]

In public, Ankara had denied approving the secret dispatch of arms to Cyprus, and the official Turkish radio station broadcast that the vessel had been fishing for dolphins, while Fazil Kuchuk doubted that the ship with its 'inflammable' cargo was even heading for Cyprus.[6]

The transportation of arms and ammunition by fishing vessels from Turkey could not achieve the aim of creating a force of 10,000 men. Beyond the slow pace of the dispatches and the small amounts that could be carried on each mission, there were dangers from the weather conditions and British patrols. The fishing boats were not capable of escaping if necessary and, if they did not sink due to the bad weather, they were sunk by the Turks themselves so as to avoid arrest by the British patrols and having their illegal operation discovered prematurely. Their main concern was not, of course, the British,[7] who, as we know today, were in on the game, but the reactions of Greece and the international community.

The case of the sinking of the *Elmas* led Ankara, as Ismael Tansu says, to the decision to use larger vessels.

In a notable part of Tansu's narrative, he reveals not only the total cover for the activities of the Turkish officer by the Turkish government but also the total support – financial, material and political – of TMT.

> When we began the dispatches of arms in larger vessels, we increased our demands regarding the quantities and types of weapon. We had a written order from the Defence Minister, Edhem Menderes, and were able to take whatever weapons we wanted. On the one hand we were collecting arms to send to Cyprus and on the other we were training TMT members coming from the island. And we had accelerated our activities.
>
> Despite all the secrecy, there were some leaks that had repercussions. Incredible rumours started going around saying, for example, that the Special War Office was preparing a secret army for Menderes and that Ismael Tansu was collecting arms for this army.
>
> After the military move of May 27 [he is referring to the military coup of May 27, 1960] I learned that I was going to be arrested. They had cast us as Menderes' Gestapo. Fortunately I knew Alpaslan Turkes. I asked for a meeting with him and went to see him. I explained the real objectives of the Office and that, additionally, we had taken on the Cyprus issue. This moved Turkes, who is Cypriot, and he told me that he would give us everything we needed. From that day on we were able to secure heavy arms such as mortars.

But what happened to the weapons when they arrived in Cyprus?

The leader of the first TMT strike force was the Turkish Cypriot Mehmet Tiremeseli,[8] a member of the Auxiliary Police Force[9] that the colonial administration had set up in order to counter Greek Cypriot moves in favour of *enosis* and which comprised entirely Turkish Cypriots.

Tiremeseli was also responsible for the group whose job it was to transport arms to Nicosia, at a time when the British had imposed emergency laws that provided for the death penalty for anyone caught carrying arms. Of course, Tiremeseli, as a member of the Auxiliary Police Force, had a permit from the British authorities allowing him to travel during curfew hours and it was unlikely that any patrol would stop and search him since he could produce his identity as a member of the Auxiliary Force.[10]

> In the middle of 1958, the first orders were to hand out the weapons to those villages in immediate need. The weapons were taken to Nicosia by the transport group and collected in the *cadir*. We received them from there and handed them out. All the weapons were covered in wax and they were all buried in the ground apart from one gun that was kept for use. We buried some in fields, some in pits, some in gardens. The places where we buried the arms were called *canak* (vessels) and each *canak* was marked by, for example, a tree. We would bury them at a certain distance from the tree or whatever marker we selected.

Another piece of evidence, from Kemal Sahilboglu,[11] notes that responsibility for the safekeeping of the arms in each *canak* in the villages belonged either to the schoolteacher or the community leader. The former received his salary from funds controlled by the Turkish Cypriot leadership and Turkey, while the latter depended on his good relations with the Turkish Cypriot leadership in order to be able to carry out his duties as community leader. Consequently, both would follow orders, either as a matter of conscience or out of need. No one could open the *canak* without the orders of the *bozkurt.*

Certain *canak* were opened for the first time at Christmas 1963, while it is certain that, following the intercommunal troubles of 1963 and the forcible movement of the Turkish Cypriots, certain *canak* remained untouched and probably remain so to this day.

The Turkish government covered all the costs of this operation. This had been Zorlu's promise to the officers who had undertaken to implement the plans.[12] The money came from secret budgets, as revealed to the officers by the then head of the Cyprus Desk at the Turkish Foreign Ministry, Adnan Bulak.[13] Whenever there was a problem, Zorlu would intervene and resolve it.

*

The First TMT Leader in Cyprus

The first person to be appointed TMT leader in Cyprus was Colonel Riza Vuruskan, who also served in the Special War Office, like Ismael Tansu. With him, another 13 officers[14] had been selected to serve in various TMT-related positions. Their names were given to the Foreign Ministry in case they needed to be provided with cover. These officers had been sent to Cyprus in the guise of consular employees, employees of the Turkish Press Office in Nicosia, clerks in a Turkish bank and teachers.

According to entries in Vuruskan's diary,[15] on July 13, 1958, the officers who were to be posted to Cyprus received their forged passports. Vuruskan himself would adopt the false name of Ali Conan.

On July 21 they applied to the passport section of the British Consulate with a letter from the Labour Bank, which confirmed that they were its employees and that they would be travelling to Cyprus on bank business.

The following day, Vuruskan and his deputy had a meeting with Foreign Minister Zorlu. He writes in his diary:

> The Minister told us that we must transform the villages into fortresses so as to enable them to defend themselves. He also said that to this end we might need to do some building work.
>
> Replying to a rather vague point in his address, as we were leaving I said to him:
>
> 'Sir, we see our mission to Cyprus as a secret mission which aims at a guerrilla war for the protection of the Turkish community and at the armed support of the government's positions. From your address, we have understood that our ultimate aim, if needs be and circumstances allow, is to bring about a general rebellion and to place the whole island under our control. Have I understood correctly? Is this our ultimate aim? Should we be preparing for this eventuality?'
>
> The Minister replied, though not especially eagerly:
>
> 'Yes, that is the aim.'[16]

Vuruskan took up his duties at a time when the British, with Sir Hugh Foot as the new governor, were attempting to find ways of reaching an understanding with the Cypriots. From the start of 1958 they had been trying to find ways of ending the armed conflict with EOKA. During the first days of August, the governor announced a temporary suspension of operations and EOKA responded in kind. Vuruskan took advantage of the truce to organise the TMT forces better and to place them under his complete control.

His attention focused mainly on the Turkish Cypriots who were serving in the colonial security forces. There he found ready human resources for manning TMT, indeed with the collusion of the British, who tried to contribute to the organisation of the Turks long before Vuruskan took up his duties. Moreover, in order to bring the two communities into conflict, the British founded the Auxiliary Police Force, which was manned entirely by Turkish Cypriots and was used to suppress the almost daily demonstrations by the Greek Cypriots, which usually ended in clashes with the force.

The Turkish Cypriot press provides an abundance of information about the British contribution to Turkish efforts to set up a secret organisation, even before TMT took on its final shape under Ankara's guidance.

From the outset, Vuruskan correctly assessed the possibilities he was being offered due to the mass participation of the Turkish Cypriots in the colonial police and security forces. And he set out to exploit this as his first aim by bringing them into the ranks of TMT.[17] The Turkish Cypriot police were already trained, they could provide him with useful information on the movements of the British and the Greek Cypriots and they were covered fully in the missions they were set.

Moreover, in this way he also resolved a serious problem that he was facing concerning the recruitment of members, since the majority of the Turkish Cypriots refused to be dragged into such adventures. 'The initiated ones,' they complained, 'approached the Turkish Cypriots and talked to them about the organisation, about being initiated, but they were not convinced.'[18]

TMT's First Targets: 'Traitors'

Until the beginning of 1958, Rauf Denktash served in the colonial prosecutor's office. Indeed he had been the public prosecutor in the trial of the crew of the *St George*, who were arrested by the British for transporting arms for EOKA in 1954.

Denktash had made a name for himself within the Turkish Cypriot community for the fanatical way in which he had prosecuted the crew of the *St George*.[19] There was, of course, no shortage of those who considered him an agent of the British.

The formation of TMT required the presence on the political level of a dynamic leader who believed in the organisation and its objectives and could protect it politically while promoting the political objectives of the organisation dynamically and persuasively. Denktash was such a man.

At the end of 1957, Denktash was elected chairman of the Federation of Turkish Cypriot Institutions, displacing its previous chairman, Faiz Kaimak.

Arif Tahsin provides important information on Denktash's rise:[20]

> With several others, I heard on two occasions from the late Faiz Kaimak how Rauf Denktash was put forward for the chairmanship of the federation. In brief, Faiz Kaimak had said the following: 'I was invited to Ankara by Edhem Menderes, who told me, 'We thank you for your contribution, Faiz, but the time has come for you to withdraw. We need a more aggressive person.' I tried to object and I was told, 'There is a trigger on the gun.'
>
> I returned to Cyprus and I decided not to stand as a candidate but I was curious to see who they would put in my place. And I went to the meeting. I told Niazi Maniera that I would not be standing. Meanwhile I saw Denktash wandering around the room and I realised that he was the one they wanted to have as chairman. I told Maniera to stand himself. 'No Faiz, don't get me mixed up in this business,' he replied. 'You mean you're going to elect that agent of the British as your chairman?' I said.
>
> The removal of Faiz Kaimak and the promotion of Denktash shows that the idea of Turkey appointing certain people to certain positions is not a new one.
>
> The name of Denktash began to be heard among the people following his rise to the chairmanship of the federation. And the talk certainly came from Nicosia. I don't know whether it is true or not but as soon as Denktash became chairman, this was heard: 'The one who abandoned us yesterday to become the prosecutor of the British, what business has he among us today?' And there followed the explanation: 'At one time Denktash was a tremendous speaker and in one of his speeches he said: "if necessary we shall take up arms and head for the mountains," and from then he received his promotion from the British.

> It is true that at the time, it was possible to get somewhere if you insulted the British enough. There were people in this country who could obtain a scholarship in England through just two newspaper articles.'[21]

1958 was a difficult year for Cyprus. On the one hand the British colonial government had launched an all-out attack against the EOKA fighters, and on the other the Turkish Cypriots had intensified the 'cleansing' of anyone who expressed opposition to their leadership's policy.

There were, of course, instances of Turkish Cypriots defying the danger and openly condemning the terrorism that was being exercised against the anti-nationalists. Moreover there was no lack of revenge attacks,[22] which essentially confirmed their accusations.

In Turkey, the internal situation was almost chaotic. (The social and political upheaval eventually led to the coup d'état on May 17 of the following year and to the ousting of the Menderes government.) The last thing that the Menderes government wanted at the time was for the situation in Cyprus to get out of control, as it would have poured more oil on the fire that had already been lit within Turkey. The government faced the possibility of having to pay the price for its incitement and abetting of the nationalist stirring up of Turkish public opinion over the Cyprus issue. That price would be, as indeed it was eventually, its power. As always happens when Turkey is facing serious internal problems, public opinion turns, with a belated rise in nationalism, to external issues.

At the end of January, the Baghdad Pact conference was held in Ankara and Zorlu told the press that on the fringe of the conference he would be discussing the Cyprus issue with his British counterpart Selwyn Lloyd who was accompanied by the governor of Cyprus, Sir Hugh Foot. The Turkish press went to town with articles in favour of partition while in Cyprus itself there were incidents between the security forces and Turkish Cypriots demonstrating for partition in Nicosia, Famagusta, Limassol and Larnaca,[23] which resulted in eight dead and more than 70 injured.[24]

The events in Cyprus thus provoked Menderes' concern. True, TMT had been formed by his decision but he had also made it clear that no action should be taken without his express orders. Now he was facing a situation in which the organisation he had supposedly set up to deal with EOKA was involved in provoking the British and murdering Turkish Cypriots, causing further trouble to his already troubled internal front. He therefore called on the head of the Special War Office of the General Staff, Danis Karabelen, for explanations. With him went Ismael Tansu, the man responsible for implementing the decision to set up and operate TMT, and Riza Vuruskan, the organisation's first leader in Cyprus.

Ismael Tansu recalled:[25]

> We discovered at once why the Prime Minister had called for us. The first to speak to him was officer Riza Vuruskan, head of TMT, who explained the situation in detail. Then it was my turn: 'Mr President, I can assure you that under no circumstances have we undertaken armed action. There is no chance of us acting outside the guidelines laid down by the government. There may have been some violence but the object of the exercise justified it. Similar incidents may occur in the future too but these are to enable us to keep the organisation secret and strong.
>
> After these explanations, he did not ask us anything further. He merely noted: 'In no case whatsoever do we wish to have an armed conflict with Greece. Be very careful. If you act alone you may harm the government's policy.'

It is also worth seeing how Ismael Tansu, from Ankara, explained the incidents caused by fanatical members of TMT in Cyprus during that year:

> In those days, TMT had been strengthened and its existence had started to become real, especially from a psychological standpoint. A strengthening of the morale of the Turkish Cypriot community and of us officers was evident. It was during this time that certain elements, having got hold of weapons, began to take part in robberies. We learned that they were collaborating with the Greek Cypriots and the British and acting against the organisation. It is a law of secret organisations that traitors are punished. But we were unable to try them or to imprison them and there was a danger of their numbers rising. There was a danger of everything being revealed. We had to remove them and that's what we did.

There was a favourite method used in such cases. Those who disagreed with the organisation were referred to as 'certain elements' and thus any action against them became justified. And when the numbers of those disagreeing grew, the accusation of 'treason' was brought in so as to justify the 'cleansing'. This occurred in the case of Turkish Cypriots.

This is also the conclusion of many Turkish Cypriot journalists, researchers, authors and historians who have dealt with the subject. One of them, Ahmed An, in a series of articles[26] provides plenty of additional details:

> In its first proclamation, on November 2, 1957, TMT gave the first command to the Turkish Cypriots concerning 'total obedience to the orders of the organisation' and announced the following: 'In this struggle there may be – though we do not wish to believe such a thing – traitors. In such a case, their extermination will be unavoidable.'
>
> With the anti-Communist campaign started by Grivas, the EOKA leader, in the autumn of 1957 and which culminated in January 1958, the left-wing Greek Cypriot union leaders and democrats faced persecution and murder. While EOKA created a special group for the assassination of Greek Cypriot Communists, TMT undertook similar activities against the Turkish Cypriot democrats.
>
> Any Turkish Cypriots who opposed the policy of *taxim*, which had been given a nationalist character, were proclaimed traitors and condemned to death. The position that the Turkish Cypriots could not coexist with the Greek Cypriots had originally been an exhortation but it gradually began to be imposed forcibly.
>
> Through a proclamation at the start of May 1958, TMT ordered all Turkish Cypriots to resign from the left-wing PEO trade union and warned that it would punish all those who continued to work with the Greek Cypriots. In their May Day celebrations in 1958, Greek Cypriot and Turkish Cypriot workers had demonstrated together and stressed their joint struggle against a common enemy, British imperialism. This fact caused concern both to the colonial administration and the Turkish Cypriot leadership.
>
> That same May Day, Kuchuk had visited the Ataturk Institute and had urged the pupils to avoid any contact with Communists. That night, the Turkish Cypriot Educational Sports Association (TEK), which was frequented by young left-wingers, was attacked and looted. *Haravghi* newspaper wrote on May 3, 1958: 'It has been noted that during the May Day events, certain Turks were photographing those in attendance. Later, in the Turkish quarter, it was

rumoured that TEK had sent a representative to the events, that their members had betrayed the Turks and that they were agents of the Greek Cypriot union leaders. And in the evening, 30 fanatical Turks attacked the association's premises and looted them, throwing into the street whatever was inside and burning it.'

Terrorism and blackmail would very soon bring results. Within a few days, the Turkish newspapers were full of announcements concerning the resignation of Turks from PEO. TMT, aiming to affect a British plan that was being drawn up[27], issued a proclamation on May 18, 1958, calling upon the Turkish Cypriots to join a mass struggle. The proclamation, which was found at Pyla,[28] said that, 'On the day when Britain gives Cyprus its own local self-government, the island will be drowned in blood.' The same proclamation gave orders for the completion of all preparations so that the Turkish Cypriots would be ready for a mass struggle within 15 days.

In another proclamation, circulated on May 20, 1958, there was a reference to the fact that in Anatolia the struggle had been carried out with sticks and axes and that the lack of arms should not affect the people's morale. And while the Turkish Cypriots were collecting sticks, stones, axes, sharp instruments and more in their homes, they were hanging pictures on their walls that showed a Cyprus divided in two under the boot of a terrifying Turkish soldier.

Another Turkish Cypriot newspaper, *Zafer Kibrisli Turkeridir* (*Turkish Cypriot Victory*), published on October 15, 1965, the results of this first round of the TMT terrorism campaign against the Turkish Cypriots themselves. The newspaper referred to it as 'Operation Annihilation of Left-wing Turkish Cypriots':

- May 22, 1958. Murder attempt against Ahmed Sadi Ergut, chairman of the Turkish branch of PEO. Sadi was injured and a few days later he escaped to London.[29]

- May 24, 1958. Brutal murder of Fazil Onder, owner and chief editor of the newspaper *Inkilapci* (*The Revolutionary*), which was closed down by the British at the end of 1955 but reappeared at the beginning of 1958.

- May 29, 1958. The barber Ahmed Yaghia, a member of the TEK board, is murdered as he sleeps. On the day of his murder, the Turkish Cypriot newspaper *Bozkurt* publishes a 'statement' by Yaghia in which he notes: 'Apart from the fact that I am not a member of the labour union, I am not a leftist either. I declare that I am and always have been faithful to the line taken by our leaders and our people.'

- June 5, 1958. Attempted murder of Hasan Ali, a member of the board of the builders' union affiliated with PEO.

- June 30, 1958. Limassol barber Ahmed Ibrahim is murdered. His 'crime' was to publicly support the coexistence of Greek Cypriots and Turkish Cypriots.

- July 3, 1958. Attack against Arif Barudi, who manages to escape. His 'crime' was working in a Greek-owned business.

The list, of course, is not complete, neither as regards the number of people who were victims of TMT's wrath nor their 'crimes'.

TMT and the British

From the start of the 1950s, the British systematically promoted in Cyprus all those elements which either provoked a direct clash between the two coexisting populations and gave the colonial administration the ability to maintain a state of mistrust among the Greek and Turkish Cypriots that London could exploit on a political and diplomatic level, or laid the foundations for a future worsening of the conflict.

Apart from the fact that Ankara was encouraged to act on an international level so as to serve British interests, in Cyprus itself the ground was being cultivated in such a way that Turkish Cypriots could be used as a balance against the Greek Cypriots' demand for *enosis* and as the 'great alibi' of British policy on Cyprus.

In its efforts, Britain was not only exploiting the terrible financial and social conditions prevailing on the island immediately after World War II but also the mistakes of the Greek Cypriot side – and mistakes most certainly were made.

The recruitment of Turkish Cypriots into the colonial security forces served British interests perfectly, but it also provided a way out for the masses of poor Turkish Cypriots, who were suffering in order to survive. A 'sure' job with the security forces meant a guaranteed satisfactory income and 'participation' in the administration.

The British 'explain' the increased presence of Turkish Cypriots in the police and security forces as something they 'inherited' from the Ottoman era, when the police was made up entirely of Turks (!) as the result of the Turkish Cypriots' response to the required disciplined behaviour in the ranks of the police, in contrast with the intractable character of the Greek Cypriots, and also as a result of the need to protect the police from the corruption of *enosis* propaganda.[30]

The Turkish Cypriots also acknowledge that their positive response to the security forces' recruitment drive essentially meant that they were taking part in the British fight against the Greek Cypriots, even though they add at the same time that, 'It is a fact that the Turkish Cypriots were joining the police not out of zeal for the fight against the Greek Cypriots but due to unemployment.'[31]

This view is shared by Dr Ibrahim Aziz,[32] who noted in a lecture[33] that the British had all the necessary forces at their disposal and could bring as many as they needed to cope with EOKA and the *enosis* movement but they did not do so, preferring to set up the Auxiliary Force. And he adds:

> The ordinary Turkish Cypriots, who were not aware of where the British were pushing them (since their leadership did not warn them but actually encouraged them), rushed to reinforce the various Auxiliary Forces, their only thought being of earning a daily wage.
>
> Thus the Greek Cypriots, who thought that they were waging a holy war against the British, found themselves facing the Turkish Cypriots.
>
> In this way, the British began to set their plans for partition before the Turkish community and we can see that, after 1956, the Turkish Cypriot leadership changed its tactics about maintaining the status quo, a line supported by the Menderes government.
>
> In order to stir up Turkish public opinion against the Greeks and to prepare the ground for the policy of *taxim* (partition), mass demonstrations were held which led to the bloody events of September 7, 1955, in Istanbul.'[34]

Despite identifying with Denktash's policy, Halil Ibrahim Salih, the Turkish Cypriot-born American professor of political science, acknowledges that the British took full advantage of the local circumstances in order to promote their policy of 'divide and rule'[35] through the recruitment of the Turkish Cypriots. Indeed, he confirms the degree to which the Turkish Cypriots were used by the British, reinforcing the indications that recruitment was carried out very carefully, so that it was essentially a 'gift' to TMT and Ankara's policy:

> The Special Branch of Cyprus, which was similar to the FBI in America, was put under the direction of expert personnel of Scotland Yard, London. The new recruits of the Special Branch from London were trained experts in police investigation, but were not as effective as had been hoped. They had little or no knowledge of the Turkish or Greek languages and were constantly frustrated by being unable to comprehend the Cypriot mentality, philosophy, or behaviour. Consequently, the Turkish Cypriots were paid attractive salaries to encourage them to leave their vocations in order to fill the gap in the British personnel. Once the Turkish Cypriot became a member of the Special Branch, he was used extensively in interrogating the Greek Cypriots[36] and witnessing their torture with the hope of obtaining information in regard to EOKA. [37]

The British also organised another special body comprising only Turkish Cypriots, about which Kemal Saliboglu[38] reveals a considerable amount of information:

> I worked at a thousand and one jobs until 1955 when the institution of the Auxiliary Forces was introduced. I joined on October 10, 1955. I was a member for about seven months. One day a British officer came from Kenya and chose some of us, including me, to be sent to Kenya for training in the art of tracking, so as to be able to locate EOKA men. The selection was made in Kyrenia. The first training took place at Platres, something like exams in which I came first and was made a sergeant.
>
> At the beginning of 1956 they sent us to Kenya to be trained in tracking. We were placed in the Africa Riffle Button School, some 90 miles from Nairobi.
>
> The army camp was four miles from Nairobi. There we trained on the

> mountains. Later we also went on safari and our training continued for another fifteen days. In all the training lasted seven weeks. On our return we were sent to Platres.
>
> When I returned to Kyrenia, the administrators did not want to recognise me as sergeant. At Paphos Gate [a Nicosia police station] there was a man called Chamberlain in charge of the Auxiliary Forces. He didn't want to make me a sergeant but all my papers said that I was one. Basing my case on this, I went to Deputy Governor Single, who gave orders for my rank to be recognised and I was placed in Number Nine Unit.
>
> The unit consisted of 600 Turkish Cypriots whom the British had recruited with the aim of fighting EOKA. They were answerable to no one. The only person we recognised was one we called 'Scotch Effendi' and he was the only one from whom we took orders. Even the Cyprus Police Chief had no authority over us.
>
> I swore the TMT oath in my unit, which was a commando unit.

The British used other methods of recruiting Turkish Cypriots, whom they prepared for action alongside TMT, thus assisting the organisation of the Special War Office of the Turkish General Staff to train its men and also offering them the means for the action they would undertake.

Omer Akai was TMT's weapons director, who used the codename Omer Usta. He was put in charge of arms in 1950. He explained:

> One day two British men in civilian clothes visited me at my workshop. They searched the workshop and left, returning later with a Turkish commando, who gave me a pistol to repair. I had a police book. 'If you sign the book,' I said, 'I'll repair it.' He did so and gave me the pistol, which I repaired. He wanted to pay me but I did not accept any money. He insisted and gave me ten shillings. He asked me if I wanted to work as a corporal in the police. I had found out that he was in charge of the CID. I refused but I asked him if there were other repairs I could undertake. From then on he would bring me work. Since military law was in force at the time, he gave me a green card with which I could travel anywhere at anytime I wished. There were 600 Turkish commandos whose guns I would service. Most of them had their own weapons or TMT guns, in addition to their service arms.[39]

The scene was set. The British would now be able to appear as the mediators in an 'intercommunal conflict', which would 'keep' them in Cyprus despite their 'wish' to disengage by granting self-government to Cyprus.

Britain's participation in the crime against Cyprus was considerable. It created, under the cloak of colonial legitimacy, an unending source of well-trained and armed members of TMT, from which Turkey could draw all the forces it needed whenever it needed them to promote its strategic objectives in Cyprus.

It was now clear that the predictions, assessments and warnings of the British Ambassador in Ankara were coming true: that, following London's encouragement of Turkish involvement in shaping Cyprus' future, a 'Frankenstein' would be created and, once it was acting of its own volition, control would be impossible. For this reason, Britain will always be accountable to history for everything it did – and everything it did not do – in Cyprus.

Chapter 10

YEARS OF FIRE

There were no restrictions whatsoever on the arms and means used by TMT so that they might achieve their two basic strategic objectives: the total control of the Turkish Cypriots and the creation of conditions of conflict between the two communities in order to 'prove' the impossibility of peaceful coexistence and to support the demand for partition. Violence, terrorism, executions of anti-nationalists, blackmail, lies, distortion, Cold War anti-Communism, disinformation – all were considered legitimate and were used on a daily basis. They were all the more necessary since the Turkish Cypriots lived scattered throughout the whole island in a harmonious and cooperative relationship with the Greek Cypriots and refused to obey their leaders' orders blindly.

The achievement of these two objectives would open the way to the implementation of Nihat Erim's suggestions for the creation of a territorial basis for the demand for partition and separate self-determination. Control of the Turkish Cypriots, combined with the gradual segregation of the two communities, would make it 'necessary' to transfer populations, precisely as envisaged by the Erim proposals.

The incidents of January 1958, sparked by governor Sir Hugh Foot's proposals for self-government, were the launch pad for regular action by TMT on the above basis. Turkish fanaticism was channelled as much against the British, whom Ankara accused of being particularly friendly (!) to the Greek Cypriots, as against the Greek Cypriots. The signal was given by Turkish Foreign Minister Zorlu[1] himself on the eve of the Baghdad Pact conference in Ankara, to which Sir Hugh Foot went with the British delegation in order to present his proposals for self-government. Turkey's policy, from a position of maintaining Cyprus as a British colony or 'returning' it to Turkey, had changed to one in support of partition (*taxim*). Self-government would bar the way to this and the issue thus needed to 'die' before any discussion could take place.

The abandonment of the old position and the adoption of the policy of *taxim* were announced by Prime Minister Adnan Menderes to the press on the night of January 26 during a meal at the Liman restaurant in Istanbul.[2]

In Cyprus, following the first bloody clashes between the British and Turkish Cypriot demonstrators, who were incited by TMT to react to the proposal for self-government and to whom the message had been given that '*taxim* has been agreed',[3] TMT circulated a leaflet in which it threatened that, 'The island will be drowned in blood and fire the very day self-government is announced.'[4]

However, the results did not satisfy the Turkish Cypriot leadership or that of TMT. Turkish Cypriot participation in the incidents had not been as great as expected. Fanaticism and racial hatred were limited and not enough to advance certain conditions for the achievement of the objectives that had been set.

At 10.00 a.m. on June 7, 1958, a bomb exploded at the entrance of the Press Office of the Turkish Embassy in Nicosia. 'The explosion served as a time signal and an excuse for Turkish rioters to invade the Greek sector of the old town,' wrote Nancy Crawshaw.[5]

The damage was enormous. The British security and armed forces could not restrain the mob. Two Greek Cypriots lost their lives, while the police restricted their action to guarding the so-called 'Mason-Dixon Line' that the British had drawn in order to delineate the two communities in Nicosia. It was the herald of the 'Green Line' which was later drawn, again by the British, at the beginning of 1964 after the Turkish Cypriot rebellion against the Cypriot state.

Nancy Crawshaw's comments are interesting, especially given that she is not known for having particularly pro-Greek feelings:

> The original explosion did little material damage. And circumstantial evidence strongly pointed to the fact that the bomb was of Turkish origin. This, however, did not deter Turkey from making a formal protest to Britain the next day, alleging that the Cyprus administration had failed to give the Turkish minority adequate protection.[6]

Denktash's Time Bombs

Rauf Denktash has admitted in a British television interview that he gave the order for the planting of the bomb at the Turkish Press Office.[7]

It is worth seeing what Arif Tahsin[8] has to say about Denktash's role after being chosen by Ankara to lead the Turkish Cypriots:

> Denktash was the most suitable man for the job. According to his own version of events, his father had always taken him along to meetings of adults even when he was a child and for this reason he had harboured a strong desire to lead from an early age. Perhaps he was able too. Those who selected him made a very good choice and certainly they could not have found anyone better. They cannot do that even today.
>
> Now the clashes among the Greeks and Turks could begin, those clashes that they had tried to start in the past but had failed with the exception of two or three skirmishes.
>
> Straight after Denktash's arrival, *taxim* was on the agenda. And we lived through the events of January 27-28.
>
> We were told that we had to let the world know of the existence of the Turks of Cyprus through bloodshed. The events of January 27-28 were in this sense a very good experience. We learned that we, the Turkish Cypriots, had to shed a great deal of blood in order to achieve the objectives that were placed before us on a daily basis in different guises, and we still have a lot of blood...

Denktash's revelations about the bomb at the Turkish Press Office led to comments by another Turkish Cypriot journalist, Kutlu Adali,[9] in a Turkish Cypriot newspaper:[10]

> On watching the documentary I felt ashamed to hear President Denktash himself speak of the secret hands and the reason they threw a bomb at the Turkish Press Office on January 8, 1958, exactly 26 years ago. I also felt ashamed upon learning that they had been distorting history for so many years. As *Yeni Duzen* [a Turkish Cypriot newspaper][11] had also published, the bomb attack was the work of a close collaborator of Denktash. And it is now clear that the aim was an escalation of the Turkish Cypriots' political fanaticism.
>
> The reason why I, as someone who lived through those days, now feel shame over these revelations is because, after that particular bomb attack, many innocent Turkish and Greek Cypriots lost their lives, many were injured and remained disabled and, for the first time, Turkish and Greek Cypriots were separated by barbed wire, resulting in a state of 'no solution' which continues to this day.

History professor Dr Fahir Armaoglu, who visited Cyprus recently and met Denktash, wrote in his book *The Cyprus Problem* that the bomb attack had been the work of EOKA terrorists. The disproving of a historian's view by Denktash is another reason for my feeling of shame. We cannot know whether Denktash told Armaoglu the truth but we can read with deep concern and shame about the bloody incidents caused by the bomb blast on page 452 of Armaoglu's book.

It is not easy to find Armaoglu's book. The new generation of progressives will never find it. Even if they do, they won't have any trouble reading it because Armaoglu uses his pen to support the reactionary forces. But let us read from it:

> The bomb that was thrown at the Turkish Press Office on the Nicosia-Kyrenia road on the night of June 6-7 by EOKA terrorists was the spark for the incidents. The following days saw clashes between Turkish and Greek Cypriots start and suddenly the situation turned into great confusion. On the 7th and 8th there were clashes in Nicosia and Larnaca, resulting in the deaths of four Greek Cypriots and five Turks, and two sustained serious injuries. On the same day some 200 political prisoners in the Nicosia central prison attacked their Turkish guards, injuring five of them. On June 7, the residents of Dikomo, a Greek Cypriot village in the Nicosia district, launched an attack on the Turkish Cypriot village of Ortakioi but the Turks saw them off. Because of this, the British administration separated the Greek and Turkish quarters of Nicosia with barbed wire and placed this border under the protection of British troops. On June 9, the Greek Cypriots of Nicosia attacked the Turks, killing a policeman and a woman. On June 12, bloody clashes broke out in three different places. The first was at Gunyeli.[12] The 300 Greek Cypriots of this village attacked the Turks in order to expel them and they burnt a farm. Two Greek Cypriots were killed and three were injured. The second incident took place in Nicosia. The Greeks attacked the Turkish quarter en masse and set fire to Turkish houses. The clashes between the two communities were only halted by the intervention of British troops. The third incident occurred in Famagusta. The clashes began when a crowd of Greek Cypriots attacked the Turks, resulting in injuries to five Turks and 12 Greek Cypriots.

The bloody incidents continued in this way. Armaoglu's book was published in 1963. Twenty years later, Denktash revealed on TV that the bomb attack that caused so many incidents was the work of Turks. If we set aside all the events described by Armaoglu and say that the real attackers were the Turks, is this treason? Since we were the ones who planted the bomb, was it not we who attacked the Greek Cypriots, who set fire to houses and caused deaths? If such revelations were to come from leftists, they would be accused of harbouring pro-Greek feelings and being traitors. Perhaps an order would be given to the TMT Fighters Association to issue statements dripping with blood.

From the history books we learn that the Greek Cypriots planted bombs at the Bayraktar mosque on March 25, 1963, and that on January 25, 1963, they blew up the mosque. If a respected figure publicly declares tomorrow that Turks planted those bombs, how could we look the accused and our young people in the eye after such a shameful revelation? Will we be able to justify the murder of the two journalist-lawyers?

Another bomb exploded in front of Denktash's law office and the Greek Cypriots were held responsible. On September 17, 1962, a shot was fired outside Denktash's office in the Turkish Communal Chamber. On both occasions Denktash was absent. If someone now says that these dark incidents were the work of one of Denktash's own close collaborators, what will become of our integrity? For my part, I am ashamed to even think about it.

Older readers will recall that on September 7, 1955, someone threw a bomb at the house in which Ataturk was born in Thessaloniki. Because of this, tens of thousands of Greek homes and shops in Istanbul were damaged or destroyed and many Greeks were killed. At the time it was claimed that the bomb was the work of Greek Cypriots, but when Menderes and his cronies were tried, following the May 27th revolution, it was revealed and written in the trial minutes that the bomb thrown at Ataturk's house was thrown by Turks.

There have been many such incidents. And now the history books reveal them as events of which we should be proud. We read them with shame. It appears that it is an infallible lesson of history: the betrayal of one's country is very close to a love of one's country.

One should not overlook the role of the British in the Gunyeli incident. They deliberately created the circumstances, probably in collusion with TMT, in which blood would be shed by the two communities as 'proof' of the impossibility of their coexistence. Denktash still uses the shedding of that blood to justify the policy he implements against the Turkish Cypriots as much as against the substance of the Cyprus problem.

'From Turk to Turk'

The June incidents brought to the surface the first actions of the Turks in the directions defined in the Nihat Erim proposals: the creation of conditions of conflict between the two communities and their separation, as happened in Nicosia with excessive haste on the part of the British, who, on the pretext of maintaining law and order, drew a dividing line for the first time. And of course the first forced transfer of Turkish Cypriots took place,[13] under the blackmailing and terrorist pressure of TMT with the evident aim of concentrating the Turkish Cypriot population in one place so as to gain a territorial and demographic basis by which to back the demand for partition. Turkish families from the villages of Assia and Vatyli were taken to the Turkish quarters of Nicosia and Famagusta, while Greek families who lived in areas that bordered on Turkish quarters, such as Omorphita, were forced to move to Nicosia.[14] The residents of the Turkish village of Akoursos in Paphos were transported to the northern outskirts of the Turkish quarter of Nicosia, 100 miles from their village.[15]

From the previous year, 1957, TMT had begun to impose a series of measures aimed at reducing the contacts between Greek and Turkish Cypriots in all sectors.[16] The campaign began slowly but was codified immediately after the events of 1958 in the slogans *Taxim veya olum* (Partition or death) and *Vatandas Turklerden mal aliniz* (Patriot, buy from Turks), which became known as 'From Turk to Turk'.

By this campaign, TMT took its intolerance into every level of Turkish Cypriot society. It was an operation that would complete the control that TMT had started to exercise through arms on the whole of the Turkish Cypriot community, whose very language it was trying to 'cleanse' of Greek influences, mainly because a large number of Turkish Cypriots spoke only Greek.

Most Turkish Cypriot traders and shopkeepers spoke Greek 38% of the time, according to the 1960 census.[17] The 'From Turk to Turk' campaign showed that the commercial-financial establishment of the Turkish Cypriot community chose to identify with TMT's aim of creating a 'separate economy' in the hope of gaining economic benefits, a fact that did not escape the notice of the ordinary Turkish Cypriots.

By this campaign, as Turkish Cypriot journalist Ozger Yiasin notes:

> The Turkish Cypriots became the object of exploitation by a group of businessmen who hid behind their nationalist masks. Many thugs, on the pretext of this slogan, beat up men and women, destroyed taverns, and knocked on doors to see whether you had Coca-Cola in the fridge [Coca-Cola was represented by a Greek Cypriot while Bel-Cola was its Turkish Cypriot equivalent]'.[18]

The Turkish Cypriot journalist actually published a photocopy of a letter signed by Rauf Denktash and sent to him on March 16, 1960, containing the following:

> We were shocked to discover that you frequent Greek Cypriot places of entertainment. At a time when we must act with particular sensitivity, even in the fulfilment of our most basic needs, a visit by intellectuals to Greek entertainment places just for fun is to be condemned and disappointing. This is our first and last warning.[19]

The Turkish Cypriot journalist also reveals how such warnings had been received by hundreds of people in his community, noting that 'written warnings were sent only to intellectuals': 'If you were not lucky enough to be an intellectual, there was no need to give you a warning. You would suddenly see three or four men outside your house and they would beat you up. Then you would need months to recover.'[20]

Another Turkish Cypriot journalist, Karem Adji, notes:

> Denktash and Kuchuk grew more brutal with their slogan 'From Turk to Turk'. Even if you bought parsley from a Greek Cypriot, armed men would beat you up. Our intellectuals were badly beaten, threatened, degraded and forced to flee abroad. Many were murdered by 'unidentified' people.[21]

Arif Tahsin argues that the Turkish Cypriot middle-class traders had always wanted a campaign of the 'From Turk to Turk' type. He considers that the opportunity arose due to the EOKA campaign in favour of Cypriot products and against those from Britain. Arif Tahsin vividly describes the situation prevailing in the Turkish Cypriot community at the time:

> We don't know where or how but Denktash brought a certain Jelal Hordan from Turkey and put him in charge of the youth organisation. This showed Denktash's weakness for Turks from Turkey. From then on Denktash would use his material from Turkey very well against the Turkish Cypriots.
>
> Hordan, with some of Denktash's friends in tow, was making the rounds of the villages and small towns. He changed the names of villages, interfered with the women's way of dressing [according to the teachings of Islam], and banned foreign words from our language. Anyone uttering an English or Greek word would pay, to avoid a beating, a fine of two shillings for every foreign word he had used. And in those days the Turkish Cypriots often used works like 'OK' or its Greek equivalent.
>
> Sometimes it would be two shillings, on other occasions it would be a beating, and our language was cleansed of foreign words. Not one was left. We had a few problems with those Turkish Cypriots who couldn't speak Turkish. We saw that they couldn't conform and we left them to time, which sorted them out.
>
> We could forgive anything except disobedience to the 'From Turk to Turk' campaign – that, never. The nation depended on that slogan. This was the real nationalism.
>
> It was not a question of whether we would buy a bunch of parsley, it was a matter of principle. Otherwise, what do you think? Didn't we know that it wasn't worth beating people for two eggs?
>
> But the ordinary people did not understand one thing: how could a Turkish trader go openly to a Greek trader, buy his wares, without getting a beating, put them in his shop and sell them to Turks? What kind of 'From Turk to Turk' is this, they asked. But to tell the truth, it was not 'From Turk to Turk' but 'From Turk to trader'...
>
> In any case, our people cannot understand serious business. We told them so many times, 'Don't buy from the Greeks because your money will be turned into bullets that will hit us.' Nothing! They didn't understand. What could we

> do? We had another solution: beat them! Then another would say to you, 'All right, mate, what about the money that the trader takes from us and gives the Greeks? How come that doesn't turn to bullets to hit us but it does when we give it directly to them?'
>
> If it were you, what would you answer? What would you do? Would you let him pay them to kill him? Some things have to be done out of goodness, don't they, mate? We were forced to save him.
>
> And what do you think?
>
> Instead of them killing him with his own money, wasn't it better for us to trick him?
>
> That's why we did it.
>
> A bit of a beating, a bit of love. What's wrong with that?
>
> How else could we have created a Turkish market in Cyprus?[22]

During that period of intercommunal clashes, the Turkish Cypriot residents of 13 Turkish Cypriot villages and one purely Turkish one were forced to move. At the same time, the Turkish Cypriots formed their own 'municipal authorities' in the urban centres (June 1958), Chamber of Commerce (October 1958) and Import-Export Board (November 1958) in an attempt to create the de facto conditions of segregation sought by the Turkish Cypriots' leadership elite.[23]

It was the start of the concentration of the Turkish Cypriots in one specific area of the island and the attempt to put together a separate and parallel Turkish Cypriot administrative mechanism, which aimed at the creation of a separate Turkish Cypriot statelet, in accordance with the plans and proposals of Nihat Erim.

An Unexpected Ally

In its efforts to get the Turkish Cypriot masses on its side, the Turkish Cypriot leadership did not hesitate on many occasions to present Turkish Cypriots as being in an active alliance with the Greek Cypriots, allegedly conspiring against the interests and rights of the Turkish Cypriots. Frequently it also turned against the colonial government, partly because it could not ignore the feelings of the masses but also because it wished to distort the reality concerning who was responsible for the denial of certain privileges and rights that had come with the transfer of Cyprus to Britain. The truth, of course, is that some of the restrictions imposed on the Turkish Cypriots were the legacy of the Ottoman Empire, which had attempted to maintain them by including them in the agreement with Britain for the transfer of sovereignty over the island.[24] The Turkish Cypriot leadership, however, could not expose the government of the country that claimed to be the heir state of the Ottoman Empire and with which it identified completely and acted as its mouthpiece.

This naturally did not prevent the colonial government from continuing to promote its plans, taking full advantage of the presence of the Turkish Cypriots on the island and the role that the Turkish Cypriot leadership had taken on as the channel for Ankara's orders. Consequently there was no reason to reveal such details.

The British administration, as has been mentioned, had its reasons for providing assistance to the Turkish Cypriot leadership and affording opportunities to TMT to promote its partitionist ambitions. But TMT also received help from the Greek Cypriot side. A series of decisions, mainly by EOKA under General George Grivas, played into the hands of TMT and Ankara.

In 1956, Grivas circulated a leaflet in which he banned Greek Cypriots working on the construction of the British bases at Dhekelia and Episkopi from going to work on Turkish-Cypriot-owned buses. In 1958, on Grivas' orders, an attempt was made to withdraw Greek Cypriot bank deposits of around £1 million sterling from the Cooperative Bank on the pretext that it was helping the Turkish Cypriots.[25] As part of his decision for passive resistance against the British, Grivas circulated on December 6, 1957, a leaflet with orders to the Greek Cypriots to avoid buying goods that were not of Greek manufacture or origin.[26]

A common characteristic of EOKA and TMT was their unrestrained anti-Communism, based on the argument that the leftists were against the 'national struggle' that each organisation was waging. This was how both organisations justified their executions of 'traitors'.

As for the 'From Turk to Turk' campaign, there were reactions from organised groups and leading Turkish Cypriot figures. For this reason the wrath of TMT focused particularly on such figures, many of whom it murdered.[27]

The situation that had been created on the island following the June 1958 murders favoured the further advancement of the Turks' plans, as always with British tolerance. Nancy Crawshaw, not known for an unbiased approach to developments in the Cyprus issue at the time, elegantly describes the British stance. But she could not avoid certain significant comments.[28]

> The burden of keeping the two communities apart fell to the British troops. Despite the presence of 30,000 or more troops incidents could not be avoided. Installations such as the oxygen factory required many guards in order to persuade the Greeks to go on working there. Large areas had to be policed by mobile patrols and units permanently stationed in the worst trouble spots. Much of the time the troops were seriously overworked and carried out their duties in an atmosphere of constant criticism.
>
> British soldiers helped to extinguish hundreds of fires, usually started by the Turks, but were accused by the Greeks of deliberate negligence in the case of every house or church which was burnt down. When the security forces searched the suburb of Omorphita they found lethal weapons in the houses of both communities; yet the Greeks insisted that the Turks had been warned of the search in advance.
>
> Partiality where it existed was dictated by political expediency and operational necessity. At policy level it could be traced to the importance which Britain and the US attached to Turkey as the last reliable bastion of Western defence in the Middle East. In the island, psychological and practical reasons entered into the question. Apart from periods of truce, the Greek Cypriots had for three years been shooting British soldiers in the back. The natural sympathies of the army as a whole were inevitably with the Turks, who were seen as loyal, courageous allies, sharing the same dangers in pursuit of the common enemy – EOKA.
>
> The British forces had their hands full; in need of Turkish cooperation, they tried wherever possible to avoid conflict with the Turks. The January riots had been a disastrous exception. It was at times difficult to keep the balance. The Turkish police who formed a vital component of the security forces as a whole favoured their compatriots, just as the Greek police turned a blind eye to EOKA's activities.
>
> The Greek complaints soon found their way to the House of Commons through members of the Labour Opposition, who attacked the Government for failing to carry out the emergency regulations with impartiality. A few of the complaints were valid. A Turkish Cypriot suspected of terrorist activity was granted bail and escaped to Turkey before trial; whereas Greek terrorists

were always held in custody. Ankara Radio broadcast its inflammatory propaganda unhindered when Athens was jammed.

Macmillan and Zurich

The bloody incidents of June 1958, in conjunction with the regional developments that were of particular interest to Britain, led London to the decision to table its own proposals that have remained known as the 'Macmillan Plan', which it intended to implement irrespective of any reaction.[29] It was essentially a plan for joint British, Turkish and Greek government of a partitioned Cyprus.

The threat of the unilateral imposition of partition by London persuaded Makarios to agree to discuss independence as a solution, and this in turn, with NATO pressure, led to secret talks between Greece and Turkey. These ended with the 'compromise' of the Zurich and London Agreements.

Through these agreements, Turkey secured a series of substantial advantages, which, compared with the situation at the start of their involvement in the Cyprus issue, amounted to a great success. Even more importantly, they opened the way to the further advancement of its plans. It gained recognition, for example, and legitimacy for its interest in Cyprus, and it secured guarantor rights, with the right to intervene and the presence of a military contingent on the island. Through the rights granted to the Turkish Cypriots, the Turkish Cypriot minority was upgraded to the status of community and it secured a veto over important decisions and a constitutional structure that promoted its partitionist plans.

A new chapter was opening as regards Turkish intentions since Ankara would be in a position to use its now 'legitimate' rights to take new steps regarding its policy on Cyprus.

Chapter 11

Developments in the Organisation of the Turkish Cypriots

In the years immediately after the end of World War II, Cyprus had been in a state of social upheaval. On the one hand, economic conditions were terrible, while the colonial government showed no particular inclination to deal with the problems that were growing all the more acute with the mass demobilisation of the Cypriot volunteers who had served in the British forces in the war against Nazi Germany. On the other hand, London revealed a clear unwillingness to keep its pre-war promises on the future of Cyprus, and the reactions this provoked were equally intense.

The Turkish Cypriot leadership elite viewed with great distrust the solidarity that was developing in the face of joint problems among the poorer Greek and Turkish Cypriots. Their common experiences in the trenches of war had forged an identity, which was now being expressed again – perhaps even more strongly – in the face of the enormous problems of demobilisation.

The colonial government's response to the militant demonstrations of the wretched masses for their rights and a solution to the enormous problems brought by the war was to join with the Church and the Turkish Cypriot leadership and suppress every demand and any questioning of its authority. A major event in the militant solidarity between Greek Cypriots and Turkish Cypriots was the miners' strike of 1948, which also revealed the tactics that the British would follow in dealing with later developments in Cyprus.[1] This strike may even have been the first mass, joint anti-colonial demonstration, which is why it caused such universal concern to the entire establishment – the colonial government, the Church and the leadership elite of the Turkish Cypriots.

But the expression of joint popular struggles coincided with other, broader developments,[2] which did not favour their growth or their transformation into a political movement. Things might have turned out differently in Cyprus had these other developments not been so decisive in the framing of the conditions that enabled things to develop as they did. In this respect it was a major historical misfortune that the coming together of Greek and Turkish Cypriots in a social movement demanding rights should have coincided with the sudden growth in the nationalist movement on the island.

Another contributing factor to the stillborn nature of this movement and the prevalence of nationalist designs concerned the circumstances prevailing around Cyprus. Greece was in the maelstrom of a bloody and destructive civil war that would lead to its total national dependence on foreign decision-makers. Turkey, on the other hand, was willing to undertake any role that these same decision-makers chose to give it in order that its 'evasively neutral' stance during the war be forgotten and so that it might identify with the victors, hoping to participate in the division of the spoils of the war. Furthermore, international relations were sinking in the expediencies of the Cold War and opposing ideologies.

Nonetheless, as mentioned above, the efforts by the Turkish Cypriot leadership elite to organise their own political party failed.[3] As Fazil Kuchuk admitted, although such a party was eventually formed in 1942 when he founded a nationalist party, Turkish Cypriot political activity did not begin until 1955.[4] And this political activity coincided with the arrival of Rauf Denktash on the scene.

The start of Turkish Cypriot political life, under a colonial regime and with the colonial power bringing Turkey into the process of shaping the future of Cyprus, coincided with Turkey's decision to show an interest in what was happening on the island for its own benefit and its own strategic plans and ambitions. A basic requirement for the success of Turkey's involvement was the total control of the Turkish Cypriots, which was not easy since they were scattered throughout the island and, in any case, they viewed this blatant Turkish interest with mistrust and they had strong ties with the Greek Cypriots.

Turkey's objectives were helped along not only by the colonial power but also by the conditions that had been created on the island after the start of the national liberation struggle. The mistakes that were made at this time by the Greek Cypriot leadership enabled Ankara to take full advantage of them in promoting its own aim of controlling the Turkish Cypriot community. Of course, these mistakes do not take away any of the legitimacy – historical, moral and political – of the demand for self-determination and *enosis*. It remains a fact, however, that the mistakes, by the political leadership as a whole, from the ethnarchy and EOKA to the leaders of the left, contributed to the way in which the Turkish Cypriot community – alone and unprotected, especially in the face of the dangers and threats that black propaganda was promoting and exaggerating – was drawn into the web of its nationalist, chauvinist leadership, which was under the thumb of Ankara.

The arrival of a young, dynamic, determined and able leader like Rauf Denktash had speeded up these processes. In the 1950s, there may not have been the possibility of organised political life but the leadership elite, through the demands it made of the colonial government, gained substantial leverage over the Turkish Cypriot community and increased its contacts with Ankara, from which it asked for guidance and assistance. The creation of illegal terrorist organisations such as *Volkan* at first and later TMT in the state of terror caused by black propaganda and disinformation, as well as the criminal activities of these organisations, aligned the Turkish Cypriot community – whether it wanted it or not – with the objectives of the leadership and Ankara.

After the formation of TMT, in fact, no activity was permitted which did not have the approval of the Turkish officers who headed the organisation. Every action, even those of the leadership elite, required TMT approval and, by extension, that of Ankara. Every position on any aspect of any problem, even more so on a political level, every demand and every way of handling an issue was shaped by Ankara and conveyed to the Turkish Cypriot leadership either through the commander of TMT or via the Turkish diplomatic mission in Nicosia.

The Zurich and London Agreements secured many of the preconditions set by Nihat Erim in his report for the 'legitimisation' of Turkish designs on Cyprus. And with these conditions secured, prospects grew for success regarding the achievement of broader and longer-term strategic Turkish objectives in Cyprus.[5]

Turkey, then, secured significant military advantages through the Zurich and London Agreements:

> Turkey was recognised legally as one of the parties to the shaping of Cyprus' future. It was turned into one of the parties to the 'dispute' over Cyprus which, from an issue of national liberation and vindication, from an issue of decolonisation and self-determination, ended up as an 'intercommunal problem'.
>
> It secured a legal military presence on the island, in the context of its status as a guarantor of the establishment that had been set up by the agreements, and with a right to intervention under certain circumstances.
>
> The Turkish Cypriot minority was upgraded and recognised as a politically

separate community, with increased rights such as that of the veto, which was turned into a way for Ankara to control the situation in Cyprus.

The separate procedures set out in the constitution that stemmed from the agreements enabled Ankara to impose and maintain total control of the Turkish Cypriot community.

The Turkish Cypriot minority was upgraded to community status like that of the Greek Cypriots, and as a result future demands took on a legal basis that moved ever further away from that which its status as a minority gave it.

With independence, the development of the political organisation of the Turkish Cypriots was favoured by Turkey, which, with TMT and the Turkish Cypriot leadership as vehicles for its policy, shaped the political expression of the Turkish Cypriots in such a way as to facilitate the advancement of its own plans.

The very same processes emanating from the Zurich Agreement also determined the structure of the political organisation of the Turkish Cypriots, at the head of which were placed Ankara's choices. Fazil Kuchuk was elected unopposed as the first Vice-President of Cyprus while Rauf Denktash became President of the Turkish Communal Chamber.[6] At the same time, the reinforcement of the Turkish Cypriot state within a state took on a new potential (see chapter 15).

The Era of Independence

The solution of independence satisfied the Turkish Cypriot masses since, despite what had happened before, the vast majority had remained moderate and succeeded in maintaining the harmonious relations that they had formed with the Greek Cypriots, the result of four centuries of coexistence. Their expectation was that the solution would also lead to an end to TMT's terrorist activity against them and to the restoration of good relations with the Greek Cypriots, which would assist in the building of a common future.[7]

Makarios' message after the agreements was one of encouragement and guarantees for such a common future: 'Greeks and Turks must cooperate in a spirit of frankness, with total respect for each other's natural rights and the community's deep understanding of our interests and rights. Fanaticism and rivalry have to end, barriers must be brought down and a spirit of unity prevail in everything we do.'[8]

Makarios could see the dangers that lay in the path of the new state and gave good warning to Greek and Turkish Cypriots: 'If, on the contrary, the foundations that we have laid are rotten, everything will collapse and fall.'[9]

Nonetheless, straight after independence the Turkish Cypriot leadership (as well as the most fanatical Greek Cypriot nationalists) began to prepare for the next phase of Ankara's plans. Fortified behind the divisive provisions of the constitution and the super-privileges granted to the Turkish Cypriots, they acted in such a way as to secure the prospects for fully realising Turkey's objectives, and as a result the operation of the state grew problematic.

The cultivation of mistrust and intransigence developed into open and public threats.

Denktash's pronouncements were provocative and inciting as he warned of the 'endless adventures' that the Greek Cypriots were allegedly preparing.[10] Denktash argued that the rights which the Greek Cypriots considered excessive:

> [...] are the same rights for which hundreds of Turks have died and thousands are ready to die. It is a pity that Makarios' political memory is short. The *bayraktars* who conquered and colonised Cyprus did not ask for 'minority rights'. We have not lived in Cyprus for centuries as a 'minority' but as governors and equals under various establishments. Why do the Greeks forget that in the Turkish, Greek and Cypriot sphere of influence they are in a minority of ten to one?[11]

It is true that the events of the preceding years had led to a climate of mistrust between the two communities and this was the 'yeast' in the policy that the Turkish Cypriot leadership would implement in the new circumstances that were being created. On the one hand, the Turkish Cypriots were enjoying a feeling of success, given the progress they had made since World War II. On the other hand, the disappointment among the Greek Cypriots took on exaggerated dimensions from the deep feeling and awareness that the Zurich and London Agreements had essentially been imposed on Cyprus. In such circumstances, certain 'EOKA-type' forces remained true to the slogan of *enosis*.

And in this they were assisted by the general stance of the Turkish Cypriot and Turkish leaderships, with official declarations even within the Turkish National Assembly, which reinforced the conviction that the Turkish side was ready to exploit the absurd and exaggerated rights granted to the Turkish Cypriot community, combined with the divisive aspects of the agreements, so as to revive and openly promote the aim of partition.[12]

The situation prevailing in Cyprus and in relations between the two communities is described elegantly by Miltiades Christodoulou:

> The Turkish Cypriots, maintaining their intense opposition to *enosis*, full of the policy of partition and encouraged by Ankara, intensified their activities with the same, albeit concealed, fanaticism and determination. Like the Greek Cypriots, they gave the impression of being dedicated to the task of reconstruction and development of the country. But they were entering a new phase of separate economic development, as they had declared and essentially planned from the end of 1959 when they brought back the slogan 'From Turk to Turk' and cultivated the maintenance or an increase in the gap between themselves and the Greek Cypriots. They cultivated their economic segregation from the Greek side, an end to all commercial exchanges among Greeks and Turks and the separate economic and more general survival of the Turkish community. [...]
>
> From the very first months after the creation of the Republic, the inability to make progress in various areas in accordance with the provisions of the agreements became evident. Constant friction and conflict were being repeated with mutual recriminations and accusations about the stance shown by each side. Almost the whole of 1961, which was the first year of the Republic's existence, passed amid tension. In Cyprus, differences grew over issues related to the implementation of the provisions in the constitution for a 70:30 ratio in the civil service, the question of establishing separate municipalities, the creation and make-up of the Cypriot army, separate majorities in the House of Representatives and other lesser or related issues. [...]
>
> The Turkish MPs began blackmailing tactics aimed at speeding up the implementation of the constitutional provisions for the civil service (70:30), the issue of separate municipalities, the Republic's army and other matters. To this end they made arbitrary use of the right to separate majorities in the House and on March 13, 1961, voted down the tax bills The country was thus in danger of being without revenue, and so Makarios called upon the Greek Communal Chamber to collect taxes on a temporary basis in the form of per-

sonal contributions, a tactic that the Turkish Communal Chamber also adopted and thus brought a partitionist situation to the very operation of the state.

On October 20, 1961, Kuchuk made use of his veto and overturned a decision of the Council of Ministers concerning the setting up of a unified Cypriot army and in December of the same year he opposed Makarios' foreign policy for Cyprus' participation in the Non-Aligned Movement, though this time without using his veto. There was intense opposition between the two sides on the question of the municipalities. Kuchuk then issued a statement that summarised the views of the Turkish side and justified the stance of the Turkish MPs and other organs of the Turkish leadership, stressing that the Greek attitude 'made the Turkish side believe that its rights are being violated'. The Turkish members of the House, convinced that they would lose this last opportunity for ever, having reminded their Greek Cypriot colleagues of their constitutional obligations towards the Turks, were obliged to exercise their right to a separate majority. [...]

On March 25 there were explosions in two Turkish mosques in the Greek quarter of Nicosia that resulted in serious damage. This caused considerable tension that led to some strongly worded articles in the Turkish press and to statements and speeches by Turkish leaders as well as mass mobilisations and rallies. The uprising by the Turkish community had been cultivated throughout the whole of the preceding period and was carrying on relentlessly. [...]

Denktash had warned of civil war just five days after the declaration of the Republic on August 21, 1960, when Cyprus became a member of the United Nations. After a telegram was sent by a group of Greek Cypriot *enosis* supporters to the Secretary-General of the United Nations, in which they condemned the agreements, Denktash sent a telegram of his own in which he spoke of the balance between the two communities based on the agreements, stressing: 'If this balance is upset in violation of the agreements or political steps are taken in favour of *enosis* or the so-called one-sided self-determination, the result will be chaos and civil war.'

When the Turks – TMT – failed to hand over their illegal arms [according to the Zurich and London agreements, both EOKA and TMT had to surrender the weapons they held] Kuchuk stated on October 5, 1960, that, 'No responsible Turk has illegal arms in his possession,' and that, 'It is not necessary to take any measures for disarming members of the Turkish community.'[13]

It was obvious that the Turks considered that by the Zurich and London Agreements they had succeeded in making Cyprus their hostage and they were in no way willing to end this situation, let alone to cooperate sincerely in the smooth running of the new Cypriot state. On the contrary, they gave the impression that they were pushing things towards new conflicts, especially if it meant achieving their objectives by political means.

The fact that the Turkish Cypriots accepted the solution of independence with relief is recognised even by the most fanatical Turkish nationalists, who acknowledge that Turkish Cypriot rights had been safeguarded. They could work and move freely and participate in the island's general prosperity.[14]From very early on, however, it was clear that Ankara had other plans. The Turkish and Turkish Cypriot press published inflammatory articles that left no doubt about what they were attempting: 'The Greeks,' wrote *Halkin Sesi*, the newspaper published by the Vice-President of Cyprus, Fazil Kuchuk, 'cannot approach us and bite us because their teeth are no longer sharp. Apart from this, we are in a position to smash the faces of anyone trying to bite us.'[15] In another article, the same newspaper warned: 'Have you Greeks heard the voice of Ankara? If you think so, come…'[16]

The Rebellion Against the State

The political unrest continued until the end of 1963. The climate that had been created heralded even worse troubles. The Turks were looking for a pretext to openly demonstrate their rebellion, again based on the Nihat Erim formula.

The situation began to come to a head in November 1963 when Makarios submitted a 13-point proposal for amendments to the constitution so as to make the state workable for the good of both communities. They were proposals for discussion. The answer did not come from the Turkish Cypriots, however, but from Ankara. Turkey, through its Ambassador in Nicosia, conveyed a statement to Makarios in which it rejected the proposals in a threatening way.

And, of course, by its stance it determined the climate in which the Turkish Cypriots were expected to react. It was an act that drove the Turkish Cypriots to extremes, despite the fact that the Foreign Ministers of Britain, Turkey and Greece, who held a joint meeting with the Turkish Cypriot leadership in Paris on December 19, 1963, had urged them to accept the principle of talking.[17] For the Turks it was already too late.

Fazil Kuchuk's newspaper had published a clear warning two months before the Turkish Cypriot rebellion: 'Whether the Greeks want it or not, Cyprus will be dismembered one day and then they will realise who is dreaming.'[18]

The clashes – now armed – began on December 23, 1963, over a trivial issue. A police patrol in Nicosia asked to see a Turkish Cypriot driver's papers and the driver refused to hand them over. He and his passengers got into a row with the patrol. Other Turkish Cypriots heard the noise and joined in and, when shots were heard, the trouble spread.[19]

This confirmed the threat made by Denktash to Makarios in a statement to *Halkin Sesi*: 'Makarios should know that if he takes action in this direction [of amending the constitution] he will find himself facing thousands more graves.'[20] He had, in any case, sworn an oath, as he himself admitted,[21] that the Turkish Cypriot community would never become a minority and he reminded all that 'the flag took its colour from the blood of 80,000 martyrs'.[22]

The Nihat Erim Formula in Practice

At the start of intercommunal conflict, Denktash and Kuchuk appeared to be competing over which of the two would make the more inflammatory statements, which, on the one hand, maintained the climate and, on the other, put pressure on their own community. The spirit of these declarations was determined once again by an article in *Halkin Sesi* – which had been turned into the mouthpiece of the Turkish Cypriot leadership – that stated the following:

> Cyprus cannot be any different from Mersin, Alexandretta or Adana. Those who are attempting to create problems will not succeed. You may be sure that, if necessary, the Turkish army and Turkish youth will overturn their efforts and strike a fatal blow there and then.[23]

Immediately after the Turkish Cypriot rebellion[24] there began a systematic implementation of the formula that Denktash and Kuchuk had proposed to Ankara.

The first aim of the uprising was to secure a territorial basis to 'legitimise' its separatist, secessionist plans. From Ankara, Denktash clarified the new objectives on Turkish radio: 'Our aim is the creation of a federation in Cyprus and, to achieve it, it will be necessary for the Turkish Cypriots to leave their villages and settle in certain areas.'[25]

The aim, then, was to secure the creation of an area in which mainly Turkish Cypriots lived and which, according to the Denktash/Kuchuk formula, would need to be defended. Under the threat of TMT arms, Turkish Cypriots were forced to leave their homes, a fact that Turkish propaganda later presented as the result of 'Greek attacks'.

By March 31, 1964, the residents of 17 Turkish villages and the Turkish Cypriots of 39 mixed villages, a total of 9,310 Turkish Cypriots, had been forced by TMT to move to predetermined areas, which were turned into enclaves.[26] Thirty-nine such enclaves were created throughout the island, the most important of which was that of Nicosia-Kyrenia. Around 60% of the Turkish Cypriot population lived in these enclaves – which covered 4% of the island's territory[27] – under the total, illegal and violent control of TMT and the Turkish Cypriot leadership. Meanwhile, Turkish Cypriot civil servants, police officers and Members of Parliament, under TMT orders, left their posts and refused to return, even when the situation allowed it.

At the same time, efforts began for the creation of a parallel 'administration'. The so-called 'General Council', whose decisions had all the force of law for the Turkish Cypriots living under TMT control, made its appearance.[28] It was the 'executive authority', while the duties of the 'legislature' were carried out by those MPs who had withdrawn from the House of Representatives and members of the Communal Chamber.

The General Council also set up a 'judiciary' comprising the Turkish Cypriot judges who had left their posts, most of them by force. For this to operate, the General Council imposed a 'tax' on all the Turkish Cypriots while Turkey reinforced its coffers with $20 million a year.[29]

The General Council essentially had the power of life and death over the Turkish Cypriots. On December 18, 1964, it announced a series of 'general rules' for the Turkish Cypriots:

Entry to the Greek Cypriot areas is not allowed to Turkish Cypriots who have not obtained special permission.

1. Anyone who breaches this rule and enters the Greek Cypriot areas with the aim of contact will be punishable with a £25 fine or imprisonment.

2. A fine will be imposed in the following instances:

   a) On anyone talking or negotiating with Greek Cypriots or accompanying any foreigner in our areas.

   b) On anyone coming into contact with Greek Cypriots on any official business.

   c) On anyone appearing in a Greek Cypriot court.

   d) On anyone visiting a Greek Cypriot hospital for examination or to obtain medicine.

3. [...]

4. A fine of £25 or another strict punishment and one month's imprisonment or a lashing will be imposed on anyone entering the Greek Cypriot areas for the purpose of:

   a) Walking.

   b) Visiting Greek Cypriots.

   c) Entertainment'.[30]

TMT's terrorism did not prevent certain enlightened Turkish Cypriots from resisting, despite the dangers they faced, speaking out publicly and condemning Denktash and his policy. The Turkish Cypriot trade unionist Dervis Kavazoglu, in a speech delivered to a mass gathering of Turkish Cypriots from the mixed village of Dhali in the Nicosia district in June 1964, referred to Denktash's aforementioned statement to an Ankara radio station and noted that this statement 'Must show everyone why the Turks were forced to leave their homes. It was not to save them from attacks by the Greeks but to promote the political ambitions of the extremists who are terrorising the Turkish Cypriot masses.'[31]

In August 1964 Ankara sent its air force to bomb the Tillyria area, where the Turks had established an enclave on the coast that they were using to bring men and arms to Cyprus illegally. Immediately after the bombing, Turkish Cypriot politician Ihsan Ali sent a letter dated August 6 to the then Turkish Prime Minister, Ismet Inonu. Its contents are especially enlightening and it is reproduced below in full:

> The Cyprus issue is at present going through a crisis. Leaning upon Your Excellency's toleration and leniency, I would like to submit that Turkey will be of no benefit to the Turks of Cyprus or of Turkey with her present attitude in this question. With her policy on Cyprus affairs, Turkey is only aiding the Mediterranean interests of the British, who have, for centuries now, exploited the humanity and also served the Cyprus Turkish leadership and their terrorists who are partners of the British. During the British rule over Cyprus for eighty years, the Turkish Cypriots were subjected to the worst treatment by the British. To verify this view, I shall give only two examples: (a) as the Municipal Law did not guarantee the rights of the Turks they frequently applied for its amendment, but British Government rejected their request, and (b) when the Turks applied for the increase of the posts in the Government service from 18% to 20%, the British again rejected their request persisting in their original decision that the Government posts should be distributed according to each community's population. Therefore, now, in view of the present adverse attitude of the British, should the Turkish Government and the Turkish public opinion not have realized the degree of their sincerity for the support of the Turkish thesis on partition or federation? But unfortunately this has not been realized, and the British have succeeded in their policy to put the two communities at each other's throat by exploiting through their agents the national feelings of the Turks, both in Turkey and in Cyprus.
>
> It has been observed by the great majority of the Turks that Denktash, who is serving the British policy of 'Divide and Rule', is cooperating with cheap

politicians in Turkey who make use of the Cyprus question in their attempt to overthrow the Turkish Government. It is indeed surprising that Turkey is insisting on the London-Zurich Agreements, which were imposed on the people of Cyprus by foreigners of bad faith. In fact, the Turkish community has not derived any benefit out of these Agreements. The only persons benefited are Denktash and his followers. Because, availing themselves of the powers secured to them by the 'separatist' nature of the Agreements, they suppressed the freedom of speech and thought by methods worse than those used by Menderes. They have misused the material potentialities in their hands. In spite of the one and a half million pounds given by the British to Evcaf, the Turkish aid on large scale, the allocation made by the Government of Cyprus out of the consolidated Fund of the General Budget and heavy taxation levied on our community by the Turkish Communal Chamber, no sound effort has been made for our community's development and, furthermore, according to a report published last year by the Turkish Communal Chamber, Evkaf is indebted to a sum of over six hundred thousand pounds. As it has already been made clear by Mr Dirvana in his article published in the *Milliyet* newspaper, Denktash was unnecessarily quarrelling with the Greeks instead of considering seriously the development of our community. I wonder what will be the feelings of the conscientious and of good-character Turks when they learn about the financial status of Evkaf as stated above.

Now, I would like to refer to the Turco-Greek relations in Cyprus. The Turks and the Greeks in the island did not let their brotherly relations spoil even during the Turco-Greek war. And, I confidently say, that, if they are left by themselves, the two communities will continue to live like brothers as in the past. The responsibility for the very tragic situation in which the Turks are now involved lies with the Turkish leadership and their gangsters, and not with the Greeks. The innocent Turkish community is now striving to get rid of the cruelty and inhuman pressure of the Turkish terrorists, and not of the Greek pressure. Nearly everyday the innocent people are wildly beaten and subjected to any kind of torture. The Turkish Government, instead of repeating their threats of invasion, thus trying to encourage and please the malevolent, should do their best to help Cyprus to become a neutral and touristic country in the Mediterranean, as once mentioned by the deceased Hussein Djahit Yalchin [a famous Turkish editor] in an article. Such efforts should be concentrated on the point of creating possibilities to secure the cooperation of the two communities. And this is exactly what the interests of Turkey and Greece demand. Is it not a historic truth that the Big Powers always get small countries to fight each other for the purpose of serving their own interests? Is it not from this historic truth that the great statesmen Ataturk and Venizelos were inspired to establish the Turco-Greek friendship? The question of the partition of Cyprus or of the establishment of federation is the result of the activities of the activities of the Anglo-Saxons, who are trying through their instruments in Turkey and in Cyprus to create a dispute between Turkey and Greece and between the Turks and the Greeks of Cyprus. Whereas, in reality, the partition of Cyprus or the establishment of federation will be destructive for both the Turks and the Greeks, it will be disastrous especially for the Turks. At a time when the Common Market has been established and all the countries of Europe try to join it, what will be the benefit if the one hundred thousand of Turks separate from the unity of the whole population? It is in the light of these realities that I have done my best to warn the Turks of Turkey and of Cyprus not to fall into the trap of the ambitious. But it has come to my knowledge that the Ankara radio station insulted me in a vulgar way for my benevolent activities. If these insults were addressed to me during Menderes' regime, I should consider them very natural. But unfortunately I was insulted over a radio station, which is supervised by a Minister of your party. It is grieving that, on one hand, Menderes was hanged as a traitor, whereas, on the other, his followers, who during his regime threatened your sympathizers, now influence the broadcasts of a radio station which is under your Minister. This station accused me of being a traitor and that I advocate what Makarios does. This is not so, I simply advocate justice. If we have now a weak case due to which we are in our present weak position, it is the result of our faulty actions in the past. If we, as a community, have made mistakes and been negligent, we may now try to adjust our position peacefully but not by force. On this occasion I must say that, as a Turk, I feel shame when I compare Makarios' mild and polite speeches with the insulting and mean language which the Ankara radio Station uses. Yes, my Pasha, the Menderes radio station continually praised Menderes' heroism and accused you of being a traitor, but the lapse of time proved who was a hero and who was a traitor. When you were insulted over the radio, I suffered a nervous crisis and, due to this, none of my family nor I listened to any broad-

> casts for many years. But now, when the station is under your Minister's responsibility, I express my sorrow at hearing that the very same putrefied tongue uses the same imputations against me.
>
> However, whatever your radio's nasty tongues may broadcast, I shall never hesitate from expressing my belief that the two communities can live in harmony as in the past. I assure you that the Turks will be happier and more prosperous in a neutral and independent Cyprus than ever before during the colonial administration.[32]

The letter is noteworthy for its clear-sightedness and its prophetic predictions. A copy was also sent to the Secretary-General of the United Nations. The result was an intensification of the Ankara radio station's attacks against Ihsan Ali and anyone else who dared to state certain truths.

A Parallel Administration

The promotion of Turkey's objectives by means of the Turkish Cypriot rebellion had not succeeded to a degree that would have allowed the start of the next phase, which was the creation of a territorial basis that TMT terrorists could defend and which would give the Turkish Cypriot leadership a seemingly legal foundation on which to proclaim a pseudo-state and to whose assistance Turkey could rush. This failure caused problems to Ankara and to the Turkish Cypriot leadership, not only on a political level but also regarding the control of the community.

Nonetheless, the General Council was formed immediately after the Turkish Cypriot rebellion, which shows that it was part of a specific plan that was gradually put into effect in parallel with the rebellion and it operated until December 27, 1967. On December 28, the Turks proceeded to upgrade their parallel 'government' in a way that was quite revealing of their intentions. The General Council was renamed the 'Temporary Autonomous Turkish Cypriot Administration'.

This political move was accompanied by a statement concerning the formation of various services, such as the postal service, the police force, local authorities, etc.

The upgrading of the 'Turkish Cypriot Administration' coincided with the consequences of the crisis at Kophinou, the Greco-Turkish meeting at Evros and the withdrawal of the Greek army contingent from Cyprus.[33]

The 'new' authority in the Turkish Cypriot community, immediately after taking up its duties, published its 'general regulations', a sort of pseudo-constitution that noted in its introduction that all the Turks living in Cyprus were subject to the Temporary Autonomous Administration.[34]

On February 25, 1968, the Turkish Cypriot leadership organised 'elections' for the post of 'President of the Temporary Administration'. Fazil Kuchuk was elected unopposed, despite keeping – and using whenever it suited him – the office of Vice-President of the Republic.

On July 5, 1970, with Denktash consolidating his position upon his return to Cyprus and imposing this on his rivals (see Chapter 14), 'elections' were held to appoint members to the 'Assembly of the Temporary Autonomous Administration'. This body comprised the 15 members of the Communal Chamber, as provided for in the constitution of the Republic, and the 15 members of the island's legitimate House of Representatives, thus giving the impression of maintaining some links with legality!

In new 'elections' that took place on February 18, 1970, Denktash replaced Kuchuk. On July 18 of the same year, Denktash removed the word 'Temporary' and his administration became the 'Autonomous Turkish Cypriot Administration' – yet another political act that revealed Turkey's intentions, as always related to the formula contained in Nihat Erim's report.

The Turkish Cypriot leadership's efforts during this period (1963-1974) aimed at leaving open a constitutional issue for the Republic of Cyprus with the obvious intention of dissolving the unified state. For this reason, the Turkish Cypriots were ordered to withdraw from their posts in government services, in the hope that the state would dissolve. At the same time, an attempt was made to form a parallel administrative mechanism so that a de facto 'post-Zurich' situation would exist.

This administrative mechanism was controlled totally by the military organisation of the Turkish Cypriots, which, in turn, was controlled by Turkish military men who had come to Cyprus illegally. These Turkish officers had under their control the seven 'district councils' that had been formed as organs of the General Council. A Turkish officer with the rank of colonel served in every district while a captain served on the 'sub-committees'.[35]

It is interesting to see how the Turkish officers made their way to Cyprus. After independence, the commander of TMT was Colonel Kenan Coygun, who arrived in Cyprus on October 3, 1962, using the false name of Kenan Coskun. He was followed by Lieutenant Colonel Orhan Orzatay, who arrived on the island by normal channels, claiming to be a tobacco expert, on November 4, 1962.[36] Another lieutenant colonel, Remzi Guven, arrived on February 20, 1963, in the guise of a representative of various charities and allegedly with the purpose of assisting in the restructuring of Evkaf. On August 6, 1963, Lieutenant Colonel Eftal Akca arrived, supposedly as an educational inspector. A mere four days later, yet another 'educational inspector' arrived, Lieutenant Colonel Girey Butak.[37]

This mass arrival of Turkish officers in Cyprus was certainly not unconnected with the Turkish Cypriot rebellion. It is clear that their arrival was part of military preparations and they certainly had the full support of 600 men from the Turkish Force in Cyprus, which was on the island in accordance with the Zurich and London Agreements.

The irregular situation that had been created by the events of Christmas 1963 contributed to the almost total dependence of the Turkish Cypriots on the military organisation that had become active by decision of Ankara. Their forced confinement within enclaves or just the presence of TMT in such a small community was virtually tantamount to the imposition of martial law, with all the consequences and aftermath that such a situation brings. In other words, through the incidents of 1963 the Turkish Cypriot community had begun a process of total surrender to Ankara, the abandonment of its own political will and identity. It was a process that was completed with the 1974 invasion and the 'herding together' of the Turkish Cypriots in the occupied areas under the 'protection' of the powerful army of occupation and the settlers.

1. Part of the infamous 'Green Line', which divides Nicosia.

2. The Secretary-General of the United Nations, Koffi Anan (centre), flanked by President Glafcos Clerides (on his right) and the Turkish Cypriot leader Rauf Denktash, at the ceremonial start of yet another round of talks between them, at Troutberg, in 1997…

3. President Makarios (left) and Rauf Denktash (right) during talks in 1977. In the middle is Prese De Cuellar, the resident UN Secretary-General's special representative.

4. Meeting between President Spyros Kyprianou (left) and Rauf Denktash (right) in 1979. In the centre is the UN Secretary-General, Kurt Waldheim.

5. Glafcos Clerides and Rauf Denktash with the S.G's special representative Ozorio Taffal, at the beginning of their talks as representatives of the two communities, in 1968.

6. The image of the 'Cyprus is Turkish' Committee.

7. Post 1974 Turkish invasion desecration of a Greek Orthodox cemetery at the Turkish occupied village of Flammoudhi.

8. Turkish tank landing on the northern shores of Cyprus in 1974.

9. Turkish invasion troops, 1974

10. The coffins of Costas Misiaoulis and Dervis Kavasoglou side by side and covered by the Greek and the Turkish flags respectively. They were both murdered by TMT.

11. Desecration of a Greek Orthodox Church.

12. The last British Governor of Cyprus Sir Hugh Foot handing over Cyprus to the first President of the Republic of Cyprus, Archbishop Makarios, in 1960. Behind Sir Hugh Foot the first Vice President of the Republic Fazil Kutchtuk.

13. The signing of Cyprus's independence. Sir Hugh Foot (centre) flanked by Fazil Kutchuk (seated right) and Archbishop Makarios (seated right).

14. Fazil Kutchuk (centre, with arm raised), with Rauf Denktash on his right, after Kutchuk's election as the Republic's first Vice President.

15. The first attempts to create a state within a state by TMT and Turkey. The Turkish military unit stationed under the 1960 agreements, parading with TMT groups.

Chapter 12

TMT: A TALE OF BLOOD

The organisation, training and reinforcement of TMT after independence took on additional possibilities. The relative freedom that prevailed enabled its members to move around more easily. In any case, there was the presence of TURDYK (the Turkish military contingent of 650 officers and men, stationed in Cyprus as part of the 1960 independence agreement), which was an important staging post in the organisation of the Turkish Cypriots' secret army. And next to TURDYK were the Turkish Cypriot men and officers of the police force and of the Cypriot army that was being formed, all of them core members of TMT.

The control of the Turkish Cypriot community by the Turkish officers of TMT's administration spread everywhere. From the smallest details of daily life to the position the Turkish Cypriots would adopt on state organs, the TMT leadership dictated everything. The political authority of the Vice-President.,Ministers, MPs and other Turkish Cypriot state and political officials had in essence come into the hands of the TMT leaders,[1] who did not accept any deviation whatsoever from their decisions.

The big problem for TMT and the Turkish Cypriot and Turkish leadership, which almost 'demolished' the basis of TMT's strategy, was the fact that, following the 1963 rebellion, the vast majority of the Turkish Cypriots lived and worked in areas controlled by the state, with which the Turkish Cypriots maintained legal relations. This was why the punishments that the TMT leadership imposed on the 'lawbreakers' were particularly harsh, with the purpose of acting as a deterrent and a model for the others.

Denktash had set himself against the Zurich and London Agreements[2] and for this reason his stance during the transition period was totally negative as regards the procedures aimed at determining the details of independence and the constitution. His aim was the maximum exploitation and safeguarding of all those divisive elements of the agreements and the upgrading of the Turkish Cypriot community into a separate political, economic and social entity. One result of this was that he found himself under fire even from the 'guided' Turkish press, doubtless because Ankara's policy was to safeguard in practice the rights that it had obtained through the agreements before moving on to the next phase of its plans. From what Arif Tahsin says[3] it appears that below the surface there was disagreement between the politicians and the military in Ankara over which tactics should be followed, with the military naturally adopting a harder line. It was with them that Denktash identified.

Denktash's differences with Ankara were also revealed in his relations with the Turkish Ambassador to Nicosia, Emin Dirvana, when Denktash decided to hold a special event in January 1961 to honour the Turkish Cypriots who had died during clashes with the British on January 27-28, 1958, as heroes of the *taxim* campaign.

The Turkish Ambassador, who had been invited, made his attendance dependent on the understanding that all references to *taxim* would be avoided, a fact that provoked a reaction and accusations from Denktash.[4] The Turkish Ambassador later wrote the following on the subject:

> Denktash also accused me of not allowing the Turks who had fallen in 1958 to be honoured or the flags to be flown at halfmast. I feel shame on his behalf for the degree to which he is distorting the truth. I regret that I must reply to him. The Turks of Cyprus honour their dead on January 28. On this day in 1958, a number of Turkish Cypriots were killed in clashes with the British. On that day I attended the ceremonies with all the embassy staff and the commanders of TURDYK. Denktash, however, also wished to mark June 7. Dr Kuchuk had reservations and asked for my opinion. I was informed that on June 7, 1958, a bomb had been planted at the Turkish Press Office by individuals who, as was later discovered, had nothing to do with the Greek Cypriots. The Turks of Nicosia had subsequently been incited to 'be filled with sacred indignation' and carried out acts similar to those of September 6-7, 1955, in Istanbul…[5]

Miltiades Christodoulou has noted his own experience of the views of the Turkish Ambassador on Denktash. He behaved, in Dirvana's view, as if he were the commander of the Turkish military forces, which he cited to back up his threats and blackmail.[6]

Arif Tahsin adds that, as a young, ambitious member of TMT, he had himself visited the Turkish embassy in order to invite the Ambassador to the aforementioned ceremony and had heard first-hand the latter's opposition to any slogans in favour of *taxim*. Referring to what Dirvana said, Arif Tahsin writes:

> 'I told the journalists too and they didn't like it but I'm going to tell you the same thing,' Dirvana went on in his address. 'The Turks are like oriental sheep-dogs, the Greeks are like street dogs. You don't know what the oriental sheep-dogs are like but they grow to be very big. When street dogs see them they walk around them and bark from a distance. They daren't attack. The oriental sheepdogs ignore the street dogs and proudly carry on their way. If they become angry, though, they will pounce on them and destroy them on the spot. And then they proudly carry on their way while the street dogs continue to bark from a distance.'[7]

Whether they understood the Turkish Ambassador's words or not, the Turkish Cypriots were in a state of confusion, mainly because of the differences that had arisen between the two factions that had developed within the ranks of TMT, the hard-core faction and the opposing 'tolerant' faction. Despite this they did not reduce their efforts to maintain a state of fear and terror in the community, threatening anyone who failed to follow orders and the organisation's policy. Arif Tahsin himself describes how a leading TMT official, Kemal Semi, invited him to undertake murders on the orders of the commander of the organisation. He also describes the clash between the head of Nicosia, Colonel Ahmed Gyotsmez, code-name Yilmaz, and other 'area commanders', clashes which led to his 'transfer' to Paphos.[8]

During the period preceding the open rebellion, there was no end to the actions that aimed at maintaining a climate of disagreement and mistrust between the two communities. On a political level, political disagreements prevailed, due to the Turkish Cypriot leadership's insistence on the total implementation of the divisive provisions of the agreements, while, on the level of action, bombs were planted at Denktash's office on September 17, 1962, at the Communal Chamber and at two mosques on March 25, 1962. Makarios condemned the bomb attacks in a statement in which he described them as 'sacrilegious and barbaric',[9] while the main event, one that was especially revealing, was the murder on April 24, 1963, of two young lawyers who had publicly spoken out against the policy of conflict and racial segregation of the two communities.

Murders and Muzzles

The case of the murder of the two young lawyers, Mustapha Hikmet and Ahmed Muzafer Gurcan, is of particular interest since it was perhaps the only case to go to court.

The two Turkish Cypriot lawyers had founded the People's Party immediately after the 1960 parliamentary elections. On August 4, 1960, Gurcan declared his party's support for the Zurich and London Agreements and for Kuchuk's foreign policy, despite vehemently opposing him, especially because of the 'dictatorial and one-party tendencies' within Denktash and Kuchuk's National Front.[10] The two lawyers also published *the Cumhuriyet* newspaper, in which they wrote passionate articles in favour of peaceful coexistence and collaboration between the two communities and against the policy of *taxim*. They were especially critical of the policy of Denktash and Kuchuk regarding their provocative actions and Denktash's persistent desire to drag Turkey into military action on Cyprus.[11]

This stance was unacceptable to the Turkish leadership, as it was to TMT. Denktash himself invited them to his office and threatened that they would come to a tragic end if they continued to behave in such a manner.[12]

Ihsan Ali states that Gurcan had visited the then powerful Minister of the Interior, Polycarpos Yiorkatzis, whom he briefed with the information that Denktash was preparing the ground for clashes and bloody incidents in both communities.[13] Leontios Ierodiaconou recalled a statement by Yiorkatzis immediately after the bomb attacks against the two mosques in Nicosia, during which Gurcan is said to have told him that, according to a Turkish embassy employee, the explosions were the work of Turkish extremists.[14]

The day after the explosions, the newspaper owned by the two lawyers revealed:

> The sad events, which provoked the intense indignation of our community, are certainly the work of a foreign power or organisation that believes that tension in bicommunal relations in Cyprus will serve its interests. It has been shown that everything was well organised. It is clear that there is a foreign hand involved since the events occurred at a time when efforts were being made to improve relations between the two communities. Consequently it appears that there are a good number of people who do not wish to see these relations improve.[15]

The newspaper returned to the subject a week later, noting that the calm and reasonable stance of the people had overturned the plans of those who aimed to turn the island into a battleground, and that reason had prevailed in the face of the efforts of those who wanted to serve their own narrow interests. It did not avoid mentioning an address to Greek Cypriot youngsters in which mention was made of 'restarting the struggle', and this time not against the British. 'We,' the two lawyers commented in their newspaper, 'do not understand such words. Is it not possible to solve our problems in a peaceful way?'

When national fanaticism and chauvinism erupted once more, causing fire in the church of Ayios Kassianos on the outskirts of the Turkish Cypriot quarter of Nicosia on April 9, 1962, the newspaper proclaimed that those responsible were 'once again the enemies of both communities'.

On April 23, 1962, *Cumhuriyet* announced that it would soon be revealing the identity of the bombers and terrorists who were planning bloody incidents in order to provoke intercommunal strife: 'We repeat for the last time. Every reasonable individual is in a position to judge who the cheap, sold-out person behind the bomb attacks against the two mosques was. The day is near when the mask will fall from that cheap, sold-out person's face.'[16]

It was the last issue of the newspaper. That same evening the two Turkish Cypriots were murdered in their homes in front of their wives.

Moe than 3,000 Turkish Cypriots attended the lawyers' funeral. Among them were the mufti of Cyprus, Ali Dana, and the Turkish Ambassador, Emin Dirvana. who was immediately recalled to Ankara. Naturally, no member of the Turkish Cypriot leadership dared attend, even as a formality. On the contrary, every effort was made – unsuccessfully – to place the blame for the murders on Greek Cypriots – Denktash's now familiar tactic.

Journalist George Spanos was one of the first to learn of Hikmet's murder:

> On hearing the tragic news, I first found myself looking over the bed of the dead 33-year-old Ayhan (Mustapha) Hikmet, in Kara Pupa Street. Gurcan was murdered the same evening in his yard at 12, Volos Street, Omorphita. Ayhan Hikmet, I remember, bore a wound that went right through his forehead, since he was shot at almost point-blank range, like Gurcan, who was found dead by his wife in his car.
>
> Hikmet and Gurcan had been planning to bring out their newspaper on a

> daily basis, despite the threatening telephone calls that they were receiving from TMT agents.[17]

The wives of the two murdered Turkish Cypriots said that the threatening telephone calls had been a daily phenomenon. At the inquest, which took place on July 4, 1962, they gave evidence that can only be described as harrowing. For example, reference was made to the presence of a military jeep a few hours before Gurcan's death outside a neighbour's house, the tenants of which took an hour and a half before finally deciding to respond to the heart-rending cries of Gurcan's widow that they call the police. Another notable reference was to the appearance of the photographer of *Halkin Sesi*, which Kuchuk published, who photographed the victim long before the police arrived on the scene and then disappeared, only to turn up later in Turkey.[18]

From the statements, Turkey's involvement became clear, with the participation of Turkish soldiers of TURDYK in the planning and execution of the murder.

A statement was also given by the then Interior Minister Polycarpos Yiorkatzis, who confirmed the information about his meetings with Gurcan. He also provided a tape of their conversation. Gurcan described the contacts of the Turkish Colonel Remzi Tirban with Kemal Ahiz Kal, regional commander of TMT in his neighbourhood of Neapolis in Nicosia, who had revealed to Gurcan that TMT forces had been armed and placed on alert. He also mentioned information given by an official of the Turkish Embassy about those responsible for the explosions in two mosques and the moves of Rauf Denktash, who was in court as Evkaf's lawyer 'to protect the interests of the Turkish Cypriot community'.

During his cross-examination of Yiorkatzis, Denktash attempted to defame the two murdered men, Gurcan in particular, calling him a degenerate. He declined to respond to one of the judges' remarks that his funeral had been attended by distinguished citizens and the Turkish Ambassador.

In their book *Polycarpos Yiorkatzis, the Houdini of EOKA*, Panayiotis Papademetris and Andreas Neophytou mention the following in connection with the case:

> Denktash tried to present the murder of Gurcan as being linked to 'woman trouble'.
>
> In his repeated questioning he would mention a Turkish woman's name and

attempted to discover whether Gurcan's widow knew that her husband had a girlfriend, that he maintained two homes and would go home late.

She replied in the negative and the court denied Denktash's request to be allowed to refer to Gurcan's past.

From what was said in court, instead of being the protector of the Turkish Cypriot community, Denktash found himself being accused...

Denktash also tried to prove that Gurcan was a Communist, saying that he had originally been employed at the American radio station in 1944 after a personal recommendation but had been dismissed later because of his leftist beliefs.

During the state of emergency [1955-1959], he said, Gurcan was attacked by young Turks because of his views, so they said, against the Federation of Turkish Associations [of which Denktash was chairman].

'I personally expressed my sorrow,' Denktash said, 'for the incident, which I condemned. Later I sued him for publishing libellous reports against me.'[...]

Under cross-examination by Cacoyiannis [Yiorkatzis' lawyer] about the character of Ayhan Hikmet, he replied that he had known him as a youngster 'as a good boy' until he 'discovered that he had left-wing tendencies'.

CACOYIANNIS: A person with left-wing tendencies is a bad character?

DENKTASH: Of course, he is as dangerous as a thief.

CACOYIANNIS: So you believe that leftists ought to be locked up?

DENKTASH: No, I don't mean that.

CACOYIANNIS: How can you not mean that? Since thieves are locked in prison, why not leftists? Did you not say that people knew who Gurcan was and that no one felt sorrow at his death?

DENKTASH: Yes. Not so much for his bad character as for the deceitful methods he used.

When Cacoyiannis presented the latest edition of *Nacak* [Denktash's newspaper, the issue referred to being that of May 24, 1962] and asked if a specific article was his, Denktash answered in the affirmative.

CACOYIANNIS:	Was it right, Mr Denktash, to write a leading article in which you attack two murdered journalists today when the Interrogating Committee is still carrying out its work?
DENKTASH:	The work of the Interrogating Committee has nothing to do with the murders.

In Denktash's article, entitled *We have a letter for the grave*, he accused the two journalists of being agents of the Greeks.

He also described them as traitors who gave everything to the Greeks in order the gain their favour and concluded:

> When your coffin passed in front of the bust of Ataturk, did you not feel a tremor of emotion? According to a Bulgarian newspaper, you collaborators with AKEL were to save Cyprus.[19]

The Interrogating Committee sessions were used by Denktash not only to blacken the names of the two Turkish Cypriot anti-nationalists but also to send messages to the rest of the Turkish Cypriots concerning the punishment that awaited anyone failing to align himself with his leadership's policies. They were also used to reinforce his efforts to sow the seeds of mistrust among the Turkish Cypriots and, of course, to present himself as a courageous leader who did not hesitate to clash with the Greek Cypriots if it meant 'protecting' the rights of his community.

Kavazoglu and Misiaoulis

Following the incidents of Christmas 1963, despite the obvious failure of the Turkish side to create on the ground the conditions it considered necessary in order to promote its demands on a political level, a situation had been created which helped TMT and the controlled Turkish Cypriot leadership to brutally impose their authority on the Turkish Cypriots, mainly on those who lived in the small areas that were under armed control.

But the denial of the expectations that they were cultivating in the Turkish Cypriots, the smoothing out that was attempted, the inability to prevent the movement of more and more Turkish Cypriots to the state-controlled areas, despite their terrorist methods, and the contacts they were having with the Greek Cypriots encouraged to a significant degree those Turkish Cypriots who rejected the policy of racial segregation.

One such individual was Dervis Kavazoglu.[20] A leading unionist with the PEO trade union federation and a member of the politburo of AKEL, he was a focus of resistance for the progressive Turkish Cypriots against the racist policy of Denktash and Ankara. With speeches in the villages and Turkish neighbourhoods, with articles first in *Cumhuriyet* newspaper and later in *Inkilapci*, he revealed the deceitful role of Denktash and his cronies and Ankara's plans, and he analysed the advantages of peaceful coexistence and cooperation.

TMT and Denktash focused their hatred on the person of Dervis Kavazoglu, on whose head they frequently put a price while on many occasions they tried, unsuccessfully, to kill him.[21]

Kavazoglu's articles, his interviews in the local and foreign press, his speeches and his statements were a strong indictment of the policy of terrorism that the Turkish Cypriot leadership was following and implementing. They were a source of encouragement to those Turkish Cypriots who were being oppressed by their leadership, to such a degree that leadership began to feel itself threatened and its authority questioned.

> In order to promote their terrible plans, the imperialists and no one else created the myth that it is supposedly impossible for the two communities in Cyprus to live together peacefully. With the help of their agents, they uprooted 20,000 Turks and herded them together in places that are no different from concentration camps, thus laying the foundations of a future territorial dismemberment. Today thousands of Turks live like nomads in tents and in the countryside, far from their homes, their villages, their fields, and their peaceful activities. Turkish primary and secondary schools are closed and thousands of children are being denied their education in order to further this immoral aim – dismemberment. A handful of fascists, helped by the imperialists and

> using arms and fascist methods, have seized the leadership of the Turkish community. They are responsible for the woes of the Turkish Cypriot population. It is they who prevent the Turkish population from expressing its true feelings and its thoughts, which are clearly against imperialism. It is no exaggeration to compare these Turkish Cypriot refugee camps with Hitler's concentration camps. In the darkness of night, they shoot and kill democratic journalists and progressive figures of our community. They arrest, abduct and imprison anyone daring to speak freely and express their thoughts. They torture them with mediaeval devices of Hitler-like invention. We are in a position to prove these terrible things with irrefutable evidence.[22]

The attempts on Kavazoglu's life finally succeeded on April 11, 1965. Kavazoglu was travelling from Nicosia to Larnaca with Costas Misiaoulis, his Greek Cypriot friend and colleague, who was likewise a trade unionist. It was a Sunday morning, around 10.30. The killers had planned their ambush well, on a public road too. They used automatic weapons to attack the two men, who died in each other's arms.

The Turkish Cypriot leadership attempted at first to lay the blame on the Greek Cypriots but they later hailed the 'success', describing Kavazoglu as 'a Communist who was *persona non grata* in the Turkish Cypriot community'.[23]

Kavazoglu and Misiaoulis remain to this day symbols of intercommunal cooperation and friendship and their memory is honoured every year on the anniversary of their death. Unfortunately their sacrifice did not prevent worse for Cyprus.

Kutlu Adali

Kutlu Adali[24] was a friend and collaborator of Denktash from 1954. In 1959 he was appointed director of *Nacak*, the newspaper that Denktash published. After independence, he was the head of Denktash's office in the Turkish Communal Chamber and, of course, a member of TMT. He had first-hand knowledge of the methods used by Denktash and TMT and he gradually grew to dislike them, to such an extent that he could no longer accept them. After the 1974 invasion in particular, when, through the intervention of the Turkish leader Deniz Baykal, he was appointed director of the so-called Office of Births, Deaths and Emigration in the occupied area, he had the opportunity to experience closely the drama of the Turkish Cypriots who, due to the conditions prevailing in the occupied part of the island, were forced to emigrate while their place was taken by settlers from Turkey. Kutlu Adali was mature enough to realise that the presence of Turkey in Cyprus was a source of trouble and he began to write daily articles in *Yeni Duzen* newspaper, the mouthpiece of the Turkish Republican Party, against the policies followed by Denktash and Ankara.

On July 7, 1996, 'persons unknown' waited for Adali outside his home in the Turkish quarter of Nicosia and, when the opportunity arose, opened fire on him with automatic weapons. It was yet another Sunday morning. Hit in the head, Adali died instantly. His attackers later telephoned *Kibris* newspaper to assume responsibility for the murder on behalf of the Turkish Revenge Brigade, a unit of the 'Grey Wolves'.

On June 8, 1996, *Yeni Duzen* had revealed that the same organisation was behind the murder of the Turkish journalist Ferhad Tepe of the pro-Kurdish newspaper *Ozgur Gudem*.

Adali's murder caused a storm of protest among the Turkish Cypriots. Parties and organisations condemned the killing and demanded that the perpetrators be caught and punished, declaring at the same time that terrorism would not gag them.

Adali's funeral turned into a rally in support of the peaceful coexistence of the two communities and against Denktash's fascist methods and Ankara's policy on Cyprus, despite the gloomy presence of Denktash's 'police' and the Turkish armed forces, who surrounded the mosque in which the funeral service was taking place and checked everyone approaching it.[25] Those present shouted slogans such as 'We will not be silenced', 'If you keep quiet, it will be your turn next' and 'We are not a district of Turkey'.

What was it that had caused so much fear within the racist occupation regime that it decided to execute Kutlu Adali?

Claire Palley, the British Professor of Constitutional Law and adviser to the Cyprus government on constitutional matters, revealed that Adali was to have given evidence against Turkey to the Human Rights Committee of the Council of Europe.[26] Adali, she said, intended to prove Turkey's settlement of the occupied area and the way it had forced the Turkish Cypriots to emigrate.

Adali's wife Ulcay also said that her husband had been murdered because of the revelations he was about to make concerning the occupation regime.[27] She spoke of the threatening telephone calls that her husband had received and said that the names of the two killers, members of the Turkish Secret Service (MIT), had been given to the 'police', who had naturally taken no action.

Kutlu Adali was passionate about safeguarding the Turkish Cypriots' identity, which he saw as having nothing to do with that of the mainland Turks. Over and above Denktash's choice of racial segregation, which he criticised harshly, he believed that the presence of the Turkish army and settlers was destroying this Turkish Cypriot identity. He also considered that the settlers were transforming the occupied area into a haven for criminals, whom the Turkish Cypriot leadership needed in order to stay in power:

> The bad politicians have lost the confidence of the Turkish Cypriots and have therefore turned to the tens of thousands of settlers from Turkey in order to secure their votes. They tell them: 'For God's sake save us and we'll give you the Greek Cypriots' properties.[28]

His great fear was the total annihilation of the Turkish Cypriots. The changing of their identity, the privileged treatment of the settlers and the economic conditions prevailing in the occupied area were forcing the Turkish Cypriots to leave the island:

> I remember as a boy that the number of Turkish Cypriots, which barely reached 65,000, was claimed by the Turkish leadership as 85,000. When the official 1960 census showed our population to be 104,320, the Turkish Cypriot leadership claimed that it was 120,000. The 1974 population must have been 115,000 but it was presented as 140,000. When it was announced as 180,000 it was finally revealed that people had been transported from Turkey.[29]

Also worrying was the character of the settlers. With them came crime and they used the island as a base for broader criminal activities:

> While the chauvinistic Turkish administration cultivates in our hearts the fear of the Greek Cypriots, the Turkish Cypriots live in fear that they will be killed

> by the criminals living among us who pay no heed to human life. [...] These criminals are not Turkish Cypriots but they attempt to fool us by saying that they are the same as we are. There can be no doubt that the Turkish administration is guilty of every crime perpetrated here. Through their mistaken policies they have abandoned our poor people to the hungry wolves. In the name of their own petty interests and demands they have transformed our beautiful country into a battlefield. And when we write the truth, they get angry. Were crimes committed in Cyprus before July 20, 1974? Anyone who is 40, 50, and 60 years old has known very few crimes in half a century. No one was ever killed for a bracelet, no woman's head was ever shattered for a few pounds, nor was her throat cut for a necklace or her wrist slashed for a bracelet.[30]

He saw the occupied part of Cyprus gradually being integrated into Turkey and he expressed the Turkish Cypriots' nostalgia for the old days when the two communities lived together:

> Annexation by Turkey and not independence will be the basis of Turkey's relations with North Cyprus. [...] I have noticed when walking the streets that the idea of annexation has already brought changes before it has been officially implemented. The streets, the shops, post offices and banks are unbelievably full of soldiers. It is as if there are more soldiers than citizens. There are many houses in Nicosia where Turkish Cypriots are no longer living. Children no longer play in the narrow streets of the neighbourhood, nor do the Turkish Cypriot women clean their pavements or talk to their neighbours. Filth and spit, not to mention urine, are everywhere. [...] The Turkish Cypriots no longer sit outside their front doors. People from Anatolia in multicoloured clothes have replaced them. Some speak in an incomprehensible fashion. Others speak Kurdish, Arabic, and Persian. [...] Yes, annexation cannot be achieved overnight. This corrupt situation, which is forcing us Turkish Cypriots to emigrate to Britain, Canada and Australia, has also not come about overnight. We have been weeping and leaving this country for the past 31 years. A good friend tells me that 44,000 Turkish Cypriots have asked the Australian High Commission for permission to settle in Australia. This means that in the immediate future the number of Turkish Cypriots will fall to precisely 64,000.[31]

The infiltration of the occupation regime's services by settlers has been systematic and aims at transferring authority from the Turkish Cypriots to the settlers so that the Turkish Cypriots may be controlled more easily:

> When I spoke with a retired policeman, he shared my concerns. In the police, he told me, the Turkish Cypriots are no longer the majority. Settlers from Turkey make up more than half the force. Yes. Just as the demographic character is changing, so too is the police force. I note that everything is being 'Turkified' in the Turkish Republic of Northern Cyprus. Only judges and lawyers maintain the Turkish Cypriot identity. Within the next twenty years it will be very hard to find a Turkish Cypriot. Denktash is justly proud of his achievement…[32]

Chapter 13

The Years of Hope

The policy followed by the Turkish Cypriot leadership and Ankara following the apparently premature and unplanned Turkish Cypriot rebellion[1] was intended to prevent things from returning to normal on the island, to maintain everything achieved so far – the transfer of Turkish Cypriots, the creation of enclaves, a climate of abnormality and conflict, etc. – and to bring about negotiations, not on a return to legitimacy but on the building of a new constitutional order, based on the further development of the partitionist image that the Turks were attempting to promote. They considered the fact that they had managed to create such an issue, with which the international community was concerned, as a success and a new starting point from which either new actions or mediation efforts by third parties could be launched. Any attempt at bringing calm or starting talks with the aim of resolving differences and overcoming the causes of the conflict were viewed in a completely negative manner.

On March 4, 1964, the Security Council approved the appointment by the United Nations Secretary-General of a mediator whose mission was 'to promote a peaceful solution and an agreed settlement of the problem faced by Cyprus'.[2] The UN Secretary-General appointed Galo Plaza to the post on September 16, 1964. According to Plaza's report, which was submitted on March 26, 1965, the Turkish positions as set out by Fazil Kuchuk in a memorandum to the mediator were the following:

The basis of the Turkish arguments was that the situation created by the events of Christmas 1963 placed the security of the Turkish Cypriots in immediate danger. The Turks tried – and are still trying today – to justify their every position by the claim that their security is threatened. They spoke then of genocide and always presented themselves as the side under threat, in spite of the fact that Turkey's involvement and policy actually reversed the relationship. That is to say that it was the Greek Cypriot side that was under constant threat due to Turkey's status as a guarantor power.

The conclusion drawn from this position was that Turkey's guarantees were essential for the security of the Turkish Cypriots, thus preventing any attempt at amending the guarantee system contained in the Zurich and London Agreements, which the Greek Cypriots insisted was necessary within the context of the process of completing Cypriot independence based on UN principles and international law. Arguing that by the 1960 agreements their community was no longer a minority but a community with its own separate political and constitutional rights, the Turkish Cypriots asked for additional guarantees in the shape of their geographical segregation from the Greek Cypriots. And since they recognised that such a situation would not be acceptable to the Greek Cypriots, the only compromise solution that they were willing to discuss was that of a federal state. Their proposal for geographical separation provided for a necessary 'exchange of populations' and a dividing line that started at the village of Yialia in the north-west of the island, passed through Nicosia and ended in the Turkish quarter of Famagusta, behind which would lie 38% of Cypriot territory.[3]

These positions were also supported by Turkey, which insisted on an additional dimension. It argued that the 1960 agreements had created an 'acceptable' balance between the two communities on the island and also between Greece and Turkey, one that had to be safeguarded in the context of any solution. It is clear that this was an essential requirement for the further promotion of its military objectives.

It is no coincidence that it is still using this same argument today: that, if these balances are upset by a solution, it will be necessary to 'reopen' the agreements by which they were created (Zurich, London and Lausanne) and renegotiate new balances that are acceptable to both sides. It was clearly using blackmailing tactics in order to maintain what it had already claimed and to make further demands against Hellenism.

The position of the Greek Cypriot side was that the Republic of Cyprus had been founded by the Zurich and London Agreements, not as a result of the will of the Cypriot people. The constitution was an extension of the agreements and had never been put to the people. It insisted on the implementation of democratic principles and the removal of those elements that either meant or encouraged political division, or restricted Cypriot independence, such as the treaties of guarantee.

Nonetheless, in order to contribute to a peaceful settlement, the Greek Cypriots were willing to make two concessions: Cyprus, as an independent state, could be demilitarised and remain non-aligned over and above any guarantees aimed at maintaining the rights of the minority, and additional measures in the favour of the minority could be taken.

According to the Galo Plaza report, President Makarios agreed to the following guarantees for the minority:

1. Provisions should be made in the constitution for the exercise of human rights and fundamental freedoms not less than those set forth in the European Convention for the Protection of Human Rights and Fundamental Freedoms, to which Cyprus is a party, and in conformity with those set forth in the Universal Declaration of Human Rights. The constitution should declare these rights and freedoms to be immediately applicable in the internal law of Cyprus.

2. Each of the 'minorities' should be permitted to continue to enjoy a broad autonomy, to be guaranteed by the constitution and by legislation, in special matters of religion, education and personal status.

3. Provisions should be made by the government of Cyprus to prevent discrimination on account of race, ethnical origin or religion in the appointment and treatment of members of the public service.

4. For the purpose of restoring confidence between Greek and Turkish Cypriots, the government of Cyprus, as one of its first official acts after agreement was reached, should decree a general amnesty in respect of all crimes and offences related to the events beginning in December 1963.

5. For a purely transitional period of defined duration and again for the purpose of helping to restore confidence between the Greek and Turkish Cypriots, the government of Cyprus should invite the United Nations to appoint a Commissioner who, assisted by a staff of observers and advisers, would observe on the spot the application of the foregoing provisions.[4]

The Turks, however, were adamant in their positions, and the Turkish position was taken seriously by the Western allies, whose interventions tended to satisfy Turkey's demands.

Nonetheless, certain truths did not escape the United Nations mediator, who showed the necessary courage to include them in his report. He viewed, for instance, as a natural development the constitutional impasse caused by the 'inflexible provisions of this unique constitution', which, he noted, he could not ignore 'due to their link with the present situation in Cyprus and the circumstances under which a new arrangement may be found'.[5] With this position, he justified Makarios' attempt to amend the constitution and the submission of the 13 points:

> Several of the most important amendments proposed by the President reflected deadlocks that had actually occurred in the functioning of the constitution. For example, in proposing that the right of veto of the President and the Vice-President should be abolished, he referred to the fact that the latter had vetoed a majority decision of the Council of Ministers that the organisational structure of the Cyprus army should be based on mixed units comprising both Greek Cypriots and Turkish Cypriots, since the Vice-President had favoured separate units.[6]

The mediator dared further to note in his report that a solution to the Cyprus problem could not be sought in a return to the situation as it was before the incidents through the complete implementation of the agreements. And this because, as he explained, the unworkable constitution was the root of the problem and the guarantees did indeed restrict Cyprus' independence. Both of these elements affected developments and thus had to be dealt with. His view was that geographical segregation would not only cause a mass of economic and social problems but would perpetuate antagonism and thus the crisis, and he dared also to point out that geographical segregation and the guarantee system agreed in Zurich was not the only way of safeguarding the security of the Turkish Cypriots. A solution to these problems, he noted, could be achieved by the implementation of the principles of the United Nations Charter.

Ankara and the Turkish Cypriot leadership, as expected, rejected his report. But they could not react to the views of the United Nations Secretary-General himself as expressed in his report to the Security Council on the situation in Cyprus, particularly regarding the intentions and demands of the Turkish leadership. The UN Secretary-General would repeat these views in reports until 1974:

Nonetheless, the absence of movement by the Turkish Cypriots outside their areas is thought to be dictated by political expediencies, specifically in order to reinforce the assertion that the two main communities in Cyprus cannot live together peacefully without some kind of geographical partition.[7]

The Turkish Cypriot leaders are following an inflexible policy against any measures that would mean that members of the two communities live and work together or which could lead the Turkish Cypriots to recognise the authority of representatives of the government. Indeed, from the moment that the Turkish Cypriot leadership is tied to the policy of physical and geographical separation of the two communities as a political objective, it is not possible to encourage activities on behalf of the Turkish Cypriots, which could be interpreted as promoting the advantages of an alternative policy. [...] The result is a clear policy of differentiation on the part of the Turkish Cypriots. [...] The suffering imposed on the Turkish Cypriot population is a direct result of its leadership's policy of isolation, which is being imposed on the ordinary people by force.[8] The Turkish Cypriot policy of self-isolation has led the community in the opposite direction to that of normality.[9]

With rare exceptions, the Turkish Cypriot leadership has banned entry to areas under its control to all Greek Cypriots, whether they are government employees or ordinary citizens. This ban appears to have been imposed as a matter of political principle with only the slightest attempt to justify it.[10]

For a long period the government called upon the refugees to return to their homes, assuring them of their safety, while in certain villages it had repaired or rebuilt abandoned Turkish Cypriot houses in the hope that this would encourage some Turkish Cypriot families to return home. [...] It is well known that the Turkish Cypriot leadership does not favour the return of the refugees to their homes in the government-controlled areas. To justify this position, it cites the security of the refugees, in spite of the fact that there is no doubt that the main reason is political.[11]

While the Turkish Cypriots may move freely throughout the island, apart from certain military areas, access to the Turkish Cypriot enclaves, to certain Turkish Cypriot villages and to certain main roads is not permitted to the Greek Cypriots. [...] If this abnormal situation, the result of the policy of the Turkish Cypriot leadership, is not dealt with, it will destroy the favourable climate that has been created...[12]

A Return to Normality

After the crisis at Kophinou in November 1967, and in spite of the treacherous action of the Junta, which led to the withdrawal of the Greek division from Cyprus, the government proceeded with a series of steps aimed at normalising the situation on the island. Many police and National Guard posts were removed, the movements of the Turkish Cypriots were facilitated, the public services responded to their obligations towards eligible Turkish Cypriots, and a review took place of the list of materials whose sale had been restricted because they might be used by the Turkish Cypriots for military purposes.

At the same time measures were announced for the relief of needy Turkish Cypriots, including state aid for repairs to Turkish Cypriot houses that had been damaged during the clashes, and conditions were created for the productive employment of Turkish Cypriot workers.

The masses of the Turkish Cypriots responded positively to the measures and the period from 1967 to 1974 was one of intense economic activity throughout the island. In the tourism sector, progress was spectacular as new hotel units sprang up daily, chiefly in the Nnrth-east of Cyprus. The numbers of foreign visitors rose impressively, bringing valuable foreign exchange, which was used to fund developments in other sectors of the economy. Through the government's five-year plans, agriculture gained a significant infrastructure, which stabilised and developed the rural economy. The transport system was improved, communications developed, education was adapted to fulfilling the requirements of the economy and Cyprus gradually turned itself into a financial and commercial centre for the whole region.

The picture of wealth certainly worked as one of the factors in the positive response by the Turkish Cypriot masses to the normalisation measures announced by the government and it reinforced significantly the resistance of the average Turkish Cypriot to TMT extremists who were trying in every way to maintain their control.

Resistance to Misery

The denial of the expectations created by the Turkish Cypriot leadership in the

Turkish Cypriot masses over supposed partition through the intervention of the Turkish army also contributed to the reaction of the ordinary Turkish Cypriots against the conditions imposed on them by their leadership. With the rebellion against the state, 99% of the Turkish Cypriots, according to one Turkish Cypriot newspaper,[13] were convinced that Turkey would invade Cyprus and, when this did not happen, their disappointment was huge. Especially since their situation was deteriorating due to the economic measures imposed for military reasons by the government, which badly affected the ordinary people.

Life for the Turkish Cypriots in the areas controlled by TMT was hard. As one Turkish Cypriot newspaper wrote,[14] living conditions were particularly bad for some 10,000 'refugees', i.e. those who had been forced to abandon their homes. Their monthly income was no more than £15 and they lived in tents – so that the Turkish Cypriot leadership could use this fact for propaganda purposes – without water, electricity, telephones, postal services, etc.

During this same period the situation in Turkey was in a state of flux with economic, social and political problems worsening, military coups and popular struggles, questioning and ideological clashes. It was a period during which the left dared to raise its head and did not hesitate to clash with the right and the establishment, promoting another view of the problems facing the country and proposing alternative solutions to them.

Many young Turkish Cypriots, in Turkey for studies, found themselves caught up in these circumstances. On their return to Cyprus, either during vacations or at the end of the studies, these people could not accept the brutal violence and terrorism that had been imposed on their community by TMT. And so, with boldness and in spite of the dangers, they highlighted the need for political expression by the Turkish Cypriots by means that were not controlled by TMT.

During this period, the Association of Revolutionary Youth (and the Turkish Cypriot students in Istanbul) had grown active and many of its members had been arrested and imprisoned by TMT for their activities against the policy of the Turkish Cypriot leadership on the Cyprus issue.

These circumstances, combined with a similar development of anti-nationalist thinking on the part of the Greek Cypriots, mainly due to the imposition of the dictatorship in Greece and the anti-national activities of the Junta in Cyprus, had contributed to a rapprochement among the masses, especially in the trade union sector, which was creating favourable prospects for the country.

The Turkish Cypriot students even reached the point of doubting the ability of Kuchuk to represent the Turkish Cypriot community.[15]

Nonetheless there were also negative elements, which, through their activities, complicated the situation and made it incredibly difficult for the progressive forces of the Turkish Cypriots to demonstrate openly against the policy of their chauvinistic leadership. For instance, the appearance of unofficial, chauvinistic armed organisations within the Greek Cypriot community reinforced the efforts of TMT to maintain the Turkish Cypriot community under its control.[16]

Arif Tahsin rightly questions the actions of the Greek Cypriots that helped Ankara's partitionist plans and which concerned the refusal of the Turkish Cypriot leadership to allow the Turkish Cypriots it had turned into refugees by force of arms to return to their homes and properties during the period of normalisation:

> What served best those who wanted the division of the island or the concentration of the Turkish population in one place was the ban on the Turkish Cypriots returning to their villages. In this light, the stance of the Turkish side is understandable. What is quite incomprehensible is the stance of the Greek side, which said that it was against *taxim.* On the one hand it was against partition and on the other it assisted substantially in the realisation of the plans of those who wanted *taxim* and helped towards concentrating the Turkish population in one or a few areas.[17]

Chapter 14

Rauf Denktash: Life and Times

In an address to the Rotarians in 1972, Rauf Denktash spoke of his childhood and his time as a pupil at the English School in Nicosia:

> Coming back to our school years, I don't think that our generation, the children of that age, had any reason to worry about their future. [...] They were years when people of our age knew that there was British 'oppression' on the island. [...] We were just English School pupils. Greek and Turkish kids who lived opposite one another in the same neighbourhood, who played together, argued. [...] I remember, when I was a boy, I would go with my father to Greek monasteries all over Cyprus, to Greek houses, we enjoyed ourselves as friends with the Greeks, as good friends. They came to our homes too, and I think reason was that we had no political differences.[1]

From his graduation from the English School and afterwards, Denktash contributed more than anyone to the creation of 'political differences' between the Greek and Turkish Cypriots. And on the creation and handling of these 'political differences' he based his career as leader of his community, a position for the obtaining and maintenance of which he has used every fair and foul means, indifferent to the consequences and the cost to his community.

Denktash's ambitions were unrestrained all along. He always viewed with envy any reference to Ataturk, whom he wanted to imitate. He grew up with an acute sense of rivalry with the Greeks, to whom he attributed an air of superiority, probably to compensate for the feeling of inferiority that runs through his generation.

His adulthood coincided with the dramatic events in Cyprus, which appear to have marked his 'philosophical' approach to the island's problems. He would later write:

> In 1931, when Greek Cypriots under the leadership of the Greek Orthodox Church burned down the Government House in the name of *enosis*, I was seven years old.

> I was twenty-one, in 1945, when all leaders who had been banished from the island for having organised that revolt, were allowed to return, carrying higher banners for *enosis*.
>
> I was twenty-six in 1950 when the Church organised what they called a plebiscite for *enosis*, which the British Government rightly regarded as a sham, and which Turkish Cypriots took as a calculated threat and a provocation.
>
> Four years later Colonel Grivas landed in Cyprus as part of a conspiracy with Archbishop Makarios and the Greek Government in order to start a terrorist campaign for *enosis*. I was 30 by then and a prosecuting counsel in the Attorney-General's office, able to see, from day to day, how terror affected my Greek-Cypriot friends, who began to declare that they were all for *enosis*.[2]

From very early on, Denktash had created, developed and maintained – to this very day – contacts with the most reactionary, chauvinistic circles in Turkey, contacts which he used on the one hand in order to impose himself on the Turkish Cypriot community and on the other, however implausible this may seem, to make Ankara toe the political line that served his own plans.

His first involvement in public affairs concerned the education of the Turkish Cypriots, with the planned aim of integrating this into the educational system and programme of Kemalist Turkey. The British colonial government of Cyprus approved the setting up of a special committee made up exclusively of Turkish Cypriots, to study the problems of the Turkish Cypriots, including education which until then had remained firmly attached to its Islamic character.[3] Denktash's presence on the committee was decisive and was even expressed in its report: 'We do not wish for greater control than that of the Greeks over educational matters. On the other hand, we do not accept – for any reason – less control.'[4]

This position represented from then on the character of his political positions against the Greeks: copying their every demand, claiming and protecting whatever had been gained that was identical to whatever the Greeks had gained, etc.

Throughout his career, Denktash has made his choices on the basis of certain fixed criteria. He has exaggerated to an extraordinary degree his concept of the power of the Church, and as a result its every decision is, to him, part of an imaginary conspiracy against the Turks with the aim, as he still believes, of realising the 'Great Idea'. Every development in Cyprus was for Denktash a copy of the developments in Crete with the aim, as he still believes today, of giving the

Turkish Cypriots a future similar to that which the Turks of Crete had. He still shares the most fanciful suspicions of the Panturanist groups of the Greeks' intentions and everywhere he sees slaughter and blood, genocide and annihilation. Even today his exaggerations concerning the victims among the Turkish Cypriots are enormous – and he has managed to brainwash the community – while his political arguments have been based, since his early days, on the myths about massacres that he himself has cultivated and maintained.

Denktash took on a substantial role in the leadership of the Turkish Cypriot community immediately after independence. From his position as Speaker of the Turkish Communal Chamber he essentially controlled the community from the top down. He opposed the Zurich and London Agreements, which he was nonetheless obliged to accept, but he never stopped planning and pressing for the next stage. On the one hand, under his guidance, all the Turkish Cypriot officials of the Republic of Cyprus maintained a provocative stance, with the systematic promotion of the divisive elements of the agreements, while, on the other, he reinforced the climate of conflict between the two communities. Arif Tahsin writes:[5]

> During this period [immediately following the Zurich and London Agreements] rumours grew about Denktash and the newspapers in Turkey started to attack him openly. According to the rumours, Denktash was against the agreements and he was also directing the community against the agreements, saying that, 'The Greek Cypriots are not sincere.'

Denktash's career as a lawyer began and ended in the colonial prosecutor's office, where he demonstrated a singular fanaticism in the persecution of the Greek Cypriot freedom fighters. And of course the colonial government wanted nothing more than this…

Denktash's special political relations with the British have not been revealed fully but even his own people considered him a man of the British at the time.[6]

His first big legal case as a prosecutor was the trial of the crew of the Greek-flagged boat *Saint George*, which was arrested on January 25, 1954, as it unloaded arms for EOKA. The trial began in Paphos on March 17 with Denktash playing the role of public prosecutor for the colonial establishment – the arrested men were accused of attempting to overthrow it – with particular warmth and enthusiasm. There followed other fighters who found themselves in the British courts facing Denktash the prosecutor.

His political activity, however, was overshadowed by the presence of Dr Fazil Kuchuk, the sole and unopposed leader of the Turkish Cypriots. It took many years and a great deal of deception and bloodshed before he had succeeded in brushing Kuchuk aside and taking over the reins of the community.

The Flight to Ankara

Denktash represented the young generation of Turkish Cypriot intellectuals who had no memories of the Ottoman Empire beyond the Turkish Republic and Kemal Ataturk. He had dynamism, which, combined with the fanaticism that marked him out, brought him into conflict on many occasions with the far more moderate and acceptable first leader of the Turkish Cypriots, Fazil Kuchuk. The two men had more than a few disagreements and clashes. After all, Kuchuk was the only obstacle in the way of Denktash being recognised as the sole and undeniable leader of the Turkish Cypriots.

Turkey may have created TMT but Denktash had begun to prepare the way for armed conflict much earlier. In any case, Ankara's decision was implemented at a pace dictated essentially by Denktash, on whom the Turkish officers entrusted with the mission of organising, training and arming TMT members depended.

Although there has never been adequate evidence, many Turkish Cypriots believe that the incidents at Christmas 1963, due to which developments in the Cyprus issue took on their present form, were provoked – and at the wrong time – by Denktash in order to force the implementation of the plans for partition.[7]

Ihsan Ali refers to Denktash's stance towards Makarios' proposals for constitutional changes:

> Instead of suggesting to Turkey that it deal with the proposal in good faith, Denktash did the opposite. He exploited this proposal in such a way that the bloody incidents of 1963 took place. There is evidence to confirm this. For example, some time before the incidents, he forced the Turks in the towns to abandon their homes in the Greek Cypriot neighbourhoods. He also obliged the Turks living in mixed villages to leave them, on the pretext that the Greeks

> were going to attack. The purpose of this plan was to create faits accomplis in order to bring about dismemberment. He tried through terrorism to keep the Turkish community away from the Greek community.[8]

From Arif Tahsin's references, it is evident that the untimely rebellion against the state caused a major clash between Kuchuk and Denktash, who immediately afterwards left Cyprus with his family and settled in Ankara.[9]

Others claim that Denktash was taken before a TMT 'military court', the session of which was presented to the Turkish Cypriots as a meeting 'for an exchange of views after the truce', following the incidents of Christmas 1963.[10] The 'military court' comprised, among others, the *bayraktar*, *sadakar* (regional commander) and *serdar* and its real purpose was to restrict the authority of Kuchuk and Denktash – something that Denktash had realised and he preferred to leave Cyprus.

Others say that, after the 1963 incidents, the morale of the Turkish Cypriots was low and, even among the military and political leadership, the prevailing view was that they should surrender – a position attributed to Denktash which explains his flight from Cyprus.

His flight was presented publicly as a mission to the Security Council for the debate on the Cyprus issue. However, Arif Tahsin notes that Denktash had declared from abroad that Makarios had banned him from returning to Cyprus, long before the government announced such a move, a fact that is interpreted as an attempt by Denktash to give another dimension to his flight.[11]

The decision to have Denktash arrested should he return to Cyprus was taken in March 1964 for offences connected to the rebellion against the state. Denktash could, of course, have returned, been arrested and undergone a trial, which could have been used as an opportunity for him to promote his positions in an international court and to become a hero to his community, managing at the same time to push aside his rivals. He responded to this suggestion thus:

> Certainly…I would have enjoyed the trial. But in those days once you were arrested in Cyprus there was no telling if you would ever be seen again. So I had to stay in Turkey, Prime Minister Inonu telling me that once the UN came to Cyprus he would see to it that I entered Cyprus safely, in the proper way.[12]

Before settling in Ankara, Denktash did indeed address the United Nations

Security Council for the first time in his career, thanks to the mediation of the Turkish delegation. His address was totally in line with the policy of abolishing the Republic of Cyprus that Ankara was promoting and the recognition of the 'existence of two peoples', which would have to be segregated by population and territorially. And, all the while, he kept repeating the word 'genocide'.

The failure to achieve the initial objectives of the Turkish Cypriot rebellion against the state forced him to backtrack slightly and oppose the sending of a peacekeeping force to the island, arguing that, 'the guarantor powers, on the basis of the agreement that is being attacked in this chamber, could undertake this mission jointly,' to maintain peace.[13] The obvious aim was to increase the number of 'official' Turkish forces on Cyprus, which could be entrusted with the task of maintaining peace.

He also attempted to neutralise the principles of international law and the UN as criteria for examining the situation in Cyprus, claiming that, 'Every country, every state has its own special characteristics and the implementation of general principles is dangerous.'

The distortion of historical facts and realities has always been a perfectly legitimate weapon for Denktash, who would claim that the communities in Cyprus 'each lived as autonomous communities together, yet always separate. Down to the smallest village there have always been and there are Greek and Turkish authorities looking after the affairs of their communities separately.'

He presented the Zurich-London Agreements as a compromise 'reached fairly and responsibly.' 'It was a settlement between equals, not between the majority and the minority. The notion of majority and minority would have arisen if there had been a Cypriot nation.'

Ankara 1964-1967

Denktash's presence in the Turkish capital helped him – in spite of the fact that it had essentially been imposed on him so that he would be under the control of the Turkish government – to obtain important experience but mainly to make acquaintances, which would later prove useful in forcing Ankara to adopt his choices. Not that Ankara was against this. It was simply that, in every case, it was obliged to take other factors into account, which Denktash rejected.

It remains a fact that from Ankara he was safe to play the role of the 'exiled' leader of a 'liberation' movement. And he sought this through interviews, speeches and statements, and in correspondence with foreign political figures.

Always appearing in his capacity as Speaker of the Turkish Communal Chamber, he promoted his ideas passionately and always focused on the same points: the weakness of the other Turkish Cypriot leaders on the one hand, his dynamism on the other and the undeniable abilities that made him the central figure in the promotion of the Turkish positions.

Denktash reached the point of launching attacks in all directions, even at the Attorney-General of Cyprus, Criton Tornaritis, to whom he addressed a letter on July 17, 1964, and in which he requested that the latter condemn the Cypriot government and move abroad:

> I wish to advise you to get out of the impasse in which you find yourself before it is too late. Ask for your pension and settle abroad if you do not wish to be considered an accomplice in the crimes of the Archbishop and his clique. I shall say no more. I have said enough to warn you of the forthcoming developments.[14]

From that time he advanced the claim that recognition of the government of Cyprus was 'illegal', demanding that the United Nations accept this position and, consequently, give the relevant orders to its peacekeeping force. In a letter to the then UN Secretary-General, U Thant, on September 5, 1964, he wrote:

> The first point to be cleared up is that Makarios has ceased to be President of the island of Cyprus and that the constitutional government of the Republic of Cyprus does not exist. Once this is accepted, it will be clear to all that the duty of the UN peacekeeping force is to prevent the Greek Cypriots from ill-treating the Turkish Cypriots. This force must have the right to take responsibility for internal security in the island [i.e. to end the sovereignty of the Republic of Cyprus and the authority of its government] and must be able to impose its will on all sections of the population.[15]

To blame for everything was the policy of *enosis*, according to Denktash, who fanatically supported partition as the 'antidote' and 'medicine' to this policy. And he had no problem with stating from that time, however much embarrassment he may have caused to Ankara:

> The problems of Cyprus are due to the policy of *enosis*, a policy which is nourished by Greece, which was fabricated and planned by Greece. Turkey and the Turkish Cypriots are against *enosis.* The issue, however, is what concerns Greece and Turkey. They must come to an understanding and sort it out. And the fairest and most realistic arrangement is the creation of Greco-Turkish borders in Cyprus.[16]

To those who pointed out that he was making propaganda for partition from the safety of Ankara while the Turkish Cypriots were in a difficult position on the island and their morale had received heavy blows, he would reply: 'Turkish morale may be low but it is invincible. If we are given the means, we can finish the job. It may take time but we have patience.'[17]

Despite these views, which were tantamount to admitting his ambitions of abolishing the Republic of Cyprus, a recognised member state of the UN, he had no moral scruples – and this was to become a permanant feature of his political practice, which he still follows faithfully – about asking the Secretary-General of the UN to mediate for his return to Cyprus, as if nothing had happened:

> For over three years I have lived in Turkey, far from my work and my responsibilities, while Greek Cypriot propaganda accuses me daily of every crime under the sun, including cowardice and desertion in the face of danger. Unable to defend myself in exile, I have been unable to reply decisively to my accusers. If you were to put yourself in my place, you would realise, I am sure, the spiritual and psychological agony in which I have lived for the last three years.
>
> In the name of justice and to justify the principles of the UN Charter, I look forward to a final effort from you to secure my safe return to Cyprus. Until now I have avoided taking the law into my own hands and returning of my own volition to Cyprus with a number of volunteers whose return to the island has also been banned. If, however, there is no justice and the Greek Cypriot administration insists on claiming the force of law, I regret to inform you that I shall resort to measures that I consider necessary, for the consequences of which I am not responsible.[18]

Nonetheless, only four months later, in the light of charges published in the Turkish Cypriot press by his political rivals, that he was living a life of luxury in Ankara while the Turkish Cypriots suffered, Denktash was showing signs of wanting to flee and abandon his 'struggle'. This was encouraged by his inability to persuade Ankara to adopt a dynamic policy on Cyprus, a fact that brought disappointment to himself and to those Turkish Cypriots whom he had managed to stir up at Christmas 1963 with promises and assurances that Turkey would intervene.

The denial of these expectations, as was only natural, had an effect on his own dependability in the eyes of the Turkish Cypriots, and he was aware of this. For this reason he considered giving up everything and settling in London. He even sent a letter to the British Bar Association in which he asked for information on the circumstances under which he would be able to exercise the profession of lawyer in England. Having given a brief biographical note and explained the reasons for his being in Ankara, he writes:

> A solution to the Cyprus problem is not yet visible and I am now considering the possibility of restarting my career in the legal profession in England, if circumstances permit, until I am able to return to Cyprus. I am considering such a possibility for both moral and health reasons. I am sending this letter because a Turkish Cypriot client of mine who resides in London has requested my services in a case in the Appeals Court. I should like to reply to him on the basis of your response to my questions.[19]

All the time he was in Ankara, Denktash felt that his rivals in Cyprus were acting to create a gulf between him and the Turkish Cypriots, that an entire campaign of disinformation had been carried out based on the fact that he was living safely in Ankara, and that he had to decide either to give up everything or risk returning to Cyprus illegally, getting away even from the surveillance of the Turkish authorities, and thus becoming once more the 'hero' of TMT and its members.

Strange though it may seem, compared with the image of the determined man that he always presents, Denktash was unable to come to a decision. But he was bothered by the fact that in Cyprus, without him being able to react, his standing had received a heavy blow.

Complaints about Ankara's Stance

His situation led him to a permanent state of complaint. Everything and everyone was at fault but he was especially annoyed with the Turkish government, which he held responsible for developments, accusing it of being slow, indecisive and afraid of accepting responsibility.

These complaints are described in a book that was published in Ankara on October 29, 1966, entitled *Cyprus at the Eleventh Hour – The Motherland will have the Last Word* (*Notes, thoughts and recollections of the Cyprus struggle*).[20]

The book's introduction shows the conditions prevailing in Ankara and views on Cyprus at the time. Denktash's Panturanist ideas are also evident, both with reference to the situation created in Cyprus and in relation to his ambitions and vision. He writes in the introduction:

> I feel the need to explain to the 'happy minority' that is wondering whether 'it is right to send 32 million people to war for the sake of 120,000 individuals' that the Cyprus problem is not a question of saving the 120,000 Turks of Cyprus. The Cyprus issue determines the future of Turkey. Behind this issue the Great Idea lies craftily in wait. The Kurdish question, the Hatay issue, even that of a new Armenian question, all await the outcome of the Cyprus issue. A victorious conclusion to the Cyprus issue is completely necessary for Turkey's national interests. [...]
>
> I have a few words for those who say, 'The Turks of Cyprus are to blame for the situation.' [...] On this I have said as much as I can under the present circumstances. The day will come when circumstances will enable us to tell the whole truth. [...]
>
> I also have a few words for those who say that 'we have lost Cyprus'. The struggle we are waging is not yet over. We can win it. We are confident that we will win it. But are we doing everything we can to win it? That is another matter. I felt the need to speak about this too.
>
> There are some who say that 'nothing more can be done'. For their sake I cry that the world has never called 'halt' to the right and the strong. And it never will.[21]

Denktash's major complaint was that, from the outset of the Cyprus issue, the

Turkish side had allegedly not clarified its objectives and the way in which it would achieve them. The Greeks, he said, from the day the British arrived, were asking for *enosis*; when they burnt down Government House in 1931 they demanded *enosis*; in 1955-1959 they demanded *enosis*:

> When the 1959 agreement was being signed, Makarios was thinking about *enosis*. As soon as the Republic of Cyprus was founded in 1960, the secret Greek organisation for the realisation of *enosis* was created, the blood of the Turkish Cypriots was shed for *enosis* in 1963, 102 Turkish villages were burnt down for *enosis*, 203 Turks were killed so as to break the resistance of 120,000 Turks, and even today Makarios says, 'Our aim is *enosis*.'
>
> We said 'maintenance of the status quo' and we did not want to believe it possible that one day the British would abandon the island. Ignoring international changes, we followed a blind policy of friendship with Britain. So as not to upset the British, the Foreign Ministry declared that there was no Cyprus question. There were times when the official doors were closed to delegations coming to Turkey to explain the situation. We should not forget this. [...]
>
> We have said that Cyprus is Turkish and will remain Turkish and once we founded associations called 'Cyprus is Turkish' in Cyprus and Anatolia. But we had no plan for keeping Cyprus Turkish or such a policy.
>
> Then we said 'partition or death'. Today there are hundreds of unburied Turks who fell because they believed in their motherland, they desired their freedom, loved their flag. But again there was no plan or a specific policy to bring about partition.
>
> The Republic of Cyprus was founded to safeguard peace, to establish Turkish-Greek friendship, to protect NATO. Turkey guaranteed the existence of this Republic.[22] But no policy was ever formulated to realise this obligation, there was never any plan drawn up in this direction. Blindly we believed in Makarios' good faith and we forgot Cyprus amid the worries over internal problems.
>
> The constitution was being trampled on, line by line.
>
> 'Show goodwill. Don't be negative, everything will be fine,' they told us. And there were official declarations that, 'The constitution will be implemented to the letter and the rights of the Turks will be safeguarded.'
>
> From the foundation of the Republic of Cyprus on August 16, 1960, to

> December 22-23, 1963, when the troubles began, Turkey could have done a lot to save the situation. But Turkey was not following developments and fell victim to Anglo-American-Greek friendship.
>
> Finally, the events of 1963 illuminated what would follow. Turkey awoke.
>
> We took part in the London Conference saying that, 'A federal administration on the basis of geographical division is the least of our demands.' It was a national aim, not merely a nice request. It was the least of our demands for the protection of our rights.
>
> Today we do not even mention federation. Soon it will be a crime to mention a satisfactory solution on the basis of geographical division. It seems that we are afraid and faint-hearted due to a lack of confidence in our own matters and in the Turkish Cypriots...
>
> The Cyprus issue has been turned into a Turkish-Greek conflict. Turkey, having imposed its policy on the Turkish Cypriot community, has taken all the initiatives and shouldered its historical responsibilities for the result of the struggle. The supporters of the *Megali Idea* will use the results of this conflict to begin new cases. We have to realise this.[23]

Denktash's danger warnings about the *Megali Idea* (the 'Great Idea', a doctrine adhered to by Greek nationalists at the beginning of the 20th century, which aimed at expanding Greece's borders), about 'new Greek claims against Turkey' and about a repeat of Greek policy on Crete, aimed to create conditions for the adoption of extreme choices on the part of Ankara, choices that were eventually made on the pretext of the coup against Makarios in 1974.

The continuity in Denktash's demands is clear from these extracts. It is also worth noting some of Denktash's references to instances such as the 'From Turk to Turk' campaign because they contribute greatly to an understanding of Turkish tactics and their relationship with their ultimate objectives, something which still applies today.

> During this period [1958-1960] we had begun the 'From Turk to Turk' campaign with the aim of creating solidarity among the Turks. This had annoyed the Greeks. It was not at all good for them to lose a market of 120,000 people. We also affected the interests of certain Turks who bought from the Greeks and sold on to the Turks. We aimed to create a new Turkish market in which

> the importers and exporters would be Turks. [...] In six months, deposits in the Turkish banks had doubled...
>
> Some of those whose interests had been harmed attempted to place obstacles in the way but we cast them aside...
>
> We asked for help from an economist and diplomat who had come to Cyprus. We explained the situation to him and asked for his advice for carrying out the campaign more scientifically. He laughed. 'Such a thing is not possible. What you are trying to do does not exist in any book or in any regulation. It is against science and reason.'[24]

What Denktash was fighting for with such passion was to persuade people that, without military intervention by Turkey, the Cyprus issue could not be resolved in accordance with Turkish designs. At every opportunity he would argue in favour of a military solution:

> Negotiations are taking place at the UN on the Cyprus issue. Certain politicians come and find me with the aim of attacking their political rivals. Until now they did not know me. Some of them say: 'If we were in power, we would follow a more active policy.' I ask them: 'Would you intervene on the basis of the agreements?' Some reply: 'That depends on the international circumstances and our military situation.' Others say: 'We would intervene immediately.'
>
> In many places I am asked, 'Should there be an intervention?' I reply:
>
> 'The agreements exist, we have the right to intervene. But I don't know whether there should be an intervention.' They don't like this answer. They want me to say: 'The intervention should have taken place, we have missed opportunities,' etc. After so long, only now was the army able to say that it was ready. Were there other opportunities? History alone will give the answer. Only those who hold the reins of this state can give the answer. But one thing is clear: Cyprus cannot be saved and our rights cannot be secured without intervention. I say this to some people and they call me a warmonger.[25]

Since then...

Denktash also complains that not enough 'volunteers' were sent to the island, but he notes that the 'fighters' have been organised into an army of 15,000 men.[26]

Chapter 14

Illegal Return and Arrest

Denktash attempted to return to Cyprus illegally on two occasions. The first was in July 1964. Unknown to the Turkish government, he claimed, he succeeded in boarding a Turkish launch carrying Turkish Cypriot student 'volunteers' and ammunition to the coastal enclave at Kokkina on the north-west of the island. He even managed to go ashore, and stayed there waiting for his transport to the Turkish quarter of Nicosia to be organised. However, the National Guard's operations against the enclave took place and Denktash fled with the 'volunteers' back to Turkey.

The second attempt came in October 1967. He managed to disembark on a deserted shore between Larnaca and Famagusta and tried to make his way to the Turkish quarter of Nicosia. He was recognised and arrested by an armed game warden, who led him to the coffee shop in his village, which did not have a police station. He informed a neighbouring National Guard camp and shortly afterwards, guarded by an army unit, Denktash was taken to Nicosia, where he was kept in confinement at the military police camp.[27] He was interrogated by the head of the Greek military intelligence service. Makarios then ordered the Speaker of the House, Glafcos Clerides, to visit and interrogate Denktash himself since from the first interrogation it appeared that Denktash, docile and with his morale low, believed that the struggle for *enosis* had been won and that there was no way of obliging the Greek forces to leave the island, while at the same time he considered that the Turkish Cypriots had lost the battle because of Turkey's unwillingness to become militarily involved in Cyprus.[28]

Clerides' assessment after his conversation with Denktash was that: 'He had come to Cyprus to strengthen the Turkish leadership and that, despite his protestations that he came without the knowledge of the Turkish government, this part of his story was not true.' Denktash, in Clerides' view, was neither docile nor did he consider himself the champion of a lost cause. He also concluded that Denktash was fully aware of the military advantages Turkey would have in the event of a Greco-Turkish military confrontation. 'He was sent,' Clerides writes, 'to Cyprus to assume leadership of his community because of the shortcomings of the Turkish Cypriot leaders and to promote Turkish policy, with which he was in total agreement.'[29]

Denktash's long statement to the military authorities is of particular interest and illuminates certain aspects of the relationship between the members of the Turkish Cypriot leadership but also the general situation prevailing on the island at the time. It is also of interest because it contains his views on certain historical events, with which we have already dealt, and on the methods used by the Turkish Cypriot leadership.

The Turkish Cypriots had doubts, at the very least, about Denktash's motives and methods from early on. But when their fears were proved correct, it was already too late. Denktash controlled the mechanisms, he had access and political support which made him immovable, particularly after the Turkish invasion and the restricting of the Turkish Cypriots to one area which is still under the complete control of the Turkish army and Denktash.

In spite of the unbelievable terrorism under which the Turkish Cypriots lived and still live, there have been from time to time instances of enlightened Turkish Cypriot journalists daring to reveal aspects of Denktash's character, ambitions, methods and objectives both before and after the invasion. On general lines, the views of the Turkish Cypriots, even the younger ones[30], are summarised in the following article by the journalist Kerem Adli[31] which refers to the ways in which Denktash managed to rise to the top of the Turkish Cypriot leadership:

> Some people were beaten up because they did not agree with the 'From Turk to Turk' campaign.
>
> All those who opposed chauvinism or were considered leftists or Communists were murdered. Those who could save themselves fled to London and to safety.
>
> Individuals whose 'treachery' had not been cleared up were executed in the middle of the road before people's very eyes.
>
> The murderers of people in their beds remain unknown. The 'crimes' of their victims remain unspecified.
>
> One evening a bomb was placed in Denktash's office. The identity of the bomber was never discovered. No one was arrested. Yet there are many who believe that the aim was to publicise Denktash's name. The claim that it was the work of Greek Cypriots or Yiorkatzis was never believed by the Turkish Cypriot community.
>
> Another evening a shot was fired from the street at Denktash's office in the Communal Chamber. The bullet passed through the window and hit the ceiling.

In these incidents there were no 'victims or injuries' because it always happened that Denktash was not in his office. And the Turks rushed out into the streets in anger at the Greeks who had thrown a bomb at Denktash's office.

After the events of December 21, 1963, Denktash supposedly left Cyprus to support Turkish positions abroad and his return to Cyprus was prevented in a curious way.

Suddenly a chance arose and, as if by magic, Denktash was on a boat off the coast of Cyprus. Despite the fact that the Greeks arrested him, they did not kill him. He was offered protection by his old schoolmate from the English School, Glafcos Clerides, and was given a bogus trial.

Meanwhile the Turkish Cypriot community rushed out into the streets shouting 'Denktash, Denktash'. Denktash quickly climbed the leadership ladder.

And then, at the time of his arrest, Denktash sent Makarios a statement in which he promised not to come to Cyprus illegally and without the permission of the government of the Greeks. He promised Makarios this, even giving guarantees, not seeing anything reproachable in connection with the nine rules of courage.

Denktash kept his promise and, with Makarios' permission, returned in April 1968 'to his country as leader'.

A leader had appeared in Cyprus. And it was time to remove Kuchuk's stripes.

Before long, in the shadow of arms and pressure from the government of the motherland, that happened too. Now Denktash is trying to beat the records of Franco, the Shah, Salazar and the overthrown Ottoman Sultan Hamit Khan. It has never occurred to him to resign because of his failed leadership and to bring it to an honourable end. But the voice of the Turkish Cypriots is growing stronger and it is saying that he has lived his era and ought to withdraw.'

Chapter 15

Before the Invasion

Denktash's arrest took place amid the climate that had been created in Cyprus by the seizure of power in Greece by the Colonels on April 21, 1967. The National Guard, meanwhile, had been infiltrated by officers of the Junta, who had gradually replaced those sent by the government of George Papandreou.

The coup d'état in Greece also signalled the start of the anti-Makarios activities by the so-called '*enosist*' elements, for whom the Colonels were allies backing up their actions. The military government of Constantinos Kolias presented itself as a supporter of *enosis*[1] while at the same time talking with the Turks on the basis of Acheson's partitionist plan. The Junta needed a success in order to satisfy the international community on which it was depending and in order to become accepted as the government.[2]

On September 9 and 10, 1967, a meeting was held in Evros between the Turkish Prime Minister, Suleyman Demirel, and the Junta's under-secretary to the President, George Papadopoulos, but it ended in total failure.

As time passed, the Junta, far from spreading its authority, was becoming more and more diplomatically isolated. This may have been one of the factors that tipped the balance in Denktash's decision to return to Cyprus illegally. With Makarios facing internal problems caused by the Junta, and the Junta condemned and isolated internationally, his return could bring about a positive reaction, particularly from abroad, especially if he should be arrested.

Denktash's arrest led to diplomatic pressure on the Cypriot government to free him, which placed Nicosia in a dilemma. On the one hand, the charges against Denktash for his role in the Turkish Cypriot rebellion and the attempt to abolish the Republic of Cyprus were too serious to ignore, while on the other hand it was similarly impossible to ignore the international community, on whose support Makarios was basing his efforts to complete Cyprus' independence.

The Turkish government sent a message to Makarios through the United Nations in which, apparently embarrassed by Denktash's action, it made a request that he be allowed to travel to the Turkish quarter of Nicosia so as to return to Turkey.[3]

On November 10, 1967, Denktash himself sent a letter to the Cypriot government, via the Attorney-General, in which he asked to be freed so as to return to Turkey, promising not to attempt to return to Cyprus illegally again. In his reply, the Attorney-General informed him that, 'It has been decided that for the time being the case will not proceed to trial regarding the pending charges, which will remain open, and he be sent to Turkey.'[4]

On November 12, Denktash returned to Turkey, to come back to Cyprus later under very different circumstances. Specifically, in less than a month after his attempt to return illegally, the Kophinou troubles broke out.[5] The dramatic developments that followed led Makarios to decide to try for a solution that was 'viable', noting in a statement that:

> Since the Cyprus issue recently entered its most crucial phase and serious initiatives and bold decisions are required to end the present deadlock, in search of a solution that falls within the framework of the viable, which is not always the same as the desirable, I am no longer able to continue to give my services from the position of President without a renewal of the popular mandate.[6]

The elections were held on February 25, 1968, between Makarios and Takis Evdokas, the voice at the time of the policy of the 'desirable', i.e. *enosis*. Makarios was returned with a landslide 95.45% of the vote and he immediately implemented a range of measures aimed at normalising the situation and at the same time sent a message of goodwill to the Turkish Cypriot side. Makarios was searching for means of peaceful understanding with the Turkish Cypriots and this was duly appreciated by the United Nations, which, by a Security Council resolution on March 18, called the two sides to talks.

In a new good willmove, the Makarios government responded positively to a proposal by the UN Secretary-General and gave its consent for Denktash to legally return to Cyprus. He did so on April 13, 1968.[7]

Parallel Authority

As has been noted, the Turkish Cypriot rebellion took place according to a specific plan, one with specific objectives. A day after the uprising, the Turkish

Cypriot leadership, led by Ankara, attempted to implement Nihat Erim's formula by the forced concentration of Turkish Cypriots in areas under its direct control and through the creation of a 'parallel authority', which would replace that of the Republic of Cyprus in these areas.

Immediately after the Kophinou troubles, the General Council that had been set up after the rebellion was replaced by the so-called Provisional Turkish Administration (PTA). In shaping the framework and the 'institutional' character of the PTA, a decisive role was played by the then General Secretary of the Turkish Foreign Ministry, Zeki Kuneralp, and the Ministry's legal adviser, Professor Suad Bilge,[8] who imposed the decision to create the PTA during a meeting in the office of the Vice-President of the Republic, Fazil Kuchuk, on December 28, 1967. At the same meeting the 'charter' of the Turkish Cypriot leadership was approved under the title 'Basic Provisions of the Turkish Administration of Cyprus',[9] in which there was an evident attempt to 'safeguard' a picture of 'legitimacy' while at the same time it was a political act taken within the framework of the Erim formula:

1. Until all provisions of the 16th August, 1960, constitution of the Republic of Cyprus are applied, all Turks living in Turkish areas shall be attached to the Provisional Turkish Administration.

2. The necessary legislation for Turkish areas shall be made by the House of the Provisional Turkish Administration, which shall be composed of the Turkish Members of the House of Representatives [of the legitimate House of the Republic] and members of the Turkish Communal Chamber [a body covered by the constitution of the Republic]. The Vice-President of the House of Representatives [who, according to the constitution, is a Turkish Cypriot and is elected only by the House] shall be the President of the House.

3. The members of the House shall continue to possess all the powers embodied in the constitution dated 16th August, 1960.

4. The House shall function in accordance with those provisions of the rules and regulations of the House of Representatives and of the Turkish Communal Chamber which are capable of being applied.

5. The laws enacted in accordance with the 16th August, 1960, constitution before the 21st December, 1963, shall be in full force and operation.

6. The House may empower the Executive Council to make any rules and regulations for application within the Turkish areas.

7. The executive power in Turkish areas shall be exercised by the Executive Council of the Provisional Turkish Administration.

8. The Executive Council shall be composed of the three Ministers envisaged in Article 46 of the 16th August, 1960, constitution, and of six other members. The Vice-President of the Republic shall be the President, and the President of the Turkish Communal Chamber shall be Vice-President of the Executive Council.

9. The Executive Council shall be composed of members responsible for Defence Matters (including both internal and external relations); Agriculture and Natural Resources; Health Services; Educational, Cultural and Teaching matters; Social Services, Municipalities, Vakufs (religious foundation property) and Cooperative matters; Judicial, Financial and Budgetary matters; Works and Communications; and Economic matters.

10. Vacancies occurring in the Executive Council, through the resignation of members or through other reasons, shall be filled by appointments made by the President on the recommendation of the Vice-President.

11. The President, Vice-President and the Members of the Executive Council shall not be engaged in any private work incompatible with their official duties.

12. The Executive Council shall have power to effect any changes in the administrative system and to define the function of the system.

13. The Defence and Security Services of the Provisional Turkish Administration shall be ensured by an organization to be established for the purpose by the Executive Council.

14. All kinds of assistance from Turkey shall be utilized in accordance with the conditions upon which the assistance has been given.

15. The functions of the Public Service Commission as envisaged in the 16th August, 1960, constitution shall be exercised in respect of all public officers of the Provisional Turkish Administration by a commission composed of three members. The members of the Turkish Public Service Commission shall be appointed by the President upon the recommendation of the Vice-President of the Executive Council.

16. The Court matters in the Provisional Turkish Administration shall be dealt with by independent Turkish Courts.

17. Turkish judges shall be appointed by the President upon the recommendation of the Vice-President of the Executive Council of the Provisional Turkish Administration.

18. Matters concerning the establishment of Turkish Courts, their jurisdiction and duties and the status of the judges shall be regulated by the introduction of temporary rules and regulations.

19. The above provisions which have been accepted for application in Turkish areas shall remain in force until the provisions of the 16th August, 1960, Constitution are applied.[10]

From the start of the 1950s, the Turks have used a tactic of copying every move by the Greek Cypriots, whether they be political actions or institutional decisions. Thus they called elections for the post of Vice President of the Republic of Cyprus (who, according to the 1960 constitution is elected only by the Turkish Cypriots) for February 25, 1968, the same day as those for President, which Makarios had called. Fazil Kuchuk was elected unopposed and took up his position as the first Chairman of the Executive Council.

*

Denktash at the Reins

The leader of TMT in Cyprus at the start of the Turkish Cypriot rebellion was Major Kemal Coskun.[11] During this period, TMT's control over the Turkish Cypriots was total. Coskun himself controlled everything.[12] He was withdrawn from Cyprus in 1967 after organising a sabotage of the fuel stores in Larnaca ,about which the Americans were especially annoyed, and they demanded that Ankara withdraw him.[13]

Coskun was a close collaborator of Denktash and he warmly supported his return, which brought him into conflict with Fazil Kuchuk. It is said that he was the one who sent the Americans' references to Coskun to Ankara while Denktash was furious at the decision to withdraw Coskun. He wrote to friends on the island and asked them to demand copies of the references that led to Coskun's withdrawal.[14]

By the time he returned, Denktash's popularity had grown. His friends had presented him as the exiled leader returning to lead the struggle for better days. And Denktash was determined not to be restricted to a secondary role. He immediately took up the position of 'deputy chairman of the Executive Council', which was something akin to 'Prime Minister'. Prior to this there had been bomb blasts at the homes of three members of the Executive Council who were known for their antipathy towards Denktash. Two of them resigned at once.[15] From that moment a purge began so that Denktash could place his own men in the administration. Moreover, with the $20 million that Turkey was sending every year,[16] Denktash appeared generous and gave pay rises to the 'fighters' of TMT and the 'police' and to the 'civil servants', thus creating a strong political power base. And with this power, and that of Turkey, which supported him, he began talks with Glafcos Clerides on the Cyprus issue.

The 1968 presidential elections, in conjunction with the developments that had led to them and a turn towards the policy of 'the viable' which the people had been asked to approve in the elections, created circumstances in which there was a superficial, at least, opposition of political views that justified the creation of political parties.

In addition to the Democratic National Party, which had put forward Takis Evdokas as Makarios' opponent in the presidential elections, and AKEL, the only organised political force at the time, various political groups began to appear on the scene. Glafcos Clerides and Polycarpos Yiorkatzis founded the Unity Party, Vassos Lyssarides formed the Unified Democratic Union of the Centre (EDEK), Nicos Sampson the Progressive Party and Odysseas Ioannides the Progressive Wing.

These were, of course, mainly parties of the right, clearly personality-based and with the basic aim of exercising personal influence over the broader right wing, which was essentially governing.[17]

At the same time the first illegal organisations of the so-called '*enosists*' made their appearance and in March 1970 the first attempt was made to assassinate Makarios, who, in search of further proof of popular approval for his move to find a solution among the 'viable' possibilities, had called parliamentary elections for July 25, 1970.[18]

Following its familiar tactics of copying every Greek Cypriot move, the Turkish Cypriot leadership also called parliamentary elections. These 'elections' proved to be a game for Denktash, who used them to open the way to replacing Fazil Kuchuk in the highest post of the leadership of the Turkish Cypriot community. Arif Tahsin writes:

> Playing the role of the 'impartial', he would add sureness to his steady progress towards the top. Steady, sure steps. Denktash was obliged on the one hand to appear impartial and on the other to ensure that his own people won. But, even more importantly, the winners had to believe or know that they had won thanks to Denktash's help while the losers should not know that they had lost because of him...
>
> On the surface there were no significant ideological differences among the candidates, but, to be on the safe side, certain steps had to be taken in this regard. All those who wanted to put forward their candidacy went under the Denktash umbrella. He had prepared a manifesto and had presented it at the Seray Hotel. Those wishing to take part in the elections had first to accept this manifesto.
>
> The opposition, whose foundations had been laid in the previous parliament and were growing ever stronger, were wiped out in the elections. The leader of the opposition, Ayhan Berberoglu, failed to win re-election...[19]

The military coup in Turkey on March 12 was of valuable assistance to Denktash in the advancement of his plans to neutralise his opponents in the Turkish Cypriot community and be recognised by Ankara as the 'one and only'. Even more so, since the Prime Minister installed by the military was none other than the architect of Turkey's strategy on Cyprus, Nihat Erim.[20]

The new Turkish regime had begun a merciless war against all sections of the left, which Denktash viewed as his own 'instigation' to start a similar war against his opponents in the community.[21] With the removal from power of the Justice Party, which was the continuation of the Democratic Party that supported Kuchuk, the discreet replacement of the latter would be a simple business.[22]

On the pretext of sending a congratulatory telegram to Nihat Erim, Denktash called a meeting of all the organisations and parties and placed before them a written demand for the implementation of the policy of partition.[23]

At the same time, clashes were on the rise within the Greek Cypriot community. The illegal organisations had become active, Grivas had returned illegally to Cyprus to form EOKA B, relations between Makarios and the Junta were at breaking point and Makarios was warning of the looming danger.

The Berberoglu Case

It was under such circumstances that President Makarios' term of office was coming to an end. He considered that the elections would be a good opportunity to politically isolate the ringleaders of the ongoing illegality as well as his political opponents, and at the same time the result would be yet another triumphant vote of confidence for his policy. Glafcos Clerides, then Speaker of the House and representative of the Greek Cypriot side in the intercommunal talks, disagreed:

> I advised Makarios that the House of Representatives, because of the advanced stage of the intercommunal talks, should prolong his term of office for a year and elections should be postponed. I gave the following reasons for my advice:
>
> a) Mr Denktash had asked at the intercommunal talks whether Presidential elections would be held, and stated that if the Greek Cypriot side held presidential elections the Turkish side would do the same, and that he

would stand as a presidential candidate of the Turkish Cypriot administration.

b) I had no doubt that Denktash, during his election campaign, would be making public statements, which he would find difficult later to ignore as a negotiator.

c) The combination of Denktash being the elected leader of his community and at the same time its negotiator will have a hardening effect on his positions, because he would be then the only person on the Turkish side responsible for a solution to be achieved, and the target of the Turkish opposition.

With regard to the intra-Greek situation I pointed out the following:

a) It was most unlikely that Makarios' opponents would produce a candidate to contest the election, knowing very well that Makarios would win with a tremendous majority, i.e. around 90%.
They would not risk a showdown that 90% of the people were supporting the feasible solution, and only a few per cent the solution of immediate self-determination – *enosis.*

b) Inter-Greek violence would be escalated deliberately by 'EOKA B', and this would have an adverse effect on the intercommunal talks.

c) The bishops, who had waited for a year before taking action against Makarios,[24] would be forced to do so, whereas if the House, by law prolonged for a year the term of office of the President, stating that this was necessary in view of the advanced stage in the talks, they would find it very difficult, either internally or externally, to take such action.[25]

Makarios finally called elections and was returned unopposed as President.

Denktash had also called elections, in which he was standing as a candidate opposed by Ayhan Berberoglu, a lawyer and chairman of the Turkish Republican Party. Fazil Kuchuk did not seek re-election due to his 'reduced support and criticism by leading members of the community but chiefly for reasons of health and age'.[26]

The elections were set for February 18, 1973, but, two days before voting was due, Berberoglu withdrew from the race and Denktash was hailed the 'undisputed' leader of the Turkish Cypriots. Precisely what had happened was later explained in an article by the Turkish Cypriot journalist Kutlu Adali:

> From the moment that the Republican Turkish Party made known its decision to put Berberoglu forward as a rival candidate to Denktash, and even before his candidacy had been formally announced, the Turkish Ambassador Asaf Inhan began to pressurise him not to stand and asked to see him frequently. During these meetings, Inhan would ask Berberoglu to brief him on the response of the Turkish Cypriots to his pre-election activities. Berberoglu accepted and after every speech would submit a report to the Ambassador.
>
> Nonetheless, from the moment that the names of the candidates were officially announced, problems began – pressures were brought to bear, there were power cuts and bad scenes in every village that Berberoglu visited. And while these shameful activities continued, the Turkish Cypriots showed a greater interest in Berberoglu's candidacy. It was obvious that they had grown tired of unemployment, poverty, pressure and violations of their human rights [by TMT thugs] and were looking to Berberoglu for a way out, for their salvation.
>
> One evening, upon his return from a village in the Karpass peninsula where he had been speaking, Berberoglu received a visit from a Turkish Embassy official, who informed him that the Ambassador wished to meet with him. When Berberoglu told the Ambassador that he was receiving support everywhere, the latter appeared satisfied at first but at once changed his attitude and said: 'Mr Berberoglu, we wish you to withdraw your candidacy.'
>
> Berberoglu was speechless. When he realised what the Ambassador was asking him, he replied: 'Until now you have been saying that you support me and feel proud that democracy is working in the community...How now, at this stage...'
>
> 'Yes, it's true,' the Ambassador replied. 'But we have received orders from Ankara that you must withdraw your candidacy.'
>
> Berberoglu replied that he could not decide alone on such a matter. And when his party met to discuss it, it was decided that he would remain in the electoral race.

At 10 o'clock the following night, Berberoglu went to the Embassy, where the Ambassador was accompanied by another person, whom he 'forgot' to introduce. Berberoglu ignored the unidentified individual and addressed himself to the Ambassador, informing him of the party's decision.

While Berberoglu was expressing the views of his party, the unidentified man interrupted him and said: 'Ankara does not want elections. That is why you have to withdraw. Makarios was elected unopposed. Ankara considers it unacceptable that the community should be divided at such a crucial moment. Please sign this paper.'

Berberoglu refused to sign the blank sheet and told the Ambassador: 'I am here as your invited guest and I am discussing the issue with you. I see that an unidentified individual is interrupting us. It is not polite when two people are speaking for a third to interrupt them. Who is this gentleman?'

The Ambassador interrupted Berberoglu and attempted to calm him down, saying that the third man was the *bayraktar*.

Berberoglu went on, 'I am pleased to meet you but I am here at the invitation of the Ambassador. This is not a military matter. I am not under the orders of the *bayraktar*. I am a candidate for the vice-presidency of a legally operating party. I cannot sign a blank piece of paper. And, apart from that, I cannot understand why I should withdraw. Makarios was returned without elections because there was no rival candidate. On the Turkish side the previous Vice-President is not a candidate, so there is a gap that must be filled through elections. The free will of the people will judge. Put the same proposal to Mr Denktash. He may withdraw, in which case elections will not be necessary.'

The *bayraktar* reacted angrily: 'We cannot ask such a thing of Mr Denktash. You will withdraw.'

'No,' came Berberoglu's reply.

In their efforts to persuade Berberoglu to withdraw his candidacy, the *bayraktar* and the Ambassador insisted that these were Ankara's orders and that they would arrange for Berberoglu to be appointed deputy leader.

Berberoglu was adamant. 'I prefer,' he said, 'the free will of the people, expressed through democratic elections. I cannot accept duties by appointment or through orders. And since the orders have come from Ankara, I shall go there tomorrow for talks with the relevant services and then I shall decide.' The response to this was, 'No, you won't go to Ankara. We are Ankara.'

> Faced by Berberoglu's insistence, the *bayraktar* threatened him: 'You cannot go to Ankara. No one knows what might happen. On leaving here you could become the victim of a traffic accident or a stray bullet.[27]

As was only natural, information about the terrorism being exercised by TMT and Denktash against the Turkish Cypriots reached the Greek Cypriot press, which published it. And of course a great amount of information about Berberoglu's candidacy was published, not only because he was a moderate but – and mainly – because he was disputing Denktash's authority. Ultimately, this fact worked against Berberoglu, whom Denktash accused of passing on information himself to the Greek Cypriot press, hinting, of course, that he was a 'traitor'.

The day after his meeting with the *bayraktar*, Berberoglu woke up early, determined to travel to Ankara to receive an explanation. However, he noticed that his home was under 'guard' by seven armed men, the head of whom informed him that they had orders not to allow him to go out. He was essentially under arrest.

Kutlu Adali tells how, 'The news of Berberoglu's arrest came as a shock to the community,' and goes on:[(27)]

> The news also sparked the interest of foreign journalists who were prevented by armed men when they asked to speak to Berberoglu. The following day an unknown man in civilian clothes visited Berberoglu and accused him of being an agent of the Greeks. 'You have a transmitter at your house,' they told him. 'You are a spy and a traitor.' They then gave him a blank sheet of paper to sign. When the unidentified man left, one of the 'guards' began to play with his revolver, asking Berberoglu to deny that he was under arrest.
>
> The pressures, threats and blackmail continued until the day of the elections. On that day, party officials visited Berberoglu and told him of their decision that he should withdraw from the race.

Arif Tahsin, Chairman at the time of the Turkish Cypriot teachers' union, in reply to a journalist's question and commenting on Denktash's assertion that a teachers' strike in 1978 aimed at overthrowing the 'government' in the occupied area, did not mince his words:

> Since you insist, I shall answer. In reality, what I have to say is a common

> secret. The Turkish Cypriot community does not elect its leaders. Irrespective of appearances and the present picture, our leaders are always appointed by Ankara. The leadership's certificate of approval always comes from Ankara and that means that the appointed leaders must adopt and represent the views of the government of the Republic of Turkey.[28]

Denktash in His Own Words

After the Turkish invasion, Denktash naturally had no qualms about admitting that he always acted in accordance with orders from Ankara, irrespective of whether he believed it or not, or whether he considered it correct or not.[29] His ambition was to 'return' Cyprus to Turkey in one way or another, guided, as he has remarked often, by the sacrifice of the 80,000 Ottomans who fell during the conquest of Cyprus. Still, he viewed the Turkish Cypriots condescendingly, considering them to be people with neither a vision nor a strategic awareness of the aim that he had set, and as a result he saw 'a lack of fighting spirit'.[30]

The vision of the return of Cyprus to Turkey had been feasible, he argued, during the period 1955-1958. Today he still considers that there is no 'united vision'. He writes: 'Turkey was pleased with the victory it had achieved with the 1959-1960 agreements, and indeed, for the first time since 1878, Turkey could reach out and touch Cyprus.'[31]

He rejected all the accusations of oppression and terrorism, arguing that the opposition had played the role of the oppressed, as it did in Turkey, and had sent reports to Ankara in which it, 'Accused us of all the activities of TMT during the period 1955-1959, depicting us as supporters of Menderes.'[32]

He considered that the first Turkish Ambassador to the Republic of Cyprus, Dirvana, with whom he clashed constantly, had been sent to keep a check on him and his fanatical supporters, in collaboration with the opposition:

> Due to the revolutionary climate and a false accusation, the valuable TMT leader, Riza Vuruskan, was recalled overnight as a 'Menderes supporter' and in his place came his incapable assistant, who for this purpose made use of his contacts with the revolutionary government. This new TMT leader, in full cooperation with Dirvana, presented a rose-tinted picture of the situation in

> Cyprus in his reports to Ankara and requested the authority to sort out us 'disasters'. If it had not been for the commander of the Turkish regiment, Turgut Sunalp, we would have had a nasty end. In the end, this leader was transferred to headquarters and in his place came Colonel Kemal Coycun who organised and directed our resistance during the Greek attacks of 1963.'[33]

To Denktash, ever since it arose immediately after World War II, the Cyprus issue had been a matter of sovereignty. The question that concerned him and the answer, which always determined his stance towards the Turkish Cypriots and efforts aimed at resolving the problem, was whether Cyprus would come under the sovereignty of Turkey or Greece. The Zurich and London Agreements were for Denktash a 'necessary' compromise, a halfway solution, a position that meant that, finally, sovereignty stemmed from both communities – a position that is not unconnected with the demands that he is making today.[34]

Chapter 16

The Crime is Complete

The Junta's coup against Makarios on July 15, 1974, proved to be the perfect pretext – one for which Turkey had been waiting for years – for changing the situation on the island by force of arms so as to open the way to a solution to the Cyprus problem in accordance with its own plans. The coup gave Turkey the opportunity to achieve its ambition of creating a permanent bridgehead on the island.[1]

Before the first invasion was even over,[2] on July 30, 1974, the Turks announced the upgrading of the authority established in the areas under their control to the 'Autonomous Turkish Cypriot Administration of Cyprus.'[3]

The then Turkish Prime Minister, Bulent Ecevit, marking the ceasefire, publicly stated the following:

> Today there is a new Cyprus and Turkey has taken up a new position in the world from that which it held two days ago. No one can question Turkey's rights in Cyprus. The heroic Turkish forces, in collaboration with the Turkish Cypriot fighters, have achieved great victories in the space of two days. Our main aim is to make Turkey's presence in Cyprus so strong that it will be impossible to turn things back.[4]

The Geneva talks concluded with the drawing up of a declaration that the three Foreign Ministers had decided to hold new talks with the participation of the Greek and Turkish Cypriots for the discussion of constitutional issues among which was 'an immediate return to constitutional legitimacy, the Vice-President assuming the functions provided for under the 1960 constitution'.[5]

Nonetheless, the declaration referred to the fact that: 'The Ministers noted the existence in practice in the Republic of Cyprus of two autonomous administrations, that of the Greek Cypriot community and that of the Turkish Cypriot community.'[6] Thus, for the first time, the 'Turkish Cypriot Administration' was acknowledged, while at the same time the Cypriot government was downgraded to the level of 'Greek Cypriot Administration'.

Upon completion of the second phase of the invasion, Turkey had under its control 37.6% of Cypriot territory, where it proceeded to implement unhindered its policy of ethnic cleansing and 'Turkification'. Those Greek Cypriots who had been unable to flee these areas were daily faced with such terrorism and danger that their escape to the free areas of Cyprus was a matter of survival. At the same time, the Turkish Cypriots, under the threat of arms and of TMT, began to move en masse to the occupied areas. The Erim formula for the creation of a territorial and demographic basis for Turkey's claims began to take on the necessary elements regarding territory.

On September 9, 1974, Turkey announced the transfer of 5,000 settlers from the depths of Anatolia as 'seasonal workers'. As British journalist Christopher Hitchens writes, 'Turkey began to transform its "peacekeeping" presence into an occupation,'[7] which, as he notes, it achieved in the following way:

> First, the Turkish Cypriots in the south had to be induced to move to the Turkish-held north. Second, the Greek Cypriots remaining in the north had to be persuaded to move south. Third, the resulting shortfall in manpower, especially skilled manpower, had to be made up. These things had to be done quickly; more quickly than the cumbersome machinery of international disapproval could move. Already there were signs that the United States Congress was exasperated by Kissinger's private foreign policy, and that sanctions against Turkey were being sought energetically. Most of the Turkish objectives were completed within a very short span of time. Help in this process came from three other forces, all of which we have met before. These were American cynicism, British naiveté about American cynicism, and Greek chauvinism.[8]

On August 18, when the last ceasefire was agreed, 10,000 Greek Cypriots found themselves behind the Turkish lines, mainly concentrated in the Karpass peninsula. At the other side of Cyprus, most of the Turkish Cypriots of Paphos and Limassol had gathered, or, to be more precise, were forced by TMT to gather, in the British base at Akrotiri.

The Turks rejected every attempt to discuss the issue of the return of the refugees to their homes as provided for in the UN resolutions, arguing that the matter was 'political' and would affect the shape of a final agreement on resolving the Cyprus issue.[9] Denktash, meanwhile, with Ankara's help was intensifying pressure on London for the transfer to the occupied areas of the Turkish Cypriots who had taken refuge at Akrotiri:

> He increased pressure on the United Kingdom to send the 10,000 Turkish Cypriots at Akrotiri base to Turkey, whence, he made it clear, they would be sent on to northern Cyprus to populate abandoned Greek properties. Asked whether he would count this as a concession, he was evasive. At a meeting of the NATO Foreign Ministers in December 1974, Dr Kissinger had urged James Callaghan to send the Akrotiri refugees to Turkey, in spite of the fact that many of them had expressed a clear preference for remaining near their old homes. Kissinger argued that this would inspire Turkish concessions and help him in his tussle with Congress over the arms embargo.[10]
>
> On 15 January, without consulting the government of Cyprus and without linking their departure to any reciprocal Turkish action, the British authorities sent the Turkish Cypriots to Turkey en masse.'[11]

The British described their decision as 'a humane action', about which the Turkish Cypriots were not particularly enthusiastic, as the correspondent for an American newspaper noted:

> In Paphos today, where some 500 Turkish Cypriots were being transferred to the north, the main square echoed with the weeping and lamenting of the elderly women, who were leaving the homes where they had lived all their lives. Greek Cypriots and Turkish Cypriots mixed easily with no enmity amongst them. Many of the departing Turkish Cypriots handed over their house keys to Greek Cypriot refugees with evident pleasure, 'for them to look after it', as one said.[12]

On June 30, 1975, Denktash had threatened to expel all the Greek Cypriots who had remained behind the 'Attila Line' if his demand for the transportation of all the Turkish Cypriots to the area under the control of the Turkish troops was not met.[13] The announcement, following the third round of talks between Clerides and Denktash in Vienna,[14] made reference among other things to the enclaved Greek Cypriots:

> Mr. Denktash reaffirmed, and it was agreed, that the Greek Cypriots at present in the north of the island are free to stay and that they will be given every help to lead a normal life, including facilities for education and for the practice of their religion, as well as medical care by their own doctors and freedom of movement in the north.[15]

What actually happened was a completely different story, as Christopher Hitchens describes:

> What was happening has been graphically described by several independent eyewitnesses as well as by the survivors themselves. Throughout the Karpass peninsula, Turkish soldiers and police set about making life insupportable for the inhabitants. Long, arbitrary curfews were imposed. Brutal and vandalistic searches, on the pretext of 'security', were commonplace. Livestock and other property was taken at gunpoint. Villagers were pointedly offered forms 'applying' for a transfer to the south. Often, the forms came already filled in and the family was simply driven to the border and dumped. One thousand, five hundred of the 9,000 or so remaining Karpassians were removed in this way, and one year after the Vienna Agreement the survivors addressed a petition to Dr Kurt Waldheim, Secretary-General of the United Nations. They implored him to prevent their forcible expulsion. On 9 December Dr Waldheim reported to the United Nations that, 'From 7,371 on 5 June 1976 the Greek Cypriot population in the north decreased to 3,631 on 6 December.' Expulsions were continuing at the rate of forty each day. At that rate, the Karpass peninsula soon became completely empty of its former inhabitants. Today, a few Greeks remain in the village of Rizokarpasso, near the very tip of the 'panhandle'. I visited them in October 1979, without the escort on which the Turkish authorities normally insist, and found that most of them are old men, too old to move.[16]

In this way the Turks had again implemented Nihat Erim's proposal for the creation of a territorial and demographic basis which they would use for the further promotion of their strategic objectives in Cyprus. Once all the Turkish Cypriots had been transferred to the occupied areas, from which almost all the Greek Cypriots had been uprooted and to which settlers from Turkey had been brought, and while the United Nations was continuing its efforts for the continuation of talks aimed at reaching agreement for a final solution to the Cyprus issue, Denktash made a declaration that not only destroyed these efforts but revealed the real intentions of the Turkish side. It came after a joint meeting of the 'Cabinet' and the 'Legislative Assembly' of the so-called 'Autonomous Turkish Cypriot Administration'. After making the usual accusations against the Greek Cypriots, Denktash concluded that there was no possibility of the two communities being able to live together. And he added:

> [The Turkish Cypriot community] having come to the conclusion that the only way for bringing tranquillity, security and permanent peace to the island is for the two communities to live side by side in their respective regions developing their own internal structures; and
>
> Having noted the fact that the Greek Cypriot community has not made any constructive response to the proposals for the establishment of an independent Federal Republic of Cyprus on the above reasonable basis; and
>
> Having taken into consideration the necessity of putting the Turkish Cypriot community's social and economic life into a new healthy order; and
>
> Having confirmed their belief and determination to oppose resolutely all attempts against the independence of Cyprus, and its partition or union with any other state; and
>
> Believing in the necessity of the non-aligned status of the Republic of Cyprus and expressing their determination not to allow the island to become subservient to any foreign interest; and
>
> Mindful of the necessity of creating in their own region the legal basis of an order leading to the establishment of the future independent, Federal Republic of Cyprus; and
>
> Reaffirming that their final objective is to unite with the Greek Cypriot community within the framework of a bi-regional federation;
>
> Have resolved that the autonomous Turkish Cypriot administration should be restructured and organised on the basis of a secular and federated state, until such time as the 1960 constitution of the Republic, the basic articles of which were determined by international agreements in compliance with international law, is amended in a similar manner to become the constitution of the Federal Republic of Cyprus, and until the said Federal Republic is established.

> With this object in view, a 50-member Constituent Assembly will be set up under the chairmanship of the President of the autonomous Turkish Cypriot administration.[17]

The Turks today present the establishment of the 'Turkish Federated State of Cyprus' as the result of an 'historical development' emanating from the Zurich and London Agreements, which, they claim, gave the Turkish Cypriot community the right to exercise its own legislative, executive and judicial authority, and they use the drawing of the 'Green Line' in Nicosia in 1964 to claim that it separated the two communities and that this event was the beginning of the creation of two separate administrations on the island.[18] They have used a great deal of legal argument to justify the new fait accompli. The 1960 constitution, they argue, had essentially been made null and void in 1963 by the Greek Cypriots, while in 1974, by the joint statement of the Foreign Ministers of the guarantor powers, the existence of two separate administrations was 'recognised'. They also argue that there exists a 'border' between the territory controlled by each administration and that talks are held between the two administrations, and they refer to an 'agreement for the exchange of populations'. And since both sides state that their aim is a bizonal federation, and since a federation is created between 'two equal entities', the foundation of the 'Turkish Federated State of Cyprus' which is not controlled by any foreign authority was 'necessary'.[19]

Knowing full well what the international reaction to their action would be, they assured the world that they did not want partition but a federation. They also argue now that their action had 'revived' the negotiation process,[20] which led to the Makarios-Denktash and Kyprianou-Denktash meetings, from which agreements and guidelines emerged.

Towards Recognition of the 'Turkish Republic of Northern Cyprus'

By now it was clear that the Turkish side's tactics were to stall for time while remaining totally intransigent in its positions, yet always leaving a small ray of hope that it would be possible to start a dialogue on a final and all-encompassing solution to the problem, so as to prevent pressure being exerted on it and to gain valuable time in which to create such a situation as to prejudge the direction in which attempts to find a solution would inevitably lead. International tolerance of Ankara helped the Turkish side to successfully employ these tactics and also led to the Greek side being 'urged' to satisfy 'minor' Turkish demands each time, which in essence meant whittling away its own positions.

After the acceptance by the Greek Cypriot side of a bizonal, bicommunal federation, the Turkish side proceeded to demand the recognition of the existence of two peoples, with separate rights to self-determination and separate sovereignties, arguing that the establishment of a federation presupposed the existence of two separate entities which agree to the transfer of part of their sovereignty to the newly founded federation.

It was clear that, under such circumstances, the negotiation process was leading nowhere, nor could it lead anywhere. On the contrary, towards the end of 1982, Turkish threats of military action against the free areas escalated on the pretext that training camps for members of the Armenian Liberation Army (ASALA) were operating there, despite the fact that, after investigations, UNFICYP confirmed that the Turkish claims were totally unfounded.[21]

Faced by this worsening situation, the then UN Secretary-General, Javier Perez de Cuellar, decided to become personally involved in efforts to find a way out of the impasse and began soundings on both sides in order to clarify their views on how best his involvement might bring about results.

At the same time, the UN General Assembly discussed the developments and passed a Resolution[22] in which it rejected the Turkish faits accomplis, demanded the withdrawal of the occupation forces and called on both sides to avoid any action that would violate the sovereignty, territorial integrity and independence of Cyprus.[23]

By way of response, Ankara replaced the Cyprus pound with the Turkish lira as the 'official' currency in the occupied areas and established a 'central bank', thus reinforcing its economic annexation of the occupied areas. At the same time, the so-called 'Legislative Assembly' of the 'Turkish Federated State of Cyprus' decided on June 17, 1983, to hold a 'referendum' on the proclamation of a separate state, based on the argument that 'the Turkish people of Cyprus have an inalienable right to self-determination'.[24]

This fact moved the UN Secretary-General to attempt to prevent any undesirable developments and in a letter to both sides, dated August 8, 1983, he set out some 'indicators', sounded them out with a view to starting a process based on these 'indicators' and asked for their views on them. The then President of Cyprus, Spyros Kyprianou, accepted the Secretary-General's proposal while Denktash rejected it. The Secretary-General then undertook to prepare the ground for a new summit meeting based on a specific agenda that he would draw up following contacts with both sides by Hugo Gobbi, his special representative in Cyprus. Gobbi returned to Cyprus carrying a written message from the Secretary-General to the two sides on November 14, 1983.[25] On November 15, Denktash proclaimed the occupied areas to be the 'Turkish Republic of Northern Cyprus'. The Turkish action had been planned to coincide with the handing over of authority by the military to a civilian government in Ankara. Denktash also announced that he would hold 'elections' (November 6, 1983) and that the new government would take up its duties.[26]

The Turks 'explain' that their action was a reaction to UN resolution 37/253, which called for the withdrawal of the occupation forces, which, in their view, did not exist since Ankara considered the presence of Turkish troops to be lawful, based on the Treaty of Guarantee.[27]

The reference to the right of the Republic of Cyprus and its people to full, effective sovereignty and control over all the territory of Cyprus was interpreted by the Turkish side as recognition of the 'sovereignty' of the Greek Cypriots over the Turkish Cypriots,[28] who had been 'changed' into a minority, and as a result the negotiation process had been 'destroyed'. This was described by Denktash as 'the last straw' that led to the decision to declare the occupied areas an 'independent state'.[29]

The truth, however, is that Denktash brought up the question of an independent state in the occupied areas straight after the invasion and subsequently intensified his demand, which peaked during the period from the start of 1983 until the decision was implemented.[30]

His basic argument was that the regime in the occupied areas had taken on an 'identity' which, far from preventing a federal solution on the island, on the contrary contributed to the process. In spite of this, the acceptance of such a state would mean in practice the abolition of the Republic of Cyprus, and the recognition that the Republic of Cyprus was no more than the 'Greek Cypriot Administration', and consequently federation would come about as the result of an agreement between two 'equal states' which would hand over part of their separate sovereignty to the newly founded federation.

Denktash's Blackmail

The day after the last ceasefire agreement, Denktash made it his aim to create a separate Turkish Cypriot state in the occupied areas of Cyprus. He himself blames successive Turkish governments for not allowing him to proceed with such a step[31] after 1974. Not because Turkey did not adopt his demand but because, as Denktash explains, Turkey's involvement in the Cyprus issue was complicated by its own major interests:[32] 'Unfortunately, the Turkish government, having courageously taken the irrevocable decision to intervene [in Cyprus], could not establish an independent state for us because of its broader interests and obligations.'[33]

The result, in Denktash's view, was that the Greek Cypriots, having the title of government of the Republic of Cyprus, were not interested in promoting a federal solution, an attitude which, he argues, he saw for himself during the bicommunal negotiations. On the other hand, in spite of the proclamation of the 'Turkish Federated State of Northern Cyprus' in February 1975, 'They did not take us into consideration.'[34]

Denktash reached the conclusion that only through the founding of a state would the 'existence of the Turkish Cypriots' be acknowledged and that, after this state was recognised, the Greek Cypriots would have a reason to work for the reunification of the two states as a federation. And, he writes, he 'persuaded' Ecevit, who, nevertheless, asked him to wait a little longer.[35]

But Denktash began to prepare the ground for his coup:

> I first spoke of my intentions to the Prime Minister of the TFSC, Mr Chagatay, and to the ex-Prime Minister, Mr Konuk, who undertook to inform their senior colleagues. The idea spread like wildfire. With the help of a small team Mr Ertekun was to prepare and translate all statements and documents into English. And in utmost secrecy all was ready by 10 November 1983. We owe much to a handful of loyal typists who knew all but did not whisper anything even to their own families and close friends. For many nights the lights in the Presidency did not go out. In silence our supporters were working hard and bringing in enthusiastic new recruits.
>
> In the meantime I made, in passing, remarks about the inevitability of declaring statehood. Mr Kyprianou poured scorn on my warnings. Mr Clerides advised him not to take them lightly.

At last we came to know the exact date of government changeover in Turkey. On 14 November 1983 I invited all members of Parliament to dinner at my residence, where we ate and joked until about 11.30 p.m. Then I disclosed my intentions to my guests, telling them that I had a sufficient majority at the House for the next day's resolution on independence. Republican Turkish Party and Communal Liberation Party members began to put forward their views. I listened patiently but would not change my mind. If we did not act the next day we would have to wait for ever. The Greek Cypriot policy of internationalisation could only be countered by this move. Whatever the consequences by way of retaliation, we were ready to face them. There was no alternative. From 1963 to 1983 we had been deprived of all our rights by the Greek Cypriots; we were treated as outlaws and as long as we stayed dormant in our present position this state of affairs would continue. We had to break this vicious circle. The world had to see that we existed. Recognition was of secondary importance. What was important was to get on the road to recognition. The key to a federal settlement was the assertion of our statehood.

The leaders of the Republican Turkish Party and Communal Liberation Party, who were always opposed to seeking the Turkish Ambassador's views on any issue, now wanted to know what he had to say about it. I told them that I did not know and had no means of knowing because all telephone connections had been cut off to prevent the news leaking. They had until 8.00 a.m. next day to consider their positions.[36]

A State of Dictatorship

The proclamation of the 'Turkish Republic of Northern Cyprus' brought strong reactions from abroad as well as from Turkish Cypriot parties and organisations on the island, despite taking place with the unanimous approval of the 'parliament', a fact explained by threats – even of death – against the 'MPs' of the Turkish Cypriot opposition.[37] The left-wing opposition Republican Turkish Party condemned the proclamation of the illegal state as having taken place with the intention of imposing a Denktash dictatorship.[38]

On December 23, 1983, the 'Constitutional Committee' was formed and on June 8, 1984, it presented a proposed 'constitution', which was accepted by the

'Constitutional Assembly' on March 12, 1985, and approved in a 'referendum' held on May 5, 1985, with the participation, of course, of the settlers, and which still resulted in 30% voting 'no'.[39] Naturally, the result again showed the weakening of the Turkish Cypriots' political will due to the mass participation of the settlers in the decision-making process.

The new situation that was created after the founding of the illegal state is described eloquently by Ozger Ozgur, leader of the Republican Turkish Party, at a seminar on Greco-Turkish differences held in Munich from January 29-31, 1988:

> We do not know what living conditions are like in the south. But we in the north are going through difficult times. The constitution of the Turkish Republic of Northern Cyprus is a copy of the undemocratic constitution of Turkey. It contains the right to search a private house without a warrant, restriction of all rights and freedoms for subjective and vague reasons such as the public interest, public order, general morality, social justice, national security, public health and hygiene.[40] Political parties cannot be established if they are against Ataturk's principles and there can be no appeal to the constitutional court for political agreements reached with a foreign power. Citizens may be tried by military courts.
>
> According to provisional article 10, the Turkish army on the island will be responsible for the internal security and defence of the Turkish Cypriot community for as long as the international situation requires it, which means that the Turkish Cypriot police force has been placed under the administration of the General Staff of the Turkish Army. Moreover, the commander of the Turkish Cypriot armed forces is appointed by Ankara.
>
> Some 30% of the adult population in the north voted against this constitution. Around half of those who voted in favour belong to the so-called labour force that was imported from Turkey.
>
> The colonial penal code remains in force. Based on this code, on December 28, 1987, the Nicosia District Court sentenced our party's daily newspaper and me personally to pay 200 million Turkish lire to President Denktash because we allegedly described him as a 'godfather' in an article published two years ago. A labourer who receives the lowest daily wage would need to work 110 years to pay this amount. I shall need 32 years to pay the fine, provided that I

continue to be an MP and to be paid 50,000 Turkish lire per month. Now that the libel case is closed, the House will debate the issue of removing my parliamentary privilege so that I may be sent for trial and be sentenced to more than five years' imprisonment because I supposedly incited the people against the Denktash regime…

In the Shadow of the Army

Control over the Turkish Cypriot community after the 1974 invasion was total. The dependence of the occupied areas, not so much on the Ankara government but more on the generals, was also total. Not only because the so-called 'security forces' of the illegal state had been placed under the command of the head of the occupation forces but because they were integrated into the military structure created by the Turkish generals in the occupied areas. There were two further reasons, well noted by Christos P. Ioannides.[41] One was the concentration of such a large number of military personnel (more than 40,000 soldiers) in such a geographically small area and among an essentially small number of Turkish Cypriots.[42] With such numbers, the influence of the military on political life could not be avoided, especially when one takes into account the 'traditional' presence of Turkish military officers in controlling TMT and the lives of the Turkish Cypriots.

The second reason was the psychological atmosphere created after the 'liberation' of the Turkish Cypriots by the Turkish army and the role of the Turkish army as guardian of Turkey's Kemalist ideology.

Political parties and elections, notes Arif Tahsin, were a real phenomenon to the community after the Turkish invasion:

> During the period of the Republic of Cyprus, the candidates were always 'only as many as required' and for this reason elections were not necessary. For example, the first Vice-President of the Republic, Dr Kuchuk, had no rival and could not feel the joy of an election victory. The same applied to Denktash. That was how Turkey wanted things. It just wanted the people it approved of to be in the administration.
>
> Before the operation of July 20, 1974, the community was in revolt. It had

grown tired of the military administration and was asking for the rules of democracy to be implemented. But we had no results. Then came first July 15 and then July 20.

After the wars, the military did not object very strongly. It appeared that the supporters of democracy were winning. The founding parliament, the constitution and the political parties were the result of their own will. And it appeared that the political leadership would change with the first elections. How were we to know that the Turks of Cyprus were not Turkish enough? And that, to 'Turkify' them to the extent that they wished, they would have to bring Turks from Turkey? By secret decision, the necessary actions were taken. And the population brought from Turkey was placed at once on the electoral registers…

The Turks of Cyprus accepted defeat. Those who could, left. The vast majority of those who could not leave locked themselves indoors. And, with the unknown numbers brought from Turkey, the vote of the Turkish Cypriots lost its meaning…

In the north of Cyprus there is an army whose salaries are not paid by the Turkish Cypriots. Its uniforms, provisions, weapons and ammunition are not given by the Turkish Cypriots. It is an army to which the Turkish Cypriots cannot give the order 'fight' or 'cease fire'. There is an army under orders from another state, one that belongs to another society. It takes its order for war or peace from mainland Turks, not from Turkish Cypriots. And the Turkish Cypriots' borders are guarded by this army. If Turkey tells it to leave, it will leave, and if it tells it to proceed, it will proceed. And this means that the Turkish Cypriots themselves are not in a position to determine the borders that are called the borders of the Turkish Cypriots.'[3]

Towards Confederation

The Turkish side's next step was to attempt to consolidate the illegal state internally in order to create the circumstances for the next stage of its faits accomplis. Recognition of the illegal state did not interest it too much at this stage. And, since the international reaction to the proclamation of the illegal state had been restricted to verbal condemnations with no cost to Turkey, the Turkish side could take them, making every effort at the same time to limit even these verbal condemnations.

But Denktash now had the support he wanted to request the dissolution of the Cyprus Republic. Just as a child continues to live unless you kill it, so it is with a state, according to Denktash.[44] And a few years later he would note that, while his state may not have been recognised and was described internationally as 'the illegal state', the reference was always to a state as recognition is not essential for the existence of a state.[45]

To the Security Council he presented the proclamation of the illegal state as 'a legitimate exercise of the right to self-determination' and argued that the Turkish Cypriots had 'asserted their rights' by their action, which was a fact of life, whether the Council accepted it or not.[46] And of course he placed the blame for his decision on the Greek Cypriots, 'Who wanted to destroy the Turkish Cypriots whose rights they appropriated,' and on the international community, which recognises, 'The Greek Cypriot administration as the legitimate government of the whole of Cyprus and of the Turkish Cypriots.'[47] He also said:

> I repeat that if the negotiations have not yielded results…it is because one of the contestants has been given, as a gift, unjustly, what he should have achieved through negotiations in a partnership situation. By declaring that the Greek Cypriots are the government of Cyprus when they are morally, legally and constitutionally not, but are merely the Greek Cypriot wing of a bicommunal state, all the incentive, all the necessity, for re-establishing a bicommunal State has been removed. Therefore they simply continue to go around the world making propaganda for themselves, getting more and more seals of approval from international forums to the effect that they are the legitimate government; and finally in May 1983 they get the terrible seal to the effect that not only are they the legitimate government of Cyprus but they are entitled to extend their legitimacy and their rule to the north, over my people.[48]

Moreover, faithful to his tactics of carrying out an illegal action whilst presenting himself as 'flexible' and 'ready' for negotiations, Denktash argued in the Security Council that the proclamation of the illegal state did nothing whatsoever to destroy the negotiation process. On the contrary, it reinforced it because he himself was leaving the door open to the 're-establishment of the bicommunal state'.

As proof, he set out these proposals from the Council rostrum:

a) The establishment of an interim administration in Varosha under the auspices of the United Nations, without any prejudice to the final political status of the area.
   The parties may enter into discussions promptly to plan for the development of the interim administration's structure.
   There shall be no numerical limitations for the number of Greek Cypriots to be resettled in the area.
   The area of resettlement will be the same as it was defined on the Turkish Cypriot map of 5 August 1981.
   The United Nations would provide such technical assistance as may be necessary to survey and rehabilitate the city's infrastructure and buildings and to facilitate the process of resettlement.

b) The reopening of Nicosia International Airport for civilian traffic under an interim United Nations administration to the mutual benefit of both sides in Cyprus.[49]

With this manoeuvre, Denktash knew that he would restrict the verbal condemnation of his illegal state and would give the international community something to occupy itself with (the prospect of refugees being able to return to Famagusta), while he proceeded to establish his illegal state.

The condemnation did not concern him overmuch. What was important then, he writes, was that the Turkish Cypriots 'confirmed their right to self-determination' and the international community 'was discussing their action'. 'Now everyone could see that there were two peoples, two partners, and that after twenty years of hostilities there were two states in Cyprus. Recognised or unrecognised, the Turkish Cypriot state existed.'[50]

As Denktash had correctly assessed, there followed a period during which proposals were made and rejected, and efforts at restarting a dialogue failed, and as time went by the Turkish side established its demands on the ground and created the conditions for the implementation of the next stage of its plans. This in practice meant the gradual political, military, social, economic and cultural integration of the occupied areas into Turkey. Without being affected by any steps by the international community, not even the Security Council, which, in Resolution 716 of October 11, 1991, and Resolution 750 of April 10, 1992, set out the basis for the solution of the Cyprus problem:

> A Cyprus settlement must be based on a state of Cyprus with a single sovereignty and international personality and a single citizenship, with its independence and territorial integrity [...] and such a settlement must exclude union in whole or in part with any other country or any form of partition or secession.[51]

On July 3, 1990, the government of Cyprus submitted an application for the Republic's full membership of the European Union. The submission of the application was an expression of the general conviction that the EU's involvement in the process for resolving the Cyprus issue would act as a catalyst, while membership would secure the territorial integrity and the sovereignty of the Republic of Cyprus.[52]

The Turkish side reacted angrily to the submission of the application. It sent two memoranda to Brussels, on July 12, 1990, and on September 12, 1990, in which it expressed its strong objections.[53] Ankara not only linked Cyprus' accession with a solution to the Cyprus problem but – and mainly – with its own accession to the EU, a position adopted by Denktash.[54]

In his statements on the issue, Denktash has followed his familiar tactic of 'crying wolf'. He speaks of unavoidable danger, addressing mainly the isolated Turkish Cypriots, who are under his full control and whose information he also controls completely, to the extent that they maintain vividly the fears and worries that he has cultivated in them. Cyprus' accession to the European Union, he says, means the union of Cyprus with Greece – *enosis* – by the back door.

> Turkey has clear rights and powers in Cyprus. These rights and powers are the same as those of Greece and they emanate (like the rights and powers of the Turkish Cypriots) from the 1960 agreements. The equality of the two guarantor powers constitutes an important basis, precisely like the political equality of the two communities, which is in force internally. No one has the right to overturn this equality. In such a case, all rights secured by an agreement are condemned to be made void. For this reason it is impossible for the partner-

ship Republic of Cyprus of 1960 to join a union to which the two motherlands do not belong.[55]

And he provides examples:

> The return of all refugees to their former homes renders the Treaties of Guarantee ineffective; the accession of Cyprus as if it is a unified state, before border adjustments are made [a reference to the 'Attila Line' that divides Cyprus], is tantamount to neutralising the rights and powers secured by the Turkish Cypriots in 1960 and it will lead to the union of Cyprus with Greece through its membership of the EU, thus abolishing the rights of Turkey as provided for by the 1960 agreements.'[56]

While the international community's efforts continued for the creation of circumstances for a productive dialogue, Denktash was creating the impression, through frequent references to the content of any solution, that federation was the only possible answer. But all his interlocutors from the Greek Cypriot side are agreed that, when the Turkish side referred to a federation, it was actually describing a confederation of two separate sovereign states.

On August 29, 1994, the 'parliament' in the occupied areas adopted a resolution which stated precisely this position. During the same period the illegal state began handing out to the settlers 'title deeds' for the Greek-Cypriot-owned properties in the occupied areas.

On March 6, 1995, the EU Council of Ministers decided that the start of accession negotiations with Cyprus would begin six months after the Intergovernmental Conference. The response of the Turkish side was a joint declaration on December 28, 1995, by Rauf Denktash and the Turkish President Suleyman Demirel which repeated Turkey's recognition of the illegal state – showing total contempt for the international community's condemnation of the action and the efforts aimed at resolving the Cyprus issue, which would overturn the decision for the establishment of an illegal state. The position was also stated officially that a solution must be based on the 'sovereign equality' of the Turkish Cypriots while, regarding the accession of Cyprus to the EU, the position was that this should be discussed after a solution, and then only with the simultaneous accession of Turkey.

The Turkish side was openly threatening that, as Cyprus' accession progressed, so too would the annexation of the occupied areas by Turkey. By various ruses, it attempted to appear ready to discuss a final settlement of the Cyprus issue but at the same time it noted that a prerequisite to any solution was the recognition of 'separate sovereignty'. It was demanding recognition of two states in Cyprus, a fact that reveals its intentions to promote a confederal solution, not a federal one.

Chapter 17

The Illegal State and Turkey

There was never any doubt that the proclamation of the illegal state was intended to relieve Turkey of all responsibility – legal, political and military – for the occupied areas and for anything taking place in Cyprus. Indeed, it was for this reason that no one recognised the illegal state apart from Turkey. On the contrary, the international community condemned its proclamation as illegal. And Ankara could not convince anyone that, after the invasion of the island by its troops, after the violent transfer of populations, the presence of its troops and the settlers in the occupied areas, it was not in complete control of the situation in the north of the island.

There already existed the decision of the European Commission for Human Rights, according to which:

> [...] the existence of some kind of political administration in northern Cyprus does not rule out Turkey's responsibility, given the degree of Turkish control over northern Cyprus, and in particular the Commission is convinced that substantial changes in the conditions prevailing in northern Cyprus cannot be decided without the express or total approval of the Turkish authorities.[1]

The Commission essentially confirmed that control of the occupation forces belonged to Ankara, a fact from which Turkey's international responsibility for everything taking place in the area under its military control emanates. Moreover, the occupying forces are merely an extension of Turkey's military might, to whose structure they belong.

The Turkish occupation forces are thought to number a fighting force of 35,000 men, supported by 300 upgraded tanks of US origin, mainly M-48 A5, 200 M-59 and M-113 armoured personnel carriers, 144 heavy guns of 105, 155 and 203mm calibre, 114 mortars, 84 anti-aircraft guns, 8 aircraft and 12 helicopters.[2]

Moreover, with the naval and air structure created in the occupied areas, as well as the landing capability they have acquired, the Turks have the ability to transport thousands of men and military equipment from Turkey in the shortest time.[3]

All this military might is under the orders of the Turkish General Staff and is not answerable to decisions of the illegal state. The same applies to the 4,000 men of the so-called 'Turkish Cypriot Security Forces' and the 'police'. This is also the case of the estimated 80,000 settlers, most of whom are former Turkish soldiers and reservists. Consequently the assertion of one Turkish Cypriot politician that '90% of the Turkish Republic of Northern Cyprus is a military zone'[4] should come as no surprise.

The Turkish army is free to do whatever it wishes in the occupied areas and this ability was indicated in a statement to the Turkish Cypriot political leaders by the President of Turkey, General Kenan Evren, in which he stressed that it is the duty of the Turkish armed forces, 'To protect the rights and the interests of the Turkish nation, and the Turkish armed forces have the right to use this authority [of intervention] wherever they serve, including Cyprus.'[5]

In such circumstances it is obvious not only who decides what goes on in the occupied areas but also who is preventing the legitimate and internationally recognised Republic of Cyprus from exercising its authority in its northern territory. The 'government' emanating from the proclamation of the 'Turkish Republic of Northern Cyprus' and its 'President', Rauf Denktash, are nothing more than mouthpieces of the decision-making centre in Ankara, as he has himself admitted, saying: 'Whether I believe it or not, whether I consider it right or wrong, I do what Turkey says.'[6] This is also the conclusion of the Turkish Cypriot opposition: 'A leader who behaves as a civil servant in Turkey cannot live in Nicosia. He ought to be living in Ankara.'[7]

Ankara's total control and responsibilities have not escaped the notice of the Turkish press, which has published plenty of details about the 'need' to conceal Turkey's responsibility.[8]

As far as the proclamation of the illegal state is concerned, Denktash's complaint that, 'Independence could only be achieved with Turkey's approval, when Turkey felt that it was necessary,'[9] is particularly revealing. Denktash expressed his satisfaction when he noted that Ankara too was acting in the same direction as he: 'In the past, before I had even said the word "independence", the Turkish government closed my mouth. Now at least I am pleased that such a thing is not happening. They let it be understood that I am correct in what I say.'[10]

The Demographic Basis

The creation of a territorial and demographic basis for the Turkish demands, as set out in the Nihat Erim formula, concerned differentiating the political and legal situation so as to face the reality of the majority Greek Cypriot community on the island. This, however, was not an adequate requirement for the political and military control of the island by Turkey. It was necessary to create a situation in which any future arrangement would be based on realities that would make the satisfaction of Ankara's military objectives inevitable. The territorial basis thus had to be complemented by a demographic one, which would neutralise the obvious Greek Cypriot advantage. Turkey had anticipated this aspect very early on. On the pretext that the population in the occupied areas was so small that it lacked the necessary labour force to ensure its economic viability, Ankara decided, based on secret guidelines,[11] to fill this 'gap' with settlers. And the decision concerned the transport of 100,000 settlers, but, due to the problems that arose in their relations with the Turkish Cypriots, they were restricted to 40,000.[12]

The population in the occupied areas before the invasion, in 1973, was 236,962. The Greek Cypriots represented 162,041 and the Turkish Cypriots 74,921.[13] On completion of their transfer to the occupied areas, the number of Turkish Cypriots in 1975 was approximately 115,000, a figure confirmed by the census carried out by the Turkish Cypriots themselves.[14]

In an interview[15] he gave in 1984, 10 years after the invasion, Denktash claimed that, 'the Turkish Cypriots comprise 24% of the population of Cyprus,' i.e. around 159,000, which leads one to the conclusion that the settlers numbered around 35,000 at the time. Turkish newspapers reckoned the number of settlers to be around 50,000,[16] a figure which did not take into account the number of Turkish Cypriots who had left Cyprus after the invasion. This means that the number of settlers was actually much greater.

If the number of settlers was restricted, this was because the problems they caused the Turkish Cypriots were enormous. The Turkish Cypriots came face to face with backward Anatolians with different morals and habits, language and certainly different values, with whom they felt there was no cultural connection whatsoever. This resulted in such a change to the Turkish Cypriot community that it frightened them, as even Fazil Kuchuk discovered, and the international press commented on it:

The policy of transporting large numbers of settlers in order to fill a gap in the north had, as expected, divisive consequences. For example, the former leader of the community Fazil Kuchuk, in an article in his opposition newspaper *Halkin Sesi*, complained that the settlers are so uneducated that, 'They thought they would come from the forests and mountains of Turkey to Cyprus by train.'

They curse the Turkish Cypriots, calling them 'British bastards' and non-Muslims, and telling them: 'We liberated you and we took these lands.' And much more in this vein.

Kuchuk has a well-known dislike of the President of the 'Turkish Federated State of Cyprus', Rauf Denktash. Yet his accusations of serious clashes between the developed and Westernised Turkish Cypriots and their backward, superstitious and often illiterate new neighbours who have some from the wildest areas of Turkey are adequately confirmed by less biased sources.[17]

Objectives and Consequences

To all these people, the occupation regime gave so-called 'Turkish Cypriot nationality', which came, naturally, with full rights. What were the objectives of this policy?

1. To change the demographic make-up of the island so as to justify the occupation of 36.4% of Cypriot territory when the Turkish Cypriots comprised only 18% of the population, and also to have complete control of the occupied areas for reasons which, of course, were related to Turkey's military objectives. This fact did not escape the notice of foreign observers:

> According to Ankara's plans concerning settlement, the Turkish population of north Cyprus should have risen by 120,000 to 250,000. Settlers from Turkey and Turkish Cypriot emigrants who left the island long ago must contribute to the population ratio between the Greeks and Turks on the island.
>
> The aim is two Turks for every Greek. By these actions they are hoping to overturn the Greek argument that the Turkish Cypriots, who do not amount to more than 20% of the total population, ought to be asking for minority sta-

tus and never 40% of the island's territory, in which their leader Rauf Denktash has proclaimed the Turkish Federated Republic.[18]

2. Internal political control. The settlers were organised by former officers of the Turkish army into their own political party, the Renaissance Party. And in the 1985 'elections' this party won 8.9% of the vote and four seats in the 'parliament'. It later cooperated in 'government' with the National Unity Party and was represented by a 'minister'.

In other words, with the mass presence of settlers, the political will of the Turkish Cypriots could be altered in accordance with Ankara's wishes. The leader of the Republican Turkish Party, Ozger Ozgur, publicly accused, 'The Denktash regime of giving blank identity cards to elements coming temporarily to Cyprus who are not citizens but who make up an electoral force imported into Cyprus and channelled to the parties of Rauf Denktash and the settlers.'[19]

A year earlier, Ozgur had claimed that, 'The constitution was approved with the votes of those who are not Cypriots, those who returned Denktash to power in the 1981 elections. Where is this story going to end?'[20]

Arif Tahsin is even more categorical:

> The transfer of people from Turkey and the persecution of the Turkish Cypriots through unemployment and misery serve no purpose except to play the game of the governments of Turkey and those under them, in order to get what they want from the ballot box. In other words, the Turkish Cypriots are a 'disobedient' community. And the majority of them do not always vote according to orders. For this reason the Turkish Cypriots, who 'do not always vote according to orders', have to be uprooted from the land where they have lived for centuries and in their place are brought people uprooted from Anatolia. And that is what has happened. In this way, 'parliaments' and the 'governments' have been formed in north Cyprus since 1976.
>
> But the will and, by extension, the future of the Turkish Cypriots was not only mortgaged in this way. That is to say that the problem is not only that they have given dual nationality to all those they have brought from Turkey. The fact that the number of those with a nationality other than Turkish Cypriot has surpassed the number of Turkish Cypriots who have only one

nationality has created a situation in which the problem of altering the will of the Turkish Cypriots cannot be resolved even if all the Turks brought here from Turkey are sent back.[21]

3. Preventing a solution to the Cyprus problem. Turkey knows very well that the Greek Cypriot side will not accept the giving of 'Turkish Cypriot nationality' to the settlers. By controlling the settlers totally, it has the ability to decide their future, whether they will stay or leave in case of a solution. It is consequently in a position to prevent or facilitate efforts aimed at a settlement by bringing up or ignoring the problem of the settlers.

And even if, under pressure from the international community, which recognises that the settlers, while violating the human rights of others, have obtained rights of their own, there is acceptance of the presence of those who have married Turkish Cypriots or were born in the occupied areas, this restricts the refugees' right of return as to expel them from the Greek Cypriot properties that they have taken over will mean a 'violation of the human rights' of the settlers.

4. The military aspect. From the start of the implementation of the policy of settlement, 'nationality' was given in the first instance to military personnel. First were the soldiers who took part in the invasion[22] since the looting that went on had made their stay in the occupied areas attractive. Then came those who had served in the occupation forces. And to make the bait even more attractive, they were demobilised in the occupied areas so as to encourage them to stay.[23] And, of course, the retiring Turkish officers who undertook the political organisation of the settlers.[24]

In this way then, beyond the occupation army, beyond the 'Security Forces' and the Turkish Cypriot reservists, Turkey established in Cyprus a strong reserve force of trained settlers. This means that, even if, for reasons of 'goodwill', it ever decides to withdraw some troops, its military force on the island remains essentially the same.

*

The Economic Aspect

The occupation of 36.4% of the island meant at the same time the control of rich resources that were important for the economy of the whole island. Specifically it represented 46% of agricultural production, 100% of tobacco production, 47% of animal farming, 26% of industrial production, 33% of employment, 65% of the tourist industry and 87% of the tourist installations under construction. From the outset, Turkey had undertaken to exploit these resources and to create conditions for the economic activity of the occupied areas, through the creation of the so-called 'Coordinating Council for Cypriot Issues', which comprised the Prime Minister, two deputy Prime Ministers, and the Ministers of Foreign Affairs, Defence, Finance, Industry and Technology, Commerce, Manufacturing, Communications, and Agriculture and Natural Resources.[25]

At the same time, an 'Office of Cypriot Affairs' had been set up in all these 'ministries', while today coordination is the responsibility of the 'under-secretary to the President for Cypriot Affairs'.

The Turkish press has from time to time published information about the employment of hundreds of Turkish civil servants for handling cases in the occupied areas, about which decisions are taken at ministerial level.[26]

From the Turkish Cypriot rebellion against the Republic until the invasion, 95% of the budget of the Turkish Cypriot leadership was, by Denktash's[27] own admission, covered by Turkey, while since the invasion Turkey has provided 40% of the budget for the occupied areas. It appears, nonetheless, that the true figure is greater since Turkish Cypriot press reports[28] place it at 45% and British ones[29] at 70%.

Given such statistics, it should come as no surprise that British MPs[30] should have pointed out to Denktash that there is no 'state' in the occupied areas but rather a colony.

Denktash has established 'public companies' in the occupied areas modelled on those operating in Turkey. According to Alper Orhon, a Turkish Cypriot former Professor of Economics at the University of Istanbul, these 'public companies' control 50%-90% of the economic resources of the occupied areas.[31] And who controls these 'public companies'?

a) Turkish Cypriot Tourist Enterprises.[32] Shareholders: Turkish Cypriot

Communal Chamber Development Fund 50%, Bank of Tourism of Turkey 50%.

b) Turkish Cypriot Airlines. Shareholders: Turkish Cypriot Communal Chamber Development Fund 50%, Turkish Airlines 50%.

c) Turkish Cypriot Industrial Holdings. Shareholders: Turkish Cypriot Communal Chamber Development Fund 50%, Industrial Organisation of Engines and Chemistry of Turkey, Super Bank of Turkey, Petro-industrial Company of Turkey, Meat & Fisheries Organisation of Turkey 50%.

d) Turkish Cypriot Marine Company. Shareholders: Turkish Cypriot Communal Chamber Development Fund 50%, Marine Bank of Turkey 50%.

e) Turkish Cypriot Tobacco Industry. Shareholders: Turkish monopolies 51%, Turkish Cypriot Communal Chamber Development Fund 49%.

f) Turkish Cypriot Oil Company. Shareholders: Oil Office of Turkey 52%, Turkish Cypriot Communal Chamber Development Fund 48%.

In every case, whether as a majority share or not, control rests with companies belonging to the Turkish state. Of course, this is not surprising since it is part of the process of integrating the occupied areas socially, politically, militarily and economically into Turkey, which takes all the decisions on important matters. In the economic sector, annexation is proceeding in accordance with a range of agreements and is codified by the Economic Cooperation Protocol signed by Denktash and Turgut Ozal on December 5, 1986. The provisions of the protocol reveal the degree of Ankara's control over the economy of the occupied areas and are at the same time a precise indicator of the discomfort felt by Turgut Ozal's government over the cost of the occupation and of the exasperation felt by the Turkish Cypriots, who realise that through such an agreement they are on the way to disappearing altogether. In any case, it has been recognised by many Turkish newspaper analysts that this situation led to the transfer of all the ills of the Turkish economy to the Turkish Cypriot community.

Prospects of EU Membership

From the start of the 1980s, awareness was growing within the Greek camp that the accession of Cyprus to the European Union might act as a catalyst for reaching a solution of the Cyprus problem. Accession to a union of states moving towards full unification, where respect for the basic principles of human rights, the democratic functioning of institutions and international law form the base on which European society is built, could perhaps be the way forward for overcoming Turkish intransigence after so many years. All the more so since Turkey itself has ambitions of joining the EU.

It turned out, however, that things were not quite so simple. Once again it was noted that, where reason ends, Turkish policy begins. Over and above the internal requirements that Turkey needs to fulfil in order to begin its accession course, requirements to which Ankara was and still is 'allergic', Turkey itself wishes to join the EU but on its own terms. It has been shown that, even in this instance, Turkey is using Cyprus as a hostage in order to blackmail the EU regarding the terms of its own accession, without thinking twice about depriving the Turkish Cypriots, in the name of whose security and welfare it allegedly invaded Cyprus, of the prospects that Cyprus' EU membership holds for them.

Beyond its hole-riddled arguments used to prevent Cyprus from joining the EU[33], Ankara is attempting to link the prospect of accession, by the conditions it is setting, to the specific solution that it wishes to impose on Cyprus. This is being exploited by Denktash to cultivate a climate of moving away from the agreed federal solution.

On July 5, 1994, the European Court ruled that products from the occupied areas could only be exported to European countries with official documents of the Republic of Cyprus. Until then, produce from the occupied areas had been exported accompanied by documents issued either by the Turkish authorities or by the occupation authorities, which enabled the Turkish side to present this fact as 'recognition' of the illegal state.

The court's decision not only confirmed the illegal status of the occupation authorities but also dealt a serious economic blow to the already poor economy of the occupied areas, with internal political consequences, especially regarding the credibility of Denktash and Ankara towards the Turkish Cypriots.

The reaction of the Turkish leadership came via the Turkish Cypriot 'parliament', which, by a resolution passed by 30 votes to 16, essentially opened up the way for the adoption of confederation as the model for a settlement.

The rejection of the European Court's decision is presented as being part of the illegal state's 'foreign policy' and states specifically:

> The decision of the European Court, which rejects the political equality and the separate sovereignty of the Turkish Cypriot people and which goes against the basic principles of justice, as well as the obsessive and one-sided demand of the Greek Administration for full membership of the European Union, cannot have a positive effect on the talks for Confidence-Building Measures. For these reasons negotiations cannot take place. Moreover, at this point, the only negotiations that can take place concern the removal of the obstacles referred to above.'[34]

The resolution also brings up the issue of the 'recognition' of separate sovereignty and essentially announces the process of completing the annexation of the occupied areas by Turkey in the economic, defence and political sectors. The conclusion of the resolution notes the following: 'Parliamentary decisions 6, March 15, 1984, and 36, March 15, 1985, which provide for a federation as the only solution are no longer valid.'[35]

Turkey's exclusion from the present stage of European Union enlargement has been used once again by Ankara to remind everyone that Cyprus remains its hostage. The Turkish government refuses to discuss the Cyprus issue in its political dialogue with the EU, while at the same time it proceeds to draw up 'agreements' with the illegal state for the annexation of the occupied areas, moves which it presents as being similar to those of the EU on the accession of Cyprus. And, of course, it now sets out without pretence the question of recognition of a separate sovereignty in Cyprus, culminating in the statement of its official position that the only acceptable 'solution' is confederation.

Footnotes

Chapter 1

1 Turkey's complete ignorance about Cyprus is revealed by Turkish diplomat Mahmoud Dikertem in his book *Ortadoguda devrim yillari – Bir buyukelcinin anilari* (*Years of Revolution in the Middle East – Memoirs of an Ambassador*), Istanbul, 1977, cited by Neoclis Sarris in his three-volume work *The Other Side*, Grammi, Athens, 1977, volume 2, Book 1, page 61. The Turkish diplomat writes: 'Thus, in this complex situation, the Menderes government was pushed into the Cyprus issue. But there had been no in-depth examination of the matter whatsoever. No one had a proper knowledge of the legal, military, political or historical and ethnological side of the problem. We merely knew that we had seized Cyprus from the Venetians in 1570 during the reign of Sultan Selim II, that in 1878 we had handed over the administration of the island – on a temporary basis – to Britain as the price of joint defence and, finally, that with the Treaty of Lausanne we had transferred all our sovereign rights to Britain. (Neoclis Sarris, op. cit., page 62.)

2 Due to its stance during the inter-war years but mainly due to its stance during World War II, Turkey 'earned' the title of 'The evasive neutral', which is the title of a book by Professor Frank Weber (University of Missouri Press, 1979) that contains very revealing information about Turkey's ulterior motives and totally unprincipled foreign policy.

3 Turkish Cypriot nationalism, the appearance of which is placed by many in the first post-war period, was essentially non-existent at the time. The Turkish Cypriots were scattered throughout the island, and enjoyed harmonious relations with the Greek Cypriots. Typical are the points cited by Michalis Attalides in his book *Cyprus: Nationalism and International Politics* (Q Press, Edinburgh, 1979, page 89) In 1881, the Turkish Cypriots made up 25% of the population and lived in 114 entirely Turkish villages and 342 mixed ones (the same number as purely Greek villages). By 1931, the percentage of Turkish Cypriots had fallen to 19%. The number of wholly Greek villages had risen to 358 while the Turkish and mixed ones now numbered 84 and 252 respectively. In 1960, the year of Cypriot independence, the Turkish Cypriots represented 18% of the population. There were 392 Greek villages, while the number of purely Turkish villages rose to 117 and the number of mixed villages fell to 114.

The appearance of so-called Turkish Cypriot nationalism did not coincide with that of Kemalist-Turkish nationalism, which the vast majority of the Turkish Cypriot community viewed with great mistrust and essentially rejected from the outset. It is nonetheless a fact that a small group of Turkish Cypriots, who represented the elite of the community but had few links by which to identify with the masses, occupied themselves with sending telegrams to the British government containing nationalist demands that had absolutely nothing to do with the masses, their real problems and their ambitions. Many researchers have gone through the Foreign Office archives and seen copies of these telegrams, and, basing their conclusions on the content, have taken as fact the objections of the Turkish Cypriots to the

Greek Cypriot demand for national vindication. This is, however, a mistaken and misleading picture, which will be overturned by much of the evidence in the present work.

4 By the Treaty of Lausanne, Turkey, as the successor state of the Ottoman Empire, gave up all claims and rights on Cyprus. The treaty gave minority status to the Ottoman residents of Cyprus and allowed them to choose to remain on the island, as British subjects, or to be repatriated, that is to return to Turkey, and with financial aid from Great Britain.

5 The Turkish Cypriot newspapers of the time contain much serious evidence to confirm this observation. The only link between the Turkish Cypriots and Turkey was their common past under the same Ottoman establishment and a common religion. The dissolution of the Ottoman establishment, which most of the Turkish Cypriots worked for, weakened their relations with Turkey even more, since it had as a result the loss of their social position and their income, a fact for which they naturally held Kemal Ataturk responsible. Moreover, isolated on the island as they were, the Turkish Cypriots remained entrenched in their conservative mentality, rejecting Ataturk's educational reforms, for example, and sending back his school textbooks written in Latin script to Ankara as unacceptable, preferring the old Ottoman system and Arabic script. The Turkish Cypriots of Famagusta, in particular, were fanatical anti-Kemalists and the last to accept the Kemalist educational reforms in the 1930s. Typical is the fact that when, shortly before the outbreak of World War II, the then British governor visited Famagusta, the local Turkish Cypriot leadership received him as 'representatives of the Ottoman communities'.

6 M. Attalides, op. cit., page 79. The Foreign Office had submitted a report which approved the effort aimed at preventing the Ottoman residents of Cyprus from leaving the island. Indeed, the Turkish Commissioner was expelled following accusations against him by Turkish Cypriots, who described him as a 'Kemalist and a Nationalist'. It was a time when Turkey was absorbed in its attempts to annex Alexandretta.

7 In his book *Cyprus at the Eleventh Hour – The Motherland will have the Last Word* (*Notes, thoughts and recollections of the Cyprus struggle*), published in Ankara in 1966, translated and distributed in polygraph copies by Thanasis Haranas in 1998, Rauf Denktash complains that it was not until 1948 that Turkey decided to send some assistance to the Turkish Cypriots.

8 Sir George Hill, *A History of Cyprus*, Cambridge University Press, 1972.

9 A huge number of studies and publications on this period contain evidence and serious analysis of British policy in Cyprus from that time until now. Particularly useful is the five-volume work by Sir George Hill, *A History of Cyprus.*

10 This was their consistent demand of the British at the time.

11 M. Attalides, op. cit., page 40, who provides an interesting analysis of the Ottoman presence in Cyprus during the arrival of the British on the island.

12 In an essay entitled *Islam and Turkish Nationalism in Cyprus* in *Die Welt des Islam*, NS, volume 5, 1957, pages 65-83, C.F. Beckingham notes that, in one instance, the Ottomans of Cyprus had demanded the cession of Cyprus to Egypt, should the British not wish to keep it!

13 M. Attalides, op. cit., page 44.

14 For example, Halil Ibrahim Salih in his book *Cyprus, an Analysis of Cypriot Political Discord*, Theo, Gaus' Sons Inc., Brooklyn, New York, 1966, page 24.

15 For details, see the book by Andreas Sophocleous *The First Cypriot Newspapers and the Human Rights of the Greeks of Cyprus*, Intercollege Press, Nicosia, 1994, page 91.
16 Op. cit., page 101.
17 M. Attalides, op. cit., page 45.
18 Arif Hasan Tahsin was a member of the Turkish Cypriot terrorist organisation TMT and chairman of the Turkish Cypriot Teachers' Organisation. After the Turkish invasion of Cyprus, in a series of articles he expressed fierce criticism of the decisions taken by the Turkish Cypriot leadership. The most important of these were gathered in the book *We See the Future and Ignore the Past*, which was translated into Greek and distributed in polygraph copies by Thanasis Haranas in 1966.
19 It is interesting that Denktash himself in his book *Cyprus at the Eleventh Hour* notes the following: 'We did not want to believe that the British would one day abandon Cyprus and we supported the continuation of the status quo. We had not realised the changes that were happening on the international scene and we blindly followed a policy of friendship with the British. So as not to make them feel bad, the Turkish Foreign Ministry said: 'We have nothing to do with Cyprus.' At one time the doors of officials in Turkey were closed to the delegations of Turkish Cypriots who went to Ankara with the aim of explaining the situation in Cyprus.'
20 Based on the census, there were 249,376 (80.3%) Greek Cypriots and 61,339 (19.7%) Turkish Cypriots.
21 Turkish Cypriot newspaper *Soz*, March 11, 1983.

Chapter 2

1 Kemal Ataturk, quoted on the official Internet web page of the Turkish Ministry of Foreign Affairs.
2 The former Turkish Prime Minister Turgut Ozal felt the need to write a whole book in order to persuade the Europeans, whom he was addressing, about the relationship between the Turkish republic and the Ottoman Empire as well as with the ancient Greek and other civilisations that had developed in the region, which he presents as component parts of today's Turkish civilisation. (Turgut Ozal, *Turkey in Europe and Europe in Turkey*, K. Rustem & Brother, occupied Cyprus, 1991.)
3 David Hotman writes (in *The Turks*, Ioannis Floros Press, Athens, 1986, page 13): 'One cannot speak about the existence of individual rights in Turkey during any era. Even when this peculiar suspended democracy works, people disappear and the will of those in government prevails.
'The 'clan', whether represented by the Sultan or by the socialist Ecevit or by the Sergeant of the gendarmerie, represents complete authority. The worst is not that this is accepted fatalistically by the overwhelming majority of the people but that it is considered natural.
'Minority rights cannot, of course, be discussed when individual rights do not exist for the Turks themselves.
'The massacres of the Armenians and the Greeks, the oppression of the Kurds, the extermination of the flourishing Greek minority in Istanbul (Constantinople) through the 'cap-

ital tax' law of 1942 and the events of 1955, the de-Hellenising of Imvros and Tenedos are eloquent examples.'

4 This phenomenon has been the subject of study and analysis by important scholars of Turkey such as the American professor Frank Weber and Neoclis Sarris, a professor at the Panteion University of Athens, who spent his youth as a Turkish citizen.

5 The principles on which Ataturk based his foreign policy immediately after the establishment of the Kemalist state were non-alignment and independence. Nonetheless, over and above his own contradictions, his heirs at least abandoned this policy and aligned Turkey wholly with the Western camp during the Cold War. See Christodoulos Yiallourides, *Turkey in Transition*, Sideris Press, Athens, 1997, page 86.

6 Alexandretta became part of Syria after the dissolution of the Ottoman Empire and the adoption of the so-called 'National Contract'. In 1920 it was placed under the guardianship of the League of Nations. In 1921, Turkey, following an agreement of France, accepted this status. In 1937, however, Turkey claimed Alexandretta, of which more than 60% of the population were Arabs. After the systematic settlement of the area with Turks, disturbances and the violent uprooting of the Arabs, the demographic situation was altered, changing the composition of the local parliament. In 1939, the installed parliament decided that the region should become part of Turkey. The Arabs, and Syria in particular, never forgave Turkey for its cunning seizure of Alexandretta and even today the problem continues to exist between the two countries. A detailed analysis of the case of Alexandretta may be found in Frank Weber's *The Evasive Neutral*, pages 38-47.

7 *The Aegean Realities*, published by the Istanbul Journalists' Union, page 6.

8 *Milliyet* newspaper, July 20, 1978.

9 Commenting on this policy of reviewing the Treaties of Lausanne and Ataturk's contradictory stance, Frank Weber notes the following: 'But no revolutionary can cut himself off entirely from his own past. This was very obvious in Turkish foreign policy during the last decade of Ataturk's life. Officially, as Ataturk had declared on many occasions, Turkey's foreign policy aimed at peace, friendship and trade with all states. Turkey had no irredentist or territorial designs. It did not wish to rebuild the Balkan and Arab provinces of the Ottoman Empire and indeed, it considered it an advantage to have lost them. It was a healthy policy. The Turks, however, had to continually remind themselves that this policy was a healthy one, even though it had been imposed on them by necessity and was not their choice.' (Frank Weber, op. cit., pages 25-26.)

10 Jacob M. Landau, *Panturkism, the Doctrine of Turkish Expansionism*, translated into Greek by Eva Nantsou, Thetili Press, Athens, 1985, page 193.

11 The interest of Ankara in the future of Cyprus was even explained by a British newspaper, the *Financial Times*, in an article on December 6, 1983, on the occasion of the declaration of the occupied Cypriot territory as the 'Turkish Republic of Northern Cyprus'. The London paper wrote: 'By allowing Denktash…'

12 M. Attalides, op. cit., page 41.

13 The Turks have no problem with developing their theories publicly on the subject, with analyses in the Turkish press and in special publications. With the end of the Cold War, for example, the well-known Turkish journalist Sami Cohen wrote a series of articles in the English edition of the Turkish Press and Information General Secretariat's publication

Newspot, explaining the meaning of 'strategic minority'. The meaning and the importance of the recognition that 'wherever there is a Turk, Turkey must also be' was examined in dozens of articles in the Turkish press by Mumtaz Soysal, who was the most important adviser to Rauf Denktash and Foreign Minister of Turkey.
14 It is more precise to speak of a Turkish-speaking person, rather than a Turk.
15 *Terzuman* newspaper, February 23, 1980.
16 *Millyet* newspaper, October 15, 1986.
17 *Financial Times*, December 6, 1983.
18 M. Attalides, op. cit., page 38.
19 'The fact that popular revolts were frequently on class lines seems well established.' (M. Attalides, op. cit., page 39.)
20 See Halil Ibrahim Salih, op. cit., page 41.
21 Pierre Oberling, *The Road to Bellapais The Turkish Cypriot Exodus to Northern Cyprus*, Columbia University Press, New York, 1982, pages 52-53.
22 All examples from Pierre Oberling's book, op. cit., pages 52-53.
23 Iacovos Tenedios, *A Retrospective of the Turkish Cypriot Press 1878-1955* in the publication of the Nicosia Municipality, *Ta Kypriaka, 1878-1955*, Nicosia, 1986, page 76.
24 Op. cit., page 79.
25 Until 1900 a total of seven newspapers were published but none were able to survive. (Op. cit., page 81.)
26 Op. cit. page 82.

Chapter 3

1 L.W. St. John-Jones, *The Population of Cyprus*, Institute of Commonwealth Studies, Maurice Temple Smith, London, 1983, page 60.
2 Op. cit., page 51.
3 This number appears ultimately to have been no more than 5,000 and on this point Michalis Attalides, L.W. St. John-Jones and others are in agreement.
4 Iacovos Tenedios, *The Socio-political Structure of the Turkish Cypriots*, Part 1, a typescript edition of the Cyprus Ministry of Foreign Affairs, June 1988. The number of Ottomans who left the island and the large numbers who returned are presented statistically by L.W. St. John-Jones, op. cit., page 56.
5 Iacovos Tenedios (*A Retrospective of the Turkish Cypriot Press, 1878-1955*', in the Nicosia Municipality's publication *Ta Kypriaka 1878-1955*, Nicosia, 1986, page 85) includes from the Turkish Cypriot newspaper *Kibris* (March 28, 1949) a narrative by Mehmet Akif who experienced this: 'But when they arrived in Adana, Mersin, Tarsus and Antalya, since they knew no trade, they had to beg for food. In two months they went back secretly, in a terrible state, to Karpasia where they were arrested and placed in quarantine in Larnaca. After 20 days, another group of 70 people returned to Kyrenia. Like the previous group, they were in an awful state. They too were taken to Larnaca. A month and a half later I went to Larnaca where I was told that another group of 45 had come back from Mersin.'
6 M. Attalides, op. cit., page 41.

7 For the administrative structure during British rule and more on this class solidarity, see Sir George Hill, op. cit.; see also H. Luke, *Cyprus Under the Turks*, Oxford University Press, Oxford, 1921.
8 M. Attalides, op. cit., page 43.
9 Op. cit.
10 Rauf Denktash, op. cit., page 5.
11 This is how Turkish scholars have tried to present it in order to 'prove' that the 'national conflict' between the two communities dates back to this time. The bulk of historical evidence refutes these claims, which go against the conclusions of other scholars who have dealt with the issue.
12 This may be seen in the memoranda sent by the Turkish Cypriot elite to the British government in London and which have been published as part of the official British archives.
13 M. Attalides, op. cit., page 39.
14 Katia Hadjidemetriou, *History of Cyprus* (Greek language), Nicosia, 1979, page 152.
15 Dr Stavros Panteli, *The Making of Modern Cyprus*, Interworld Publications Ltd, London, 1990, page 93.
16 *Ta Kypriaka, 1878-1955*, page 132.
17 Dr Stavros Panteli, op. cit., page 93.
18 Op. cit., page 126.
19 Op. cit., page 128. Distinctions which have remained in use ever since and which have proved fatal at crucial moments of the island's recent history.
20 Op. cit., page 125.
21 Op. cit., page 129.
22 The increase in the number of Greek schools during the colonial era reinforced the ideological base of the *enosis* struggle significantly, not only because of the presence on the island of teachers from Greece but also due to the creation of prerequisites for young Cypriots to travel to Athens for studies, which strengthened their nationalist views even more.
23 This was the year in which the bi-monthly magazine *Pyrsos* was published, while in 1924 it announced that it was an organ of the Cyprus Communist Party. *Ta Kypriaka, 1878-1955*, page 136.
24 Loukas Kakoullis, *The Left and the Turkish Cypriots*, Nicosia, 1990, page 11.
25 *Ta Kypriaka, 1878-1955*, page 136.
26 Op. cit., pages 136-7.
27 The British described Necati Bey as 'a traitor to his race' and 'the 13th Greek' on the Council. (See Stavros Panteli, op. cit., page 102.)
28 In these oppressive circumstances, the demand for *Enosis* was totally identified and synonymous with freedom and social justice.
29 Katia Hadjidemetriou, op. cit., pages 152-153.
30 Miltiades Christodoulou, *The Course of Greco-Turkish Relations and Cyprus*, Proodos, Nicosia, 1995, volume 1, pages 480-481. Miltiades Christodoulou was then a close collaborator with Makarios, under whom he became press officer and later government spokesman.
31 The Greek Cypriots received a nasty shock when Eleftherios Venizelos advised against mak-

ing a substantial issue of their demand for *enosis*. For details, see Yiannis P. Pikros' book *Venizelos and Cyprus*, Philippoti, Athens, 1980.

32 Petros Stylianou, *The October 1931 Movement in Cyprus*, Nicosia, 1984, pages 174-176.

33 It is interesting that a Turkish Cypriot newspaper should confirm the harmonious relations that existed between the two communities and it is a clear response to the Turkish propaganda that insists that such a thing never existed.

34 Petros Stylianou notes in a footnote that the Governor interpreted the original anti-British stance of the newspaper 'as an indication of the anti-British feelings that have started to develop and mature among the Turkish Cypriot masses, after the strong collective anti-British policy developed by the Greek Cypriot community both inside and outside parliament.' (Petros Stylianou, op. cit., page 175, footnote 1.)

35 At the same time, the Istanbul newspaper *Milliyet* – the director of which was the Turkish Cypriot Ahmed Shukry – noted in an article that 'as official Greek policy stresses that there is no Cyprus Problem between Great Britain and Greece, in the same way there is no similar problem between Britain and Turkey.'

36 Petros Stylianou, op. cit., page 176.

37 *Ta Kypriaka, 1878-1955*, page 86.

38 In Iacovos Tenedios' study *The Socio-political Structure of the Turkish Cypriots*, Part 1, op. cit., page 23, the author states the following: 'Language is a very interesting element in the harmonious contacts between the Greek Cypriot and Turkish Cypriot masses. A survey by the Turkish Cypriot researcher Ahmed An reveals the following: "On the basis of the 1921 census, in the Nicosia district 1,019 Turkish Cypriots had Greek as their mother tongue. In Paphos, the number was 350. According to the 1934 statistics, in Nicosia 1,004 Turkish Cypriots had Greek as their mother tongue while those in the Paphos district whose mother tongue was Greek numbered 521. In some villages, the Turkish population spoke both Greek and Turkish but preferred Greek in their personal dealings. Moreover, in Nicosia, Famagusta and Paphos, Turkish Cypriots whose mother tongue was Turkish used Greek words and expressions in their speech. Until 1955, the Muslim villages speaking Greek were spread throughout Cyprus. In these villages, the Muslims had the same customs and morals as the Greek Cypriots." (newspaper *Soz*, March 11th 1983) The same researcher mentions that, in 1911, 139 Greek Cypriots had Turkish as their mother tongue. In 1921, the number had fallen to 68 while in 1946 it had risen to 146.'

39 M. Kemal Dizdar, *The Origins and Administration of the Cyprus Efkaf in the minutes of the First International Cyprological Conference* (Nicosia, 14-19 April, 1969), published by the Cyprus Studies Association, Nicosia, 1973, volume 3, page 67.

40 The Council was founded in 1878 and 'modernised' in 1882. It comprised 18 members, of whom six were appointed by the British governor from the ranks of the colonial administration, three were chosen by the Turkish Cypriots and nine by the Greek Cypriots. The governor presided over this body and he held the casting vote whenever the three Turkish Cypriots and the six appointees of the governor voted together and tied with the nine Greek Cypriots, as happened 'traditionally'.

41 Iacovos Tenedios, op. cit., page 22.

42 Pierre Oberling, op. cit., page 54.

43 Iacovos Tenedios, op. cit., page 22.

44 Nancy Crawshaw, *The Cyprus Revolt*, George Allen & Unwin, London, 1978, page 43. The author writes that the Turkish Cypriots at the time 'preferred silence rather than risk becoming alienated from the British administration, their only protector against the demands of the Greek majority.'
45 Fazil Kuchuk was born in 1906 and was studying medicine at the University of Istanbul at the time when Turkish nationalism was on the rise. He later transferred to the Universities of Lausanne and Paris and returned to Cyprus in 1937 where he immediately became involved in the attempts to create a 'national conscience' in the Turkish Cypriots.
46 As noted by Ihsan Ali in his, *My Memoirs*, Nicosia, 1980, page 4.
47 Iacovos Tenedios, op. cit., page 38. Information about the groups and the foundation of KATAK has been drawn chiefly from this work.
48 Turkish Cypriot newspaper *Soz*, March 9, 1943.
49 Turkish Cypriot newspaper *Soz*, March 10, 1943.
50 Fazil Kuchuk's observation also replies to the Turks' attempt to distort the truth, by making the Turkish Cypriots appear to be victims of a double 'persecution' by the Greek Cypriots and the British.
51 Turkish Cypriot newspaper *Soz*, March 19, 1943.
52 This was a time when the Turkish Cypriots and foreigners alike had no illusions about the status of the Turkish Cypriots as a minority.
53 H.H. Gurkan, *Bir Zamanlar Kibris'ta*, Nicosia, page 134.
54 Turkish Cypriot newspaper *Soz*, April 10, 1987
55 *Kibris Postasi* newspaper, October 26, 1986.
56 Iacovos Tenedios, op. cit., page 38.
57 The British were 'generous' to Munir, who was knighted for his services.
58 Ihsan Ali, op. cit., pages 5-6.
59 *Kibris Postasi*, 29.10.1986
60 Iacovos Tenedios, op. cit., page 42.
61 The son of a judge, he was born in Paphos and later graduated from the English School in Nicosia before working as a journalist on Kuchuk's *Halkin Sesi*. In 1944 he went to London to study law on a British scholarship and returned in 1947.
62 *History of PSE-PEO, 1941-1991*, PEO Publications, Nicosia, 1991, page 13.
63 Grigoris Grigoriades, *History of SEK*, SEK Publications, Nicosia, 1994, volume 1, page 54. The same page contains an extract from the 1941 'annual report' of the colonial Labour Office, which states the following: 'During the first fifty years of British rule in Cyprus, the need for protection of workers was not felt. The public conscience saw nothing lacking in the fact that men and women worked 12-15 hours a day for a wage that covered the very basic requirements of their lives. The British Administration was content not to interfere with the country's traditions.'
64 *History of PSE-PEO, 1941-1991*, op. cit., page 14, which includes an extract from a newspaper article in which it is argued that 'a socialist-labour question as such does not exist for Hellenism and particularly for Cyprus. [...] Our supreme duty is nationalism and nationalism alone.'
65 Op. cit., page 17.
66 Op. cit., pages 13-14.

67 Pantelis Varnavas, *Joint Labour Struggles by Greek Cypriots and Turkish Cypriots*, Nicosia, 1997, page 7.
68 *History of PSE-PEO, 1941-1991*, pages 36-37.
69 *History of SEK*, op. cit., page 55.
70 Grigoris Grigoriades, pages 62-64.
71 Op. cit., page 66.
72 Loukas Kakoullis, op. cit., page 18.
73 *History of PSE-PEO, 1941-1991*, op. cit., page 84.
74 Grigoris Grigoriades, op. cit., pages 62-68.
75 *History of PSE-PEO, 1941-1991*, page 84. On the same page reference is made to the fact that, according to official statistics for 1944, when SEK was formed it had 25 unions with 758 members, compared wit PEO's 89 unions representing 10,596 members.
76 Ploutis Servas, *Joint Homeland*, Proodos Press, Nicosia, 1997, pages 138-140.
77 Op. cit., page 141.
78 Loukas Kakoullis, op. cit., page 37.
79 Op. cit., page 38.
80 Official figures of the Cyprus Ministry of Labour.
81 Iacovos Tenedios, op. cit., page 45.
82 H.A. Mapolar, *Turk isci hareketi, Kibris Postasi* newspaper, August 27, 1984.
83 *Kibris Postasi* newspaper, August 28, 1984.
84 *Kibris Postasi* newspaper, August 28, 1984.
85 *Kibris Postasi* newspaper, August 28, 1984.
86 Pantelis Varnavas, op. cit., pages 16-17.
87 *Kibris Postasi* newspaper, August 30, 1984.
88 *Kibris Postasi* newspaper, August 30, 1984.
89 Pantelis Varnavas, op. cit., pages 31-32.
90 *History of PSE-PEO, 1941-1991*, page 252.
91 Op. cit.,

Chapter 4

1 This is supported in all the official Turkish publications about Kemal Ataturk. For details of the Kemalist ideology, see the book by Lord Kinross, *Ataturk, the Rebirth of a Nation*, K. Rustem and Brother, Nicosia, 1985.
2 Panturanism: a political movement aimed at the unification of the Turanic (Turkic) tribes in a unified state.
3 For details of the appearance of Panturanism, its organisation and development, as well as its contemporary nature and activity, see the book by Professor Jacob landau of the University of Jerusalem, *Panturkism, the Dogma of Turkish Expansionism*, translated into Greek by Evi Nantsou, Thetili Press, Athens, 1983, page 36 onwards.
4 Turkey has made a science of its theory of 'vital territory' in order to promote its aims. The 'national security' argument is a basic one on all the 'open fronts' – Cyprus, the Aegean, Thrace, the Caucasus and its borders with the Arab countries.

5 For details, see *The Evasive Neutral* by Professor Frank Weber.

6 It is remarkable how easily the Turks can on the one hand distort the truth regarding their stance during the war and how, on the other, the West forgets Turkey's stance during World War II and accepts Turkish 'arguments'. In his introduction to a seminar on 'Turkey-Greece, Questions of Foreign and National Security Policy' (Munich, November 15, 1985) the Turkish Ambassador Haluk Bayulgen argued that 'through its wise foreign policy during World War II, Turkey prevented damage to the Free World in the Middle East which it would not have been able to repair afterwards' (*Turkish Review*, a Turkish Foreign Ministry publication, volume 1, issue 2, 1985).

7 As Frank Weber notes, during the war Ankara attempted to come to an understanding with Nazi Germany concerning the post-war future of Cyprus in the case of a Nazi victory.

8 *Turkish Review*, volume 1, issue 2, 1985-1986, page 14.

9 'In the general context of international relations, Greece's policy of gradual expansion against Turkey is one of the ingredients, in reality the most important ingredient, of the foreign policy being followed by Greece. [...] Since its foundation, Turkey has been obliged to follow a very difficult policy, maintaining on the one hand good relations with Greece as a neighbour, based on justice and mutual rights, and on the other facing Greece's expansionist policy.' (Oral Santer, Professor of Political Science at the University of Ankara and scientific adviser to the Turkish Foreign Ministry, in an article in *Turkish Review*, volume 2, issue 1, entitled 'Turkish-Greek Relations after World War I: A Vicious Circle of 60 Years'.)

10 Jacob M. Landau, op. cit. Interesting information on Panturanism is provided by C. P. Ioannides in his book *In Turkey's Image*, published by Aristide D. Caratzas, New York, 1991.

11 An article by Altan Deliorman entitled *Bugunkyu manasi ile Bozkurt* (*The Contemporary Meaning of the Grey Wolf*) in the magazine *Turk Kulturu*, volume 5, issue 55, May 1967, pages 470-475, as included in Christos P. Ioannides' book, op. cit.

12 Miltiades Christodoulou. op. cit., page 610, where a footnote contains an extract from the introduction of Pavlos Hidiroglu to the 6th Cretological Congress: 'Ataturk appointed his Members of Parliament to Professorial chairs at universities so that his theories about Turkic tribes and the antiquity of Turkish civilisation would prevail, while the theory on Panturanism, which presupposes an expansionist policy, became huge during Ataturk's time and is the creation of his collaborators.'

13 Jacob M. Landau, op. cit., page 132.

14 The phrase 'Turkish Culture' or 'Turkish Civilisation' is used to this day almost exclusively by the Panturanist groups and their publications.

15 These were centres of fascist activity in Turkey, which were transferred after the 1974 invasion to occupied Cyprus.

16 Christos P. Ioannides, op. cit., page 75. It is worth noting that, in 1951, the then Prime Minister of Turkey, Adnan Menderes, received a delegation from this association headed by the two Turkish Cypriots.

17 The members of this organisation were known as *Milliyetcis* (Nationalists).

18 Jacob M. Landau, *Radical Politics in Modern Turkey*, Leiden E. J. Brill, Boston, 1974, page 201.

19 Christos P. Ioannides, op. cit., pages 75-91.

20 In Turkey, and also in the view of the leadership elite of the Turkish Cypriots, it is consid-

ered that the interest of Turkish governments in Cyprus was sparked by the crusade that *Huriyet*, under Hikmet Bil, had undertaken at the start of the 1950s.

21 As far as the Turkish press's anti-Greek crusade is concerned, Christos P. Ioannides refers, among others, to reports by the American Embassy in Ankara and in particular to telegram no. 228 to the State Department.

22 Christos P. Ioannides, op. cit., page 78.

23 Orhan Birgit's description of the meeting of the committee with Menderes was published in the magazine *Akis* on February 11, 1956, and included in telegram 306 sent by the American Consul in Istanbul.

24 He was born in Izmit (the old Greek town of Nicomedia) and studied law before becoming involved in journalism.

25 Christos P. Ioannides, op. cit., page 84.

26 Op. cit., page 85.

27 Op. cit., page 86.

28 He was born in Alexandretta in 1925. In 1946 he graduated from the Military Reserve School with the rank of Infantry Captain. After leaving the army he turned to journalism.

29 Christos P. Ioannides, op. cit., page 86.

30 Bernard Lewis, *The Emergence of Modern Turkey*, Oxford University Press, London 1969, page 300.

31 Christos P. Ioannides, op. cit., page 87.

32 M. Attalides, op. cit., page 47.

Chapter 5

1 With the participation of Greek and Turkish troops in the UN force.

2 Robert Stephens, *Cyprus, a Place of Arms*, Pall Mall Press, London, 1966, page 132.

3 In November 1951 Greece had tabled the Cyprus issue before a UN committee while the same month, according to Stephens (op. cit., page 133), Evangelos Averof had a meeting in Rome with the British Foreign Minister Antony Eden during which Averof proposed maintaining bases in Cyprus and in four other areas in Greece for a period of 99 years in return for granting *enosis*.

4 It is worth noting that around 800 Turkish Cypriots voted in favour of *enosis*, despite the fierce campaign against it by the elite leadership of the Turkish Cypriots.

5 For details of this crusade, with extensive references to inflammatory articles in the Turkish press, see Neoclis Sarris, op. cit., volume 1, Book 1.

6 'Turkey played a leading part in the formation of the Baghdad Pact. Whereas in NATO, although an important contributor of troops, Turkey was a junior partner, the Baghdad Pact made her a senior member of what the British regarded as very much their own special alliance. Turkey assumed a greatly increased – indeed, a vastly exaggerated – political and military significance in the eyes of the British government. It saw the pact not so much as a defence against Russia as a means of maintaining friendly governments in the oil countries of the Middle East. With the evacuation of Egypt and the creation of the Baghdad Pact, British policy began to show signs of reverting, after more than 70 years, to the orig-

inal idea which had inspired the Cyprus Convention: protection of and support for Turkey as the shield for British interests in the Middle East, seen once more as lying chiefly in the Persian Gulf and what is now Iraq.' (Robert Stephens, op. cit., page 138.)

7 The mouthpiece of the then Turkish government, *Zafer*, typically put forward the argument in an article on August 26, 1954, that 64% of the Greek population of Cyprus were Communists in order to justify its position that 'Turkey cannot allow the creation of a front-line outpost of the Cominform sixty kilometres from its shores since the *Enosis* movement is a Communist provocation', with the clear aim of gaining the favour of the leaders of the anti-Communist hysteria of the time.

8 E.N. Tzelepis, *The Cyprus Issue and its Conspirators*, Themelio Press, Athens, 1965, page 38.

9 All the Turkish authors and scholars of the Cyprus issue are agreed that this was the British suggestion.

10 Foreign Office document WG 1081/11.

11 It is worth noting the reply of the British Ambassador to Ankara, Sir James Bowker, to London's orders, as set out in document WG 1081/13. The Ambassador warned his superiors, prophetically it might be said, of the consequences of Turkey's involvement in Cyprus: 'You have no doubt taken the following considerations into account. Such an approach to the Turkish government might well give the impression that Her Majesty's government were not only unable to deal with the Greeks unaided in a matter primarily of Anglo-Greek concern, but also that we were not confident in the efficacy of our own representations in Washington to move United States government to take the desired action with the Greeks and thought the Turkish approach would cut more ice. Apart from this possible effect on our standing with the Turks, the latter might feel that, if they responded to our request for their help, it would entitle them the right to expect that we should give them henceforward something of the status of partnership in the Cyprus question vis-à-vis the Greeks. I feel that I should point out possible far-reaching consequences of this; although as you know some such development in this direction would not necessarily be unwelcome from our point of view here [in Ankara], it may not suit the [colonial] Cyprus government if the Turks were given pretext for thinking that they would now be entitled to have more say in Cyprus affairs.'

12 Document WG 1081/23, February 17, 1954.

13 As reported in Nicos Kranidiotis' book *Difficult Years*, Estia Publications, Athens 1981.

14 Greece's presence at the London Conference had catastrophic consequences for the progress of the Cyprus issue, even though it was essentially the result of its national dependence on foreign decision-making centres. Before independence, Cyprus was claiming its liberty from London, on whom the Athens government depended almost totally during the first, post-civil-war period. After independence, Cyprus faced the hostility of Western decision-makers in Washington and London, who, on the one hand, imposed the criteria of their foreign policy on their allies so as to serve the strategy of facing the Soviet camp, and on the other were exercising substantial financial and military control of their allies, the smaller satellite states. For more details, see a host of titles, one of which is *Contemporary Greek History from the Civil War to the Junta* by Spyros Linardatos, Papazisis Press, Athens, 1986, and others are *The Rape of Greek Democracy* by Alexis Papachelas, Estia Publications, Athens, 1997, and *British and American Policy and the Greek Problem* by B.

Kontis, Paratirisis Press, Salonica, 1986.

15 Antony Eden, *Full Circle*, Cassell, London, 1960, page 414.

16 The interview was granted to the author in London immediately after the Turkish invasion of Cyprus in the summer of 1974 and was reproduced in full in the Greek Cypriot newspaper *Phileleftheros*, on December 8 and 9, 1976. It was further reproduced in the Athens newspaper *Kathimerini* on December 11, 1976.

17 Robert Stephens, op. cit., page 137.

18 Mahmut Dikerdem, *Ortadoguda devrim yillari – Bir buyukelcinin anilari* (*Years of Revolt in the Middle East – Memoirs of an Ambassador*), Istanbul, 1977, page 123, as referred to by Neoclis Sarris, op. cit., page 61.

19 Op. cit., page 62.

20 Op. cit., pages 65-68.

21 The committee comprised, in addition to Zorlu, the Deputy Joint Chief of Staff, General Rustu Erdelhun, the General Secretary of the Foreign Ministry, Muharem Nuri Birgi, the Turkish Ambassador to Athens, Setar Iksel, the Director General of the Foreign Ministry, Orhan Eralp, and Mahmut Dikerem.

22 It is worth noting that Hikmet Bil, chairman of the 'Cyprus is Turkish' committee, states that the white paper was the work of his committee precisely because the Foreign Ministry had nothing with which to help Turkish diplomats learn about the Cyprus issue.

23 E.N. Tzelepis, op. cit., page 30.

24 Nancy Crawshaw, op. cit., page 133.

25 Twenty years later, in order to justify their invasion of Cyprus, the Turks were drawing 'arguments' from the London Conference. In the publication of the Committee for Peace in Cyprus entitled *The Facts on the Turkish Intervention in Cyprus* in September 1974, they wrote, ' The importance of Cyprus to Turkey, as William Shakespeare put it in Othello, has a long historical background. It is quite obvious from the map that who controls Cyprus, controls the southern approaches of Turkey. The Ottomans were therefore compelled to conquer the Island from the Venetians in 1571. (Cyprus, by the way, has never belonged to Greece.) It remained in Turkish hands until 1878, when the administration of the Island was turned over to Britain as a base, with the condition that it would contribute to the defence of the Ottoman Empire against Russian encroachments. Britain made Cyprus a crown colony in 1919, a fact which was later confirmed by the Lausanne Peace Treaty in 1923. This, however, did not put an end to Turkish interests in Cyprus. Its strategic importance increased especially vis-à-vis the revival by the Soviet Union of the Old Tzarist ambitions over the Turkish Straits and in the Mediterranean during the Stalin era.'

Exploiting the Cold War concerns of Western public opinion which they were addressing, the Turkish propaganda leaflet stated the following:

'Cyprus, at the crossroads of the Mediterranean, is of vital importance to super powers, but it is of more importance to the security of Turkey. Turkey cannot entrust her long-term security to Greece, even if she is a NATO ally. Even now, Turkey's Western Aegean approaches and her Aegean interests are in jeopardy due to Greek control of the Dodecanese Islands. [...] Who could guarantee that Greece would always remain in NATO, and would not one day join another camp to fulfil her *Megali Idea* ambitions?'

In 1955 the argument was set out by Menderes and Zorlu. In 1974 by Ecevit and Erbakan.

And in 1983 the then Prime Minister Turgut Ozal repeated: 'Cyprus is an island which cuts the underbelly of Turkey like a stiletto. The island must not find itself in enemy hands.' (*Miliyet*, December 3, 1983.)

Chapter 6

1 Antony Eden himself wrote: 'We knew how great the difference was in the views of the Greeks and the Turks but the world did not. Very many saw our problems as a result of British colonialism. By securing an exact definition of these differences, we hoped to be able to determine the real nature of the problem. And then we would be able to set out our precise proposals for the future." (Antony Eden, *Full Circle*, op. cit., page 400.)
2 Miltiades Christodoulou, op. cit., volume 1, page 615.
3 Miltiades Christodoulou, op. cit., page 615. Archbishop Makarios spoke publicly on the matter on August 26, 1955: 'The Cyprus issue is purely one of self-determination and for a resolution of this matter the London Conference is not the competent body. If the British government were genuinely interested in resolving this matter, it should have invited the directly interested Cypriots to talks. The negotiations ought to be bilateral between the British government and representatives of the Cypriot people or between the British and Greek governments, acting for the vast majority of the Cypriots. What is Turkey's position that it can participate in the London Conference with equal rights? The Cyprus issue is not a Greco-Turkish dispute, nor is it a dispute among the three powers at the London Conference. It is first and foremost an Anglo-Cypriot dispute and by extension an Anglo-Greek dispute. The British government has gone to a lot of trouble to stoke up Turkish interest in Cyprus.' (Speech to the 3rd National Pancyprian Congress, from the *Complete Works of Archbishop Makarios III of Cyprus*, published by the Archbishop Makarios III Foundation, Nicosia, 1992, volume 2, page 71.)
4 Report of the British Embassy to the Foreign Office, August 19, 1955. (PRO, FO371/11680/RG 1084/13.) It is included in the book by D. Michalopoulos, *Greece and Turkey, 1950-1959 – The Missed Opportunity*, Roes Press, Athens, 1989, page 68.
5 E.N. Tzelepis, op. cit., pages 48-49.
6 Neoclis Sarris, op. cit., volume 1, Book 1, page 71.
7 Miltiades Christodoulou, op. cit., page 617.
8 Neoclis Sarris, op. cit., pages 77-79.
9 Nancy Crawshaw, op. cit., pages 130-131.
10 Op. cit., pages 132-133.
11 Neoclis Sarris, op. cit., pages 86-93.
12 At the time, according to Neoclis Sarris (op. cit., page 247), Nihat Erim was one of the main officials of the opposition party and the thinking behind his acceptance of the proposal was its 'national character'.
13 Neoclis Sarris, op. cit., page 275.
14 All the information concerning Nihat Erim's report is taken from Neoclis Sarris' book, op cit.
15 ARTICLE 16: Turkey hereby renounces all rights and title whatsoever over or respecting the

territories situated outside the frontiers laid down in the present Treaty and the islands other than those over which her sovereignty is recognised by the said Treaty, the future of these territories and islands being settled or to be settled by the parties concerned. The provisions of the present Article do not prejudice any special arrangements arising from neighbourly relations which have been or may be concluded between Turkey and any limitrophe countries.

ARTICLE 20: Turkey hereby recognises the annexation of Cyprus proclaimed by the British Government on the 5th November, 1914.

16 Lord Radcliffe, Constitutional Proposals on Cyprus, HMSO, London, 1956.

17 Turkish researchers and writers claim that, when Cyprus was handed over to the British, the Muslim population of the island was 60,000 and the Greek 20,000!

18 See page 102.

19 The extraordinary thing is that, from a simple reading of Erim's text, one grasps the link between the report – which was adopted from then on as official Turkish policy – and Turkish practice from that time to the present, as well as the link between the report and Turkey's present-day positions on Cyprus and Greco-Turkish relations. My italics in the report were to assist the reader to note these points.

Chapter 7

1 Robert Stephens, op. cit., page 139.

2 Nancy Crawshaw, op. cit., page 44.

3 It is particularly significant that Kuchuk, who later played a role as leader of the Turkish Cypriots and as Vice-President of Cyprus, confirms that Ankara's efforts to take over the Republic were restricted to the level of the Turkish Cypriot leadership, which confirms indirectly at least that the Turkish Cypriot leadership elite was a tool in the hands of Ankara.

4 M Attalides, op. cit., page 46.

5 The Turkish Cypriot journalist, teacher union activist and politician Arif Tahsin wrote on November 26, 1982, in the Turkish Cypriot newspaper *Soz*: 'Burhan Nalbantoglu, in a discussion, had said the following about these attempts by Britain to put Turkey into the Cyprus game: The Governor had invited Dr Kuchuk and asked him if Turkey wanted Cyprus. The doctor replied that he didn't know. The Governor then told him to go to Ankara and ask. The doctor went to Ankara but the reply was still the same, that Turkey did not want Cyprus. After this, the British Ambassador in Ankara took action and Turkey changed its mind. That's how the problem was solved.'

6 Charles Foley, *Legacy of Strife: Cyprus from Rebellion to Civil War*, Penguin, London, 1964, page 30.

7 Iacovos Tenedios, op. cit., page 49.

8 H. A. Mapolar, *Kibris Postasi* newspaper, September 10, 1984.

9 *Kibris Postasi* newspaper, September 5, 1984.

10 Ahmed An in the newspaper *Yeni Cag*, February 20, 1955.

11 Op. cit.

12 Op. cit.
13 Turkish Cypriot newspaper *Vatan*, January 9, 1995.
14 Spyros Athanasiades, *The TMT File*, Nicosia 1998, pages 13-14.
15 Op. cit., page 60.
16 *The Times*, January 20, 1978.
17 Turkish Cypriot newspaper *Vatan*, January 9, 1995.
18 Turkish Cypriot newspaper *Kibris*, February 9, 1994.
19 In his statements to *Kibris* he also said that, 'If there had not been this movement of Turkish Cypriots, the governments of the time would have given up the Cyprus struggle long before.'
20 Nancy Crawshaw, op. cit., pages 273-275.
21 Spyros Athanasiades, op. cit., page 16.
22 Op. cit., page 19.
23 *Miliyet* newspaper, June 10, 1996.
24 Spyros Athanasiades, op. cit., page 28.
25 Op. cit., pages 28-29.
26 Op. cit.
27 With the pseudonym Osman Orek, who became Defence Minister in the first government of an independent Cyprus, keeping his pseudonym.
28 Christos P. Ioannides states that Vuruskan was married to a Turkish Cypriot woman named Cihan from Lapithos, near Kyrenia (Christos P. Ioannides, op. cit., page 126).
29 Statement by Fazil Kuchuk to *Halkin Sesi*, February 16, 1979.
30 Pierre Oberling, op. cit., page 60.
31 Turkish Cypriot press, May 8, 1958.

Chapter 8

1 Both documents were submitted by the Cypriot government to the UN Security Council in 1964.
2 Memorandum by the Minister of Foreign Affairs of the Republic of Cyprus, submitted to the Foreign Affairs Committee of the House of Commons, Nicosia, February 27, 1987, page 175.
3 Op. cit., page 151.
4 It is not clear why certain sentences are in inverted commas. The author assumes that they either refer to texts by those who disagreed with the policy that is proposed in the document or they are sarcastic references to their arguments.
5 Melih Ezenbel, a Turkish diplomat who took part in the talks on Cyprus in Zurich and London, was Ambassador to Washington during the 1974 invasion and subsequently served as director general of the Turkish Foreign Ministry.
6 Interview in the Turkish newspaper *Tercuman*, July 30, 1983.
7 A reference to the notorious London Conference.
8 *Tercuman* newspaper, July 30, 1996.
9 A reference to the Turkish air strikes on Tylliria in August 1964.

10 The withdrawal of the Greek division sent to the island by George Papandreou in 1964. The division withdrew following an agreement between the Junta's Prime Minister Kolias and the then Turkish Prime Minister Suleyman Demirel at a meeting in Evros the same year.
11 A reference to the deployment in Cyprus, based on the agreements, of the Turkish contingent, TURDYK) of 650 men and the Greek force (ELDYK) of 950 men.
12 *Tercuman* newspaper, July 21, 1984.
13 M. Attalides, op. cit., page 50.
14 Robert Stephens, op. cit., page 174.
15 *Halkin Sesi* newspaper, January 20, 1963.
16 Op. cit., October 11, 1963.
17 Pierre Oberling, op. cit., page 85.
18 Niazi Kizilyurek, *Cyprus Beyond the Nation*, Nicosia, 1993, page 31.

Chapter 9

1 'Many countries', Turkey's then Foreign Minister Turan Gunes told *Huriyet* on July 20, 1980, 'since it serves their interests to some degree, want to see the Cyprus problem as our desire to protect the Turkish community on the island, while the real problem is the security of the 45 million people of metropolitan Turkey and the maintenance of a balance in the Middle East. Cyprus is as necessary as a right hand for the expansionist designs of a country, if it should have such designs.'
2 *Miliyet* newspaper, August 1995.
3 Ismael Tansu, *Miliyet* newspaper, August 1995.
4 Op. cit.
5 Op. cit.
6 Nancy Crawshaw, op. cit., page 354.
7 In some instances where the British actually did arrest Turks with fishing boats carrying arms, they kept it secret and finally set the Turks free.
8 *Miliyet* newspaper, August 1995.
9 This was a force in which, as admitted by John Redaway (administrative secretary to the governor of Cyprus, Sir John Harding, whose decision it was to set up the force) in his book *Burdened with Cyprus – The British Connection*, Weidenfeld & Nicolson, London, 1986, page 90, 1,700 Turkish Cypriots and 70 Greek Cypriots served. There was also another force, the mobile reserve, that comprised entirely 542 Turkish Cypriots. It was from these two units, by Turkish and British admission, that TMT recruited its battle-ready members. In essence, they were all under TMT orders.
10 During the whole of the state of emergency imposed by the British, no Turkish Cypriot member of TMT was arrested, nor was any charged with transporting arms, despite the fact that, according to Ismael Tansu's evidence, the weapons brought to Cyprus were enough to arm 10,000 men. During the same period, dozens of Greek Cypriots were arrested and charged with carrying arms, several of whom were condemned and executed, while in certain cases the 'arms' they were accused of carrying were capable of provoking nothing more dangerous than laughter.

11 As narrated in the Turkish Cypriot newspaper *Ortam*, October 4, 1995.
12 Spyros Athanasiades, op. cit., page 29.
13 Op. cit., page 30.
14 Op. cit., page 82.
15 Op. cit., page 86.
16 Op. cit., page 87.
17 Op. cit., page 94.
18 Op. cit.
19 Nancy Crawshaw, op. cit., page 110.
20 Arif Tahsin, *Those Walking the Same Road Cannot Arrive at Different Destinations*, translated into Greek and published in Nicosia in 1996 in typescript form by Thanasis Haranas, volume 2, page 31.
21 Denktash studied law in London on a British government scholarship.
22 Details in chapter 12.
23 Neoclis Sarris, op. cit., vol.ume 2, Book 1, page 3.
24 Arif Tahsin (op. cit., page 35) mentions that these incidents took place after the announcement of a change in Menderes' policy from a demand for the return of Cyprus to its previous 'owner', Turkey, to one for partition. On the evening of January 26, he adds, it was heard that '*taxim* has been achieved'. On the incidents and the state of the injured in a private clinic, Tahsin writes the following: 'The clinic was full of injured and dead people. At one point I saw Denktash and I said to him, "For God's sake give the order for this killing to stop." He replied: "These dead are useful to us. Through them our voice will be heard in the world."
25 *Miliyet* newspaper, August 1995.
26 There were four articles published in the Turkish Cypriot newspaper *Yeni Cag* on February 20 & 27 and on March 6 & 13, 1995.
27 This was the 'Foot Plan', which basically provided for self-government for a period of five years, after which the future of Cyprus would be decided.
28 There is a certain irony in the fact that Pyla is a mixed village in which even today Greek Cypriots and Turkish Cypriots continue to live together as then, while their peaceful coexistence is only interrupted whenever Denktash's occupation regime attempts to cause problems for its own purposes.
29 Until his death in 1987, Sadi remained in London, where he was active against the Denktash regime both before and after the 1974 invasion.
30 John Redaway, op. cit., page 90.
31 Arif Hasan Tahsin, in an article published in *Soz* newspaper, November 27, 1982.
32 Well known for his opposition to the policy of Denktash and Ankara, he experienced TMT's terrorism first-hand. Today he lives in the free area of Cyprus and works at the state Agricultural Research Institute.
33 The lecture was delivered on March 24, 1981, in Nicosia as part of the Popular University series, and in 1982 was published as a brochure entitled *The past and the course of the Turkish Cypriot community*.
34 Op. cit., page 22.
35 Halil Ibrahim Salih, op. cit., page 58.

36 In fact Turkish Cypriots were used as torturers and many of them set particular 'records'.
37 Halil Ibrahim Salih, op. cit., pages 58-59.
38 In an interview published in the Turkish Cypriot newspaper *Ortam*, September 18,1995.
39 Interview in the Turkish Cypriot newspaper Olai, January 22, 1979.

Chapter 10

1 Neoclis Sarris, op. cit., page volume 2, Book 1, page 393.
2 Arif Tahsin, op. cit., volume 2, page 33.
3 Op. cit., page 34.
4 Nancy Crawshaw, op. cit., page 287.
5 Op. cit., page 288.
6 Op. cit.
7 The interview, in June 1984, was part of *Britain's Grim Legacy*, a 13-part series by Granada TV that examined London's legacy to its former colonies. The final episode, which was devoted to Cyprus, was broadcast by ITV on July 13, 1984.
8 Arif Tahsin, *We See the Future and Ignore the Past*, pages 12-16.
9 Kutlu Adali was a member of TMT and a personal friend of Denktash, serving as his private secretary. After 1974, however, in dozens of critical articles, Adali opposed Denktash's and Ankara's policy, especially that of settling the occupied areas and integrating them into Turkey. This stance would eventually cost him his life. He was murdered by 'unidentified' killers on July 7, 1996. For more, see page 263.
10 *Ortam* newspaper, July 14, 1984.
11 It was a classic case of distorting the facts for Turkish public opinion in order to promote Turkey's plans. The village of Gunyeli, which was exclusively Turkish, had never been attacked. By contrast, the British had transported 35 Greek Cypriots they had arrested in Nicosia to the outskirts of the village and left them to return home on foot. On the way they were attacked by groups of Turkish Cypriots from Gunyeli and eight were killed.
12 Nancy Crawshaw, op. cit., page 304.
13 Miltiades Christodoulou, *The Course of Greco-Turkish Relations and Cyprus*, Proodos Press, Nicosia 15, Vol. 1, page 62.
14 Nancy Crawshaw, op. cit., page 304.
15 Christos P. Ioannides, op. cit., page 128.
16 Op. cit., page 129.
17 *Kibris Postasi* newspaper, August 15, 1984.
18 Op. cit.
19 Op. cit. It is interesting to note that, while Yiasin had previously announced that more revelations would follow, they suddenly stopped and the journalist's work disappeared from the pages of the newspaper.
20 *Soz* newspaper, June 10, 1981.
21 Arif Tahsin, op. cit., pages 14-16.
22 Pierre Oberling, op. cit., page 61.
23 Nancy Crawshaw, op. cit., page 42.

24 M. Attalides, op. cit., page 50.
25 George Grivas-Dighenis, *Memoirs of the EOKA Struggle 1955-1959*, Athens, 1961, page 361. From Grivas' reference to the results of passive resistance one may gain a clear picture of the financial base of the campaign with which, as Grivas himself notes (page 364), Makarios disagreed. The boycott of foreign goods included government lottery tickets, the British football pools, various sweets, shoes, cigarettes, washing powder, soap, serviettes, material, cars, insurance, cosmetics, etc.
26 Halil Ibrahim Salih, op. cit., pages 62-63.
27 Nancy Crawshaw, op. cit., pages 293-294.
28 Op. cit., page 294.
29 Op. cit.

Chapter 11

1 A series of publications by PEO, as well as others and articles in the press at the time, refer in detail to this period and provide interesting information on the relations between Greek and Turkish Cypriots on the level of work, as well as the activities of the colonial government and its alliances with the economic establishment of the Greek and Turkish Cypriots so as to face the demands of the masses.
2 As was to be expected, the Cold War conditions that were beginning to be felt around the world also affected Cyprus, while the interest of the imperialist forces was focused on the region with its oilfields, which increased the importance of the island to these forces.
3 This is indicated further by the fact of the different priorities of the Turkish Cypriot masses at the time.
4 M. Attalides, op. cit., page 47.
5 Discussion of the pros and cons of the Zurich and London Agreements has continued since then and is exhausting. It concerns all aspects of the issue: legal, military, social, etc. However, this discussion falls outside the scope of the present work.
6 The Communal Chamber was essentially the mechanism for controlling the issues that interested the Turkish Cypriots in particular, such as, for instance, questions of education and religion, via which Turkey and the Turkish Cypriot leadership gained a legal channel for the nationalism that was essential for Turkey's plans to work.
7 These prospects are acknowledged even by those authors who identify fully with the chauvinist Turkish Cypriot leadership, such as Pierre Oberling, op. cit., page 67.
8 Speech given during his inauguration as President of Cyprus on December 11, 1959 (*Complete Works of Archbishop Makarios III of Cyprus*, Archbishop Makarios III Foundation, Nicosia, 1992, volume 4, page 138).
9 Op. cit.
10 *News Digest*, September 10, 1963, published by the Turkish Communal Chamber.
11 Op. cit.
12 Miltiades Christodoulou, op. cit., volume 1, page 142.
13 Op. cit., pages 142-145.
14 Pierre Oberling, op. cit., page 67.

15 *Halkin Sesi* newspaper, January 23, 1962.
16 Op. cit., January 11, 1963.
17 E.N. Tzelepis, op. cit., page 143.
18 *Halkin Sesi* newspaper, October 11, 1963.
19 Polyvios G. Polyviou, *Cyprus, Conflict and Negotiation, 1960-1980*, Gerald Duckworth & Co., London, 1980, page 34.
20 *Halkin Sesi* newspaper, April 2, 1963.
21 Op. cit., April 8, 1963.
22 A habitual Denktash reference to those killed during the conquest of Cyprus by the Ottomans in 1573.
23 *Halkin Sesi* newspaper, January 29, 1963.
24 The rebellion broke out prematurely through a chance event. Developments would probably have been even more negative had the rebellion started according to a specific timetable.
25 *Cyprus Today*, published by the Greek Communal Chambers, supplements 1-9, July 9-October 15, 1964, Nicosia, parts 3-4, volume 2, page 19.
26 Op. cit., parts 3-4, volume 2, page 25.
27 Christos P. Ioannides, op. cit., page 131.
28 Z.M. Nedjatigil (who goes under the title of 'Attorney-General' in the occupied areas of Cyprus), *Our Republic in Perspective*, occupied Nicosia, 1985, page 9.
29 Halil Ibrahim Salih, *Cyprus, the Impact of Diverse Nationalism on a State*, The University of Alabama Press, Alabama, 1978, page 75.
30 This was included in the report by the Secretary-General of the UN to the Security Council on December 20, 1964.
31 *Cyprus Today*, June 1964, page 1.
32 Op. cit., August 1964, pages 17-18.
33 Much has been written about the Kophinou crisis, which developed when the National Guard organised an operation against the Turkish Cypriots in the area of the villages of Ayios Theodoros and Kophinou. Many – among them Yiannis Katris in his book *The Birth of Neo-Fascism* (*Greece 1960-1974*), Papazisi Press, Athens, 1974 – believe that this pointless operation had been devised by the Junta in Athens so as to lead the situation into the developments that followed, in other words it was part of an understanding between the Junta and Turkey.
34 The organisation of the Turkish Cypriot rebellion, based on the Nihat Erim report but also on the Turkish Cypriot leadership's proposals for action as presented to Ankara, is confirmed by the fact that in June 1965 the then Turkish Prime Minister, Ismet Inonu, admitted Turkey's intentions to the Americans. Specifically, there is a particularly revealing urgent, top-secret report by the British Embassy in Washington (No. 2081, June 4, 1964, coded PREM II 4710) which notes the following: 'I have just returned from a meeting with Rusk [then Secretary of State for Foreign Affairs]. The views of the President on the prospects of action by the Turkish government were contained in a message from Rusk to the American Ambassador in Ankara. Based on this message, Mr Hare attempted to arrange a further meeting with Inonu [Prime Minister of Turkey at the time] and he managed to get the Prime Minister out of a cabinet meeting and to put the American views to

him in the strongest possible manner. Inonu confirmed that Kuchuk will proclaim part of Cyprus as Turkish and that Turkish forces will rush to its aid tomorrow, June 5.' Inonu asked the United States to show 'understanding' for the de facto situation they intended to create the following day. There followed the well-known letter from US President Lyndon Johnson in which he warned Turkey not to proceed with its plans. This plan is included in the document of the Turkish Cypriot leadership (see Chapter 8).

35 Christos P. Ioannides, op. cit., page 134.

36 Op. cit.

37 Op. cit., page 135.

Chapter 12

1 Christos P. Ioannides, op. cit., page 142.

2 Arif Tahsin, *Those Walking the Same Road Cannot Arrive at Different Points*, translated into Greek and published in Nicosia in 1996 in typescript form by Thanasis Haranas, volume 2, page 51.

3 Op. cit., page 60.

4 Op. cit., page 53.

5 *Miliyet* newspaper, May 15, 1964.

6 Miltiades Christodoulou, op. cit., page 148.

7 Arif Tahsin, op. cit., volume 2, page 55.

8 Op. cit., page 64.

9 Leontios Ierodiaconou, *The Cyprus Problem, the Road to Bankruptcy*, Papazisis Press, Athens, 1975, page 366.

10 Op. cit., page 365.

11 Miltiades Christodoulou, op. cit., volume 1, page 148.

12 Minos Kyriakou, *Siesta on a Volcano*, The Aegean Foundation Publications, Athens, 1987, page 109.

13 Ihsan Ali, op. cit., page 39. Ihsan Ali beleived that both Yiorkatzis and Denktash had connections with the CIA and that they collaborated with each other. Yiorkatzis had secretly recorded his conversation with Gurkan and the tape was presented at the trial for the murder of the two Turkish Cypriot lawyers. The Turkish Cypriot leadership, Ihsan Ali says, had exploited the contents of the tape to present the two lawyers as Greek agents and traitors, in a desparate effort to contain the reactions to their murder.

14 Leontios Ierodiaconou, op. cit., page 367.

15 *Cumhuriyet* newspaper, March 26, 1962.

16 Op. cit., April 23, 1962.

17 *Haravghi* newspaper, February 18, 1996.

18 *Agon* newspaper, July 14, 1996. The Interrogating Committee was made up of Judge Wilson, the President of the Constitutional Court, and the Supreme Court judges Michalakis Triantafyllides and Mehmet Zekya.

19 Panayiotis Papademetris and Andreas Neophytou, *Polycarpos Yiorkatzis, the Houdini of EOKA*, Nicosia, 1997, pages 305-307.

20 Born in 1924 in the village of Peristeronopygi, he was a carpenter by trade before becoming a professional official of PEO.
21 *Chronicle of the Modern Cypriot Tragedy*, AKEL publication, Nicosia, 1975, page 194.
22 Op. cit., page 195.
23 Op. cit., page 196.
24 Born in Nicosia in 1935. Three years later his family moved to Antalya, where he attended high school before returning to Cyprus in 1954.
25 On the day of the funeral (July 11, 1996), the author was in the occupied area to cover a meeting between Denktash and Sir David Hannay, then Britain's Special Envoy for Cyprus. In the presence of the British diplomat, he asked Denktash to explain why he had not allowed any Greek Cypriot journalists to attend Adali's funeral. Momentarily embarrassed, Denktash mumbled that the author and two other Greek Cypriot journalists (Paris Potamitis and Pavlos Xanthoullis, with their TV film crew) could attend the funeral 'but with police protection'. At the mosque, the thousands of Turkish Cypriots who had gathered there applauded the Greek Cypriot journalists.
26 *Cyprus Weekly*, August 23, 1996.
27 Interview with the magazine *Aktuel*, reprinted in *Haravghi* on August 25, 1996.
28 *Yeni Duzen* newspaper, December 19, 1992.
29 Op. cit., March 3, 1993.
30 Op. cit., June 16, 1993.
31 Op. cit., August 30, 1994.
32 On July 29, 1996, hundreds of Turkish Cypriots gathered outside Denktash's 'police headquarters' and demanded the arrest of Adali's murderers. They shouted persistently, 'You will not gag us'.
The American Committee for the Protection of Journalists, whose chairperson at the time was the wife of Richard Holbrooke, US Presidential Envoy for Cyprus, included the name of Kutlu Adali on the list of journalists murdered around the world for their ideas. The same was done by the Canada-based International Committee for Freedom of Speech, which issued a statement asking for public opinion to protest to Denktash as the 'representative of the authorities in North Cyprus'.

Chapter 13

1 Arif Tahsin, op. cit., volume 2, page 89.
2 *Report of the UN Mediator on Cyprus*, republished by the Press & Information Office of Cyprus.
3 The link between this proposed line and the present 'Attila Line' is obvious.
4 *Report of the UN Mediator on Cyprus*, paragraph 93, page 27.
5 Op. cit., para. 38, page 14.
6 Op. cit., para. 40, page 14.
7 *UN Secretary-General's Report*, S/5764, para. 13, June 1964.
8 *UN Secretary-General's Report*, S/5426, para. 106, June 1965.
9 *UN Secretary-General's Report*, S/6228, para. 17, March 11, 1965.

10 *UN Secretary-General's Report*, S/7611, para. 109, December 8, 1966.
11 *UN Secretary-General's Report*, S/8286, para. 127, December 8, 1967.
12 *UN Secretary-General's Report*, S/9233, para. 55, June 3, 1969.
13 *Sabas* newspaper, December 1, 1966, included in Leontios Ierodiaconou's book *The Cyprus Problem, the Road to Bankruptcy*, page 417.
14 *Bozkurt* newspaper, October 3, 1969, noted by Leontios Ierodiaconou, op. cit., page 419.
15 Leontios Ierodiaconou, op. cit., page 431.
16 Details of the activities of these groups during the period from 1964 to the attempted coup against Makarios may be found in Makarios Droussiotis' book *From the National Front to EOKA B*, Nicosia, 1994.
17 Arif Tahsin, op. cit., volume 2, page 52.

Chapter 14

1 Rauf Denktash, *The Cyprus Problem*, published by the so-called Press and Information Office of the 'Turkish Cypriot Administration', Nicosia, 1974, page 7.
2 In the introduction to Michael Moran's book *Rauf Denktash at the United Nations – Speeches on Cyprus*, op. cit., page ix.
3 Nancy Crawshaw, op.cit., page 44.
4 Op. cit.
5 Arif Tahsin, op.cit., volume 2, page 51.
6 Op. cit., page 49.
7 Op. cit., page 51.
8 Ihsan Ali, op.cit., pages 38-39.
9 Ihsan Tahsin, op. cit., page 48.
10 Op. cit., page 50.
11 Op. cit., page 48.
12 Michael Moran, op. cit., page 33.
13 The whole of this particular address by Denktash may be found in Michael Moran, op. cit., pages 122-139.
14 Rauf Denktash in *Hatiralari, 1964-1974*, Bogazici Yayinlari A.S., Istanbul, 1996, vol. I, page 403 (Denktash's memoirs).
15 Op. cit., page 495.
16 Op. cit., volume II, page 114 (a speech to Conservative Party MPs in London, April 1, 1965).
17 Op. cit., page 75 (reply to an article by British Labour MP Noel Baker).
18 Op. cit., volume IV, page 88 (letter to the UN Secretary General, dated March 27, 1967).
19 Op. cit., page 259.
20 Excerpts have been published in Denktash's multi-volume memoirs to which we have already referred. The whole book was translated into Greek by Thanasis Haranas and published in typescript form in a limited edition in Nicosia in December 1998. The extracts referred to subsequently are mainly taken from this edition.
21 Rauf Denktash in *Hatiralari, 1964-1974*, volume IV, pages 46-47.
22 This is a significant admission regarding the guarantees. Denktash acknowledges that the

treaties of guarantee were concerned with the existence of the Republic of Cyprus and not with the 'protection of the Turkish Cypriots', as he has stated in his propaganda since 1974 to the present day.

23 Rauf Denktash op.cit., pages 49-51.
24 Rauf Denktash, *Cyprus at the Eleventh Hour,* page 26.
25 Op. cit., page 29.
26 Op. cit., page 36.
27 Glafcos Clerides, *My Deposition*, Alitheia Press, Nicosia, 1991, volume 2, page 209.
28 Op. cit., page 210.
29 Op. cit., page 212.
30 Professional obligations enable the author to visit the occupied area of Cyprus frequently and he always has the opportunity to meet and speak with Turkish Cypriot journalists, whose views are always of great interest, especially those concerning Denktash.
31 Turkish Cypriot newspaper *Soz*, October 25, 1979.

Chapter 15

1 Nicos Kranidiotis, *Unprotected State*, Estia Publications, Athens, 1985, volume 1, page 422.
2 Andros Pavlides, *Cyprus File – Top Secret*, Nicosia, 1985, volume 1, page 123.
3 Nicos Kranidiotis, op. cit., page 452.
5 In November 1967, during a visit by the Vice-President of the military government, General Spantidakis, to Cyprus, TMT caused problems for traffic on the main Nicosia-Limassol road near the village of Kophinou, while in the neighbouring Turkish Cypriot village of Ayios Theodoros it was preventing police patrols. According to Yiannis Katris in his book *The birth of neo-fascism* (*Greece 1960-1974*), Papazisis Press, Athens, 1974, Spantidakis ordered a unit of the Greek forces in Cyprus to clear out the TMT groups, which resulted in the murder of some of their members. Ankara, correctly assessing Greece's diplomatic isolation due to the dictatorship, exploited the events by demanding the immediate withdrawal of the Greek division in Cyprus and threatening to invade Cyprus if its demand were not met. 'The Junta,' writes Yiannis Katris, 'being quite aware that a foreign war would make its position shaky, appealed to NATO and to Washington, asking for assistance and advice. The American government sent Cyrus Vance as a mediator but he did not need to tire himself. With one gesture, he made the Junta bow to the Turkish ultimatum and ordered the Greek division to return to Greece at once.'
6 Nicos Kranidiotis, op. cit., pages 509-510.
7 Op. cit., page 514.
8 Halil Ibrahim Salih, *Cyprus, the Impact of Diverse Nationalism on a State*, The University of Alabama Press, Alabama 1978, page 76.
9 Op. cit., page 77.
10 Z.M. Nedjatigil, *Cyprus, Constitutional Proposals and Developments*, 'Public Information Office of the Turkish Federated State of Cyprus', Nicosia, 1977. Nedjatigil is still Denktash's chief legal adviser.
11 Arif Tahsin, op.cit.,Volume 2, page 103.

12 Op. cit., page 102.
13 Op. cit., page 103.
14 Op. cit., page 110.
15 Op. cit., page 130.
16 Halil Ibrahim Salih, op. cit., page 76.
17 A. Hadjikyriakos and C. Christoforou, *Parliamentary Elections: History, Figures, Analysis,* Intercollege Press, Nicosia, 1996, page 11.
18 Op. cit., page 12.
19 Op. cit., page 164.
20 Nihat Erim was not only the architect of Turkey's strategy on Cyprus but also an expert on the subject and was Turkey's representative during the transitional period from colonial rule to independence and the preparation of the 1960 constitution. Later he was the Turkish constitutional expert who took part in the enlarged intercommunal talks, which had come within a whisper of a solution shortly before the coup against Makarios in 1974.
21 Arif Tahsin argues that Denktash's 'anti-Communist campaign' was carried out under the guidance of an American CIA agent code-named Austrian.
22 Arif Tahsin, op. cit., volume 2, page 164.
23 Op. cit., page 165.
24 This was the so-called 'church coup', in which the three bishops asked Makarios to give up his political duties which, they claimed, were incompatible with those of the Church, otherwise they would demand that he be defrocked. This too was part of the attempt on the one hand by the Junta to weaken and control Makarios and on the other by the so-called '*enosists*' to neutralise the alleged 'obstacles' to *enosis.*
25 Glafcos Clerides, op. cit., pages 259-261.
26 Halil Ibrahim Salih, op. cit., page 77.
27 Narrative by Kutlu Adali, published in the Turkish Cypriot newspaper *Ortam* on June 4, 5 & 6, 1985.
28 Turkish Cypriot newspaper *Soz,* January 28, 1978.
29 *Yeni Duzen* newspaper, October 5, 1982.
30 Rauf Denktash, *A Vision for the Cyprus Issue,* published by the Rauf Denktash Educational Foundation, Nicosia, 1994, translated into Greek and published in typescript form by Thanasis Haranas, page 3.
31 Op. cit., page 8.
32 Op. cit., page 18.
33 Op. cit., page 19.
34 Op. cit., page 36.

Chapter 16

1 Halil Ibrahim Salih, op. cit., page 89.
2 On July 23, 1974, a ceasefire was agreed, which was not respected by the Turkish forces, while on July 24 the Junta collapsed and on July 25 the 'President' of the coup in Cyprus, Nicos Sampson, handed over power to the Speaker of the House of Representatives, Glafcos

Clerides. That same day talks began in Geneva among the Foreign Ministers of the three guarantor powers, Great Britain, Turkey and Greece.

3 *North Cyprus Almanac*, K. Rustem & Brother, London, 1987, page 43.
4 Miltiades Christodoulou, op. cit., volume 2, page 343.
5 Polyvios G. Polyviou, op. cit., page 158.
6 Op. cit., page 154.
7 Christopher Hitchens, *Cyprus*, Quartet Books Ltd., London, 1984, page 105.
8 Op. cit.
9 Op. cit., page 106.
10 By that time the process to impose an arms embargo against Turkey had began, much to Kissinger's anger.
11 Christopher Hitchens, op. cit., pages 106-107.
12 *Washington Post* newspaper, September 11, 1975.
13 Christopher Hitchens, op. cit., page 107.
14 July 31-August 2, 1975. The statement became known as the 'Third Vienna Agreement'.
15 *The Cyprus Problem*, Public Information Office, Nicosia, 1991, page 66.
16 Christopher Hitchens, op. cit., pages 108-109.
17 Glafcos Clerides, op. cit., volume 4, page 494.
18 *The Historical Background of Cyprus and the Turkish Republic of Northern Cyprus,* The Cyprus Turkish Cultural Association, Ankara, no date, page 75.
19 Z.M. Nedjatigil, op. cit., pages 31-32.
20 *North Cyprus Almanac*, page 44.
21 *The Cyprus Problem*, page 32.
22 Resolution 37/253, May 13, 1983.
23 *The Cyprus Problem*, page 33.
24 Op. cit.
25 Op. cit., page 35.
26 Z.M. Nedjatigil, *The Cyprus Question and the Turkish Position in International Law*, Oxford University Press, Oxford, 1989, page 174.
27 Op. cit., page 163.
28 Op. cit., page 164.
29 Op. cit., page 166.
30 The question of who took the decision was answered by Denktash himself in a statement made three years before the proclamation of the illegal state: 'We had decided a long time ago on the declaration of a state but we were unable to implement our decision because Turkey prevented it.' (Turkish Cypriot newspaper *Ulus*, April 12, 1980.) Moreover, on July 17, 1982, the Turkish Cypriot magazine *Ulay* published a statement by Denktash in which he said that, 'The declaration of the federated state was a temporary measure, for 6-9 months.'
31 Rauf Denktash, *The Cyprus Triangle*, published by the 'Office of the Turkish Republic of Northern Cyprus', New York, 1988, page 118.
32 Op. cit.
33 Op. cit., page 119.
34 Op. cit., page 120.

35 Op. cit., page 121.
36 Op. cit., pages 122-123.
37 *New Statesman*, January 27, 1984.
38 *Ortam* newspaper, December 11, 1983.
39 *North Cyprus Almanac*, page 45.
40 One example revealing the sources of the constitution is the issuance of a command by TMT's military commander in Paphos with orders concerning health regulations by which the Turkish Cypriot should abide! It is included in Christos P. Ioannides' book *In Turkey's Image*, page 199.
41 Op. cit., pages 163-173.
42 The Turkish Cypriots today number fewer than 90,000, according to Turkish Cypriot press reports. As there are approximately 40,000 Turkish soldiers on the island, if one takes account of the number of settlers (some 60,000), this means that there is more than one mainland Turk for every Turkish Cypriot.
43 Arif Tahsin, *We See the Future and Ignore the Past*, pages 4-5.
44 Foreign Affairs Committee, House of Commons, Third Report, Session 1986-1987, HMSO, London, page 5.
45 *Why Independence?*, published by the so-called 'Foreign Ministry' of the illegal state, occupied Nicosia, 1997, page 13.
46 Address to the Security Council, November 18, 1983.
47 The full address is included in Michael Moran's book *Rauf Denktash at the United Nations – Speeches on Cyprus*, pages 177-187.
48 Denktash was particularly annoyed by Resolution 37/253 of the UN General Assembly on May 13, 1983, which: 'Affirms the right of the Republic of Cyprus and its people to full and effective sovereignty and control over the entire territory of Cyprus and its natural and other resources and calls upon all states to support and help the Government of the Republic of Cyprus to exercise these rights.' (*The Cyprus Problem*, page 144.)
49 Rauf Denktash, op. cit., page 126.
50 Op. cit., page 128.
51 *The Cyprus Problem*, page 181.
52 See Yiannos Kranidiotis' introduction to *Cyprus-European Community*, published by the European Issues Service of the Popular Bank, Nicosia, 1994, page xiv.
53 TRNC Position Paper on European Union Membership, 1997.
54 See Yiannos Kranidiotis' introduction to *Cyprus-European Community*, page xv.
55 Rauf Denktash in *Why Independence*, page 22.
56 Op. cit., page 23.

Chapter 17

1 The Report of the Commission, applications 6780/74 and 6950/74, paragraph 83, and Appendix 1, para. 21, 10, application 8007/77, July 12, 1978, para. 21-22.
2 Aristos Aristotelous, *The Unified Defence Area, Cyprus-Greece*, Cyprus Centre for Strategic Studies, Nicosia, 1995, page 64.

3 Op. cit.
4 Alpay Durduran, leader of the Community Liberation Party (Turkish Cypriot newspaper *Soz*, May 30, 1984).
5 Turkish Cypriot newspaper *Olay*, August 23, 1982.
6 *Yeni Duzen* newspaper, October 5, 1982.
7 *Halkin Sesi* newspaper, November 6, 1983.
8 The articles published in *Miliyet* newspaper, on February 16, 1982, and in Gunaydin newspaper on November 2, 1982, are typical.
9 *Birlik* newspaper, February 12, 1983.
10 *Miliyet* newspaper, May 29, 1983.
11 Mehmet Ali Birand, *Haggling*, translated into Greek by Constantinos Hadjivergis, Ioannis Floros Press, Athens, 1985, page 105. The decision was taken on May 2, 1975, according to Birand.
12 Op. cit., page 106.
13 Memorandum by the Minister of Foreign Affairs of the Republic of Cyprus submitted to the Foreign Affairs Committee of the House of Commons, Nicosia, February 27, 1987, page 261.
14 In October 1974. The calculations were by the so-called 'Ministry of Justice and the Interior' of the Turkish Cypriot administration.
15 With the weekly Arabic-language newspaper of London, *Al-Hawadith*, May 18, 1984.
16 *Aydilnlik* newspaper, August 27, 1979, refers to 50,000 while *Gunaydin* newspaper, March 3, 1984, puts the number as 45,000-50,000.
17 John Bierman, *The Middle East*, August 1977.
18 *Der Spiegel*, July 17, 1978.
19 *Yeni Duzen* newspaper, February 10, 1986.
20 Op. cit., May 9, 1985.
21 Arif Tahsin, op. cit., page 74.
22 *Gunaydin* newspaper, December 5-7, 1986.
23 *Yeni Duzen* newspaper, January 20, 1986.
24 *Ortam* newspaper, June 27, 1985.
25 Memorandum by the Minister of Foreign Affairs, page 298.
26 *Cumhuriyet* newspaper, October 25, 1981, *Birlik* newspaper November 25, 1981, and *Huriyet* newspaper, December 1, 1981.
27 Denktash's testimony to the Foreigh Affairs Committie of the House of Commons in February 1987.
28 *Bozkurt* newspaper, March 3, 1984.
29 *New Statesman* January 27, 1984.
30 In the official minutes of the FAC hearings on Cyprus, one can find many such points made by British MPs to Mr Denktash.
31 *Dunya* newspaper, September 15-19, 1978.
32 All the information comes from a study carried out by Turkologist Iacovos Tenedios for the Foreign Ministry of Cyprus, February 1986.
33 The main arguments are that the Zurich and London Agreements – which, despite tearing them up, Turkey cites when it is in its own interest – prohibit Cyprus from joining any

organisation of which Greece and Turkey are not members, that membership would mean *enosis* 'by the back door' with Greece, which is already a member, and that accession without a solution would mean an end to prospects of resolving the problem and its transfer to the EU.

34 *Kibris* newspaper, August 29, 1984.

35 Op. cit.

Index

First published in Great Britain by

ELLIOTT & THOMPSON LIMITED
27 John Street
London WC1N 2BX

ISBN 1 904027 06 7

First Edition

Book design by Brad Thompson
Printed and bound in Malta by Interprint Limited.